ANTHROPOLOGICAL PAPERS
MUSEUM OF ANTHROPOLOGY, UNIVERSITY OF MICHIGAN
NO. 13

THE PUERTO RICAN POPULATION.
A STUDY IN HUMAN BIOLOGY

by
FREDERICK P. THIEME

ANN ARBOR
UNIVERSITY OF MICHIGAN, 1959

PREFACE

In 1948-1949 the Social Science Research Center of the University of Puerto Rico sponsored an anthropological field study of the Puerto Rican population. The initial impetus for the project arose from discussions between Jaime Benetez, Chancellor of the University of Puerto Rico, and H. L. Shapiro, of Columbia University and the American Museum of Natural History. The field study was carried out by two groups of anthropologists: one in physical anthropology, under the direction of Dr. Shapiro, and the other in social anthropology, under the direction of Professor Julian Steward, then at Columbia University. The study in social anthropology was reported in 1956 in "The People of Puerto Rico," by Steward, Manners, Wolf, Padilla, Mintz and Scheele.

The publication presented here constitutes the summary report of the biological part of the field studies. Four previous publications (Thieme, 1950, 1952, 1957, and Murrill, 1955) deal with various aspects of these data. All these publications, taken together, will accomplish the original purposes of the study; namely, to describe and analyze the biological characteristics and the physical variability in the Puerto Rican population.

Field work was done between June, 1948, and February, 1949, by a team from Columbia University composed of Rupert I. Murrill, Joan Finkle, and the author. Several months were spent at Columbia University reviewing background material and co-ordinating procedures before going to Puerto Rico. Three months of surveying the island and planning the sample structure preceded actual measuring operations (see Table S-16 for date, place, and numbers measured). In the field Mrs. Elizabeth Murrill acted as recorder and was occasionally assisted by Mrs. Jean Thieme. After December, 1948, for the last four hundred individuals in the sample, Miss Carmen LaFontaine acted as interviewer. She was assigned to aid us by the Puerto Rican Department of Health and replaced Mr. Murrill, who returned to the United States. Miss LaFontaine's co-operation and competence materially aided our project and this help is gratefully acknowledged. Another indispensible person assigned to us from the Puerto Rican Department of Health, Mr. Victor Diaz, carried out all of the blood count and hemoglobin determinations. His skill in accurately handling a very large number of readings and his amiability in fitting his personal life to the demanding schedule of field work is greatly appreciated.

As anthropologists we had to rely on the technical assistance of specialists for the analysis of sample materials and to enlarge the area of our study beyond that which is traditional. Without the aid of Dr. Juan A. Pons, Commissioner of the Puerto Rico Department of Public Health, this would not have been possible. He assigned Miss LaFontaine and Mr. Diaz to us, arranged that we have entry into the health centers, approved the arrangement to have Miss Martinez and Miss Mates de Peiz do a nutritional study which would supplement our data, and, in general, assisted us in every way possible. Dr. Jose Janer furnished us with current vital statistics and gave advice as to how best to set up the sample structure. Dr. F. J. Mejias, Chief of the laboratories, gave invaluable aid. It was he who selected and assigned Sẽnor Diaz to us from his staff. The study would, necessarily,, have been much reduced in scope without this generous help by the staff of the Department of Health.

Dr. Morales Otero, Director of the School of Tropical Medicine, of Puerto Rico, and his staff, likewise, were instrumental in making our field work fruitful. Sẽnor Dobal did all the blood typing in the blood-bank laboratory of the School of Tropical Medicine and Dr. Gonzales analyzed 961 fecal samples which we submitted to him. These men made a great contribution to our study and the material in two chapters of our report in large part depend on data provided by them.

Over and above those who actively participated in the technical aspects of our study, there were innumerable people who gave us the helpful co-operation that made our work pleasant and fruitful. At the University of Puerto Rico, Dr. Lydia Roberts and Dr. Fernando Monserrate gave generously of time and wise counsel. At the health centers and from the authorities in the Municipal Hospitals, we received unfailing help. And, finally, our deep gratitude goes to the 3,562 Puerto Ricans, who with grace and friendly spirit, voluntarily submitted to the ordeal of being bled, examined, and measured.

Financial assistance in the analysis of data was provided by a Summer Faculty Research Grant from the Horace H. Rackham School of Graduate Studies of the University of Michigan. The Watson Laboratory, of Columbia University, the Computing Laboratory of the Rackham School and the School of Public Health, at the University of Michigan, freely provided time and machines for the computations. My special thanks go to Mr. John Freysinger of the School of Public Health for his help and friendly counsel.

The author's indebtedness to Dr. H. L. Shapiro should not go without special mention. He inititated and designed this project and, more personally, as teacher and friend made being his student an especially enjoyable and profitable experience.

This summary report is divided into two parts. Part 1 includes the description of the study, the results obtained, and the tabular data immediately relevant. The tables in Part 1 carry a designating letter prefix and they are listed in the Contents. Part 2 consists of 139 basic tables and 76 graphs, and both are indexed at the beginning of the section. The basic tables and the graphs, however, are the subject of repeated and separate references in the text of Part 1, but are most convenient to consult when grouped together.

In brief, Chapters I-VI describe the nature of the sample, techniques used, and the classificatory data. The remaining chapters (VII-XIV) summarize the data and the results. Since this is a summary report, little comparative data are mentioned; attention is concentrated on the particular findings of the study. Our concern has been to adhere closely to the objectives originally set and yet to organize the material so that it may serve as source data, which may be utilized by others desiring to compare the Puerto Rican with other populations.

CONTENTS

PART I: DESCRIPTION OF THE PUERTO RICAN POPULATION

		Page
I.	Introduction	1
II.	Data and Methods	4
III.	The Sample	18
IV.	Geographic Regions	38
V.	Ethnic Character of Puerto Rican Population	44
VI.	Nutritional Data and Classification	49
VII.	Anthropometric Data	58
VIII.	Anthropometric Results	63
IX.	Dental Status	85
X.	Intestinal Infestation	106
XI.	Physiological Characteristics	124
XII.	Racial and Geographic Distribution of Blood Types and Tasters	137
XIII.	Characters of Subsamples Selected to Represent Good Health in Puerto Rico	142
XIV.	The Puerto Rican Migrant	147
	Literature Cited	150

PART 2: SUMMARY TABLES AND GRAPHS

Index to Tables	153
Index to Graphs	154
Code for Indexes of Tables and Graphs	155
Reference Table for Graphs	156
Tables 1-139	(after) 156
Graphs 1-76	follow tables

ILLUSTRATIONS

FIGURES   Page

   1. Field record blank for anthropometry 7
   2. Field record blank for dental status 8
   3. Field record blank for physiology 9
   4. IBM cards and codes 10

GRAPH

   AR-1 Difference of logarithm between nutritional Classes 1 and 2 or 3 for 8 measurements . . . 79

MAPS

   1. Relief map of Puerto Rico 39
   2. The geographic and census regions of Puerto Rico .43

TABLES

Table		Page
S-1	Sample structure	19
S-1A	Summary distribution of sample by region	21
S-2	Urban percentage distribution of sample.	23
S-3	Distribution of sample by age groups and sex compared to 1940 census	24
S-4	Regional percentage distribution of sample and 1940 census populations	24
S-5	Male sample breakdown by census region for occupation and residence categories	26
S-6	Male sample breakdown by ethnic group for residence and occupation categories	27
S-7	Female sample breakdown by region for residence and residence time categories	28
S-8	Prison sample by region and for nutritional and ethnic groups	29
S-9	Prison sample breakdown by region and occupation residence, and residence time categories	30
S-10	Female sample breakdown by region and nutritional and ethnic categories	31
S-11	Male sample breakdown by region and nutritional and ethnic categories	32
S-12	Sample breakdown of University of Puerto Rico females and World War II veterans by region	33
S-13	Structure of nutritional subsamples	34
S-14	Structure of nutritional subsample by ethnic group	35
S-15	Source of sample by sex.	36
S-16	Date, place, and totals measured	36
G-1	Description of census and sample regions.	42
E-1	Frequency distribution by sex of recorded skin color.	45
E-2	Interrelationship of ethnic factor traits	47

Table		Page
N-1	Percentage frequency in each nutritional class in our study compared to Roberts' (1949)	50
N-2	Average percentage of daily requirement for each of nine nutrients in the selected sample groups studied by Martinez and Mates De Peiz	55
A-1	Comparisons Between the means of measurements on matched male and female samples measured by two different anthropometrists.	61
AR-1	Mean body weight for each inch of stature	66
AR-2	Infant mortality in 200 selected upper-class marriages	76
D-1	Mean number of noncarious teeth in males and females of sample A	88
D-2	Average rate of DMF teeth for total sample by age and sex	89
D-3	Means of age, ethnic, and nutrition values for total sample by residence.	97
D-4	Percentage of total sample showing evidence of dental attention.	98
D-5	Percentages of total sample having had dental work done by ethnic groups	98
D-6	Rates of noncarious teeth and mean age in sample A according to dental work status	99
D-7	Frequency of shovel-shaped incisors observed by region	102
D-8	Percentage frequency of crowding observed by nutritional class	104
D-9	Percentage frequency of tooth attrition observed by nutritional class.	105
I-1	Intestinal infestation in males, females, and total sample for each species of parasite tested	108
I-2	Combinations of persons positive and negative for parasites in the total sample tested	109
I-3	Positive infestation for each sex by various subgroups	110
I-4	Positive infestation frequencies by age group.	111

Table		Page
I-5	Positive infestation frequency by ethnic group	111
I-6	Positive infestation frequency by geographic region of residence	112
I-7	Incidence of positive infestation for three helminths and three protozoa	113
I-8	Chi-square tests for total helminths and protozoa between positive and negative individuals for various subsample categories	114
I-9	Chi-square tests for selected species of parasites between positive and negative individuals for various subsample categories	115
I-10	Wilcoxon sums test for sex difference for each species of parasite tested, and confidence level	116
I-11	Mean hemoglobin values of sample groups negative for all intestinal parasites and of those positive for helminths only	116
I-12	Male and female red cell counts by infestation for *Necator americanus*	117
I-13	Eosinophil count for persons with and without *Necator americanus* infestation	117
P-1	Mean values for various physiological characteristics of the Puerto Rican population	127
P-2	Mean hemoglobin measurements in grams per 100 cc. by nutritional groups	130
P-3	Mean hemoglobin measurements of high, medium, and low groups compared with the number of rural and urban residents in each	132
P-4	Mean hemoglobin measurements for high, medium, and low groups compared with mean ethnic groups	133
P-5	Mean blood pressure values for Puerto Ricans	134
P-6	Characteristics of individuals assorted according to systolic blood pressure	135
B-1	Comparison of total actual sample with total calculated sample for percentage frequencies of ABO and Rh blood types	139

Table	Page
GH-1 Characteristics of students and veterans	143
GH-2 Mean values for University of Puerto Rico students and veterans of World War II	144
GH-3 "Good Health" sample compared to total sample means for stature and weight	145

1

Description of the Puerto Rican Population

I. INTRODUCTION

THIS ANTHROPOLOGICAL STUDY is based on data gathered in Puerto Rico from June, 1948, through January, 1949. In it the biological characteristics, including the body dimensions, dental conditions, and certain physiological attributes of a selected sample of adult Puerto Rican males and females are described in the light of their environmental and hereditary backgrounds.

There were three original purposes. The first was to describe the biological characteristics of the Puerto Rican population in 1948 in order to set up a "bench mark" as a point of comparison for the future. To this end a carefully drawn sample, a miniature Puerto Rican population, was chosen to insure that our study would represent the entire island and that any conclusions drawn about the nature of the total population could be accepted with some security.

The second aim was to study the relationship between biological man and his environment; specifically, it was to analyze the physical variability in the Puerto Rican population in terms of differences in its environmental or genetic background. Inasmuch as the adult bodily structure, or phenotype, is the product of both environment and heredity, we wished to see what role each of these played in causing the physical differences observable in the island people.

The third, a subsidiary but important, purpose was to pave the way for establishing medical standards for Puerto Rico. These would give medical practitioners and health authorities average and normal values for the population to which an individual might be compared and his health status estimated. Since the island population presents a particular genetic and environmental complex, it is highly desirable that its members be judged by what is typical of their own nature and not by norms derived from alien populations.

Although we can thus outline the broad purposes briefly, it is obvious that within the confines innumerable specific problems and matters of special import appeared. The administrative officials in Puerto Rico were primarily interested in the practicality of the findings. The 1948 "bench mark" of physical characteristics furnishes data that serves to measure future change. Moreover, the effectiveness of public health institutions and expenditures can be ultimately tested by any measurable

II. DATA AND METHODS

THE PLAN of analysis was determined by the original three objectives set up. These were (1) to obtain a descriptive "bench mark" of the Puerto Rican population; (2) to investigate the causes of biological variability within that population; and (3) to establish realistic medical standards and norms for use in evaluating the health of the individual members. To accomplish these aims it was necessary to follow three systems of analysis.

For the first objective, statistics (for both sexes) were derived for each anthropological measurement in: *(A)* the total sample (Tables 1-24) and *(B)* subsamples which comprised (1) all persons who had lived over 20 years in one of the 15 geographic regions (see Chap. IV and Tables 25-61); (2) all persons included in each of the 4 nutritional classes (see Chap. VI and Tables 62-70); and (3) all persons in each of the ethnic groups (see Chap. V and Tables 71-95). From these statistics a description of the total population, and also of the ethnic, nutritional, and geographic divisions of it, was drawn up.

To meet the second objective, the variability was determined by finding the differences due to nutrition, ethnic origin, and geographic background as expressed on the adult phenotype. Health status as indicated by several measures of physical well being, such as blood count and hemoglobin level, were considered in light of the individual's background. Basically, we sought answers to the following questions:

1. To what extent do persons of similar ethnic origin (Group 3) and like nutritional background (Class 2) vary as a consequence of a lifetime residence in different geographical environments? (See Tables 96-111 and Graphs 1-15, where Sample A, representing such persons, is arrayed according to geographic region.)

2. To what extent do persons of like nutritional background (Class 2) vary according to differing ethnic origin? (See Tables 112-119 and Graphs 16-45, where Sample B is arrayed.)

3. To what extent do persons of the same ethnic background (Group 3) vary according to their nutritional status? (See Tables 120-125 and Graphs 16-45, where Sample C is arrayed.)

At this point it may be well to explain that the tables and graphs which are considered basic to the whole report, and which were done from the initial IBM tabulations, are numbered from 1 to 139 and from 1 to 76, respectively. They are reproduced in Part 2. Other tables designed to fit the discussion and analysis of various aspects of the study are designated by a letter prefix and are located in the appropriate chapters in Part 1. The significance of letter designations is as follows:

A or AR - Anthropometry or Anthropometric Results
D - Dental
I - Intestinal Parasites
GH - Good Health
P - Physiological Characteristics
S - Sample

 The fundamental sorting criteria, then, were, in addition to sex, the ethnic, nutritional, and geographic classifications. They were (and are) believed to be the major determinants of such variability as exists within the population and the anthropometric, dental, and physiological information was consistently analyzed on this basis. Additional sorting criteria, which included urban-rural residence status, age, occupation, and physical health, served to display patterns of variation for other characteristics within these groupings of the Puerto Ricans. The type of analysis used in a particular instance was that considered most appropriate.

 Answers to the third underlying problem, establishment of medical standards, were largely obtained from the results of the first two approaches. In addition, selected groups, such as students of the University of Puerto Rico, were examined as well to find out what the characteristics of the most healthy sub-sample might be. Members of these groups were deliberately chosen for superior background, to devise what standards could be used to evaluate the status of less healthy individuals. It is difficult, however, to locate any group in Puerto Rico that is *a priori* in good health and, therefore, 100 percent useful for demonstrating what all Puerto Ricans could hope to become. As a result, our standards of good health are probably minimal, but at least they show what levels some groups actually do attain. Moreover, some of our findings as height-weight-age tables, cell count, hemoglobin, and blood-pressure levels, and also many of the body measures provide useful information for health officials. Tables for these data are scattered under various subject headings but most of them are in the chapter (XIII) on "Good Health."

GENERAL PROCEDURE

Each subject in the sample population established for Puerto Rico was examined in three stages: First, by interview; second, by measurement; and third through dental and physiological observation. Samples of blood were taken either well before the initial interview or after the third stage; fecal samples were brought in subsequent to examination.

The three field-record forms are reproduced on the pages that follow. They give the outline and, in general, the order in which information was gathered. The interview data was covered in the first 16 recording spaces of each blank (and duplicated by carbon on blanks 2 and 3). The anthropometric measures were entered on sheet 1; the dental, physiological, and other data on sheets 2 and 3. The "Blood Sample Analysis Report" (A), the "Blood Typing Report" (B), and the "Feces Sample Analysis Report" (C) were attached to the samples when submitted to the laboratory; they were later coded and reattached to the field-record sheet. The IBM cards by which the data from the record blanks were coded are also illustrated, on the following pages.

A step-by-step outline of the routine followed to obtain the necessary information may prove helpful to anyone undertaking a similar investigation.

I. *The Interview.* Spaces 1-17 on the record sheets represent the data from this source. Broken down they cover the following items. The numbers preceding the information item listed refer to the column numbers on the IBM card assigned for that coded information.

1-4: Serial Number. The subject's name, sex, and municipio were recorded also in a serially arranged reference book. This was particularly useful in collating the blood and fecal reports with the primary record sheet.

5-6: Municipio. The code number for the municipio. Each of the 77 Puerto Rican municipios was given a number in which the first digit stood for the census region and the second for a particular municipio. The number assigned to a subject was for the place of his "biological residence" which was defined as "that place which was most important in determining the environment in which the individual matured." For the majority this was the place where they were born and had lived to maturity. Usually, in persons under age 30 this residence was easily ascertained. For people older the place of longest residence was the one recorded. In the analysis of regional

A STUDY IN HUMAN BIOLOGY 7

UNIVERSITY OF PUERTO RICO BIOLOGICAL SURVEY
FIELD RECORD BLANK

1-4 Serial N̲o̲.

Municipio.............................. Date.................
Name..

5-6 Municipio No.
7-8 Age
9 Ethnic factor

10 Children Living		0 to 8, 9-Nine or over (——)		: 0 for males.	
11 Children Dead		0 to 8, 9-Uncertain		: 0 for males.	
12 Occupation	1—Female	2—Hard Labor	3—Light Labor	4—Sedentary	
13 Residence	1—Urban	2—Rural-Neighbors	3—Rural-Alone		
14 Residence Time	1—All life	2—Birth to 20	3—Over 20	4—10-20	5—0-10
15 Nutritional Class	1—Upper	2—Upper Middle	3—Lower Middle	4—Lower	
16 Subject	1—Chronic-Serious	2—Slight	3—Accident	4—Preg.	5—Non-H.C.

39-40 Abdominal Fold	17 Control Number
41-42 Knee Width	18-20 Weight _____
43-45 Head Length	Acromion _____
46-48 Head Width	Radiale _____
Min Front _____	21-22 Upper Arm _____
49-51 Bizygomatic	Stylion _____
52-54 Bigonial	23-24 Lower Arm _____
55-57 Total Face	Dactylion _____
58-60 Upper Face	25-26 Total Arm _____
61-62 Nose Height	27-29 Height _____
63-64 Nose Width	Sit Height _____
65-67 Chest Circ	30-32 Leg Length _____
68-70 Waist Circ	33-34 Trunk Height _____
71-72 Biceps Circ	35-36 Biacromial _____
73-74 Leg Circ	37-38 Bicristal _____

ETHNIC FACTOR

	W				N	
Hair Form	0	4	8	12	16	0— 6-11
Nose Shape	0	2	4	6	8	1—12-17
Lip Thickness	0	2	4	6	8	2—18-23
Skin Color Index _____						3—24-29
Ethnic Factor Total _____						4—30-35

5—36-41
6—42-47
7—48-53
8—54-59
9—60-65

Fig. 1. Field record blank for anthropometry.

UNIVERSITY OF PUERTO RICO BIOLOGICAL SURVEY
FIELD RECORD BLANK

1-4 Serial Nº

Municipio.. Date................

Name ....

5-6 Municipio No.

7-8 Age

9 Ethnic factor

10 Children Living	0 to 8, 9-Nine or over (——)		: 0 for males.		
11 Children Dead	0 to 8, 9-Uncertain		: 0 for males.		
12 Occupation	1—Female	2—Hard Labor	3—Light Labor	4—Sedentary	
13 Residence	1—Urban	2—Rural-Neighbors	3—Rural-Alone		
14 Residence Time	1—All life	2—Birth to 20	3—Over 20	4—10-20	5—0-10
15 Nutritional Class	1—Upper	2—Upper Middle	3—Lower Middle	4—Lower	
16 Subject	1—Chronic-Serious	2—Slight	3—Accident	4—Preg.	5—Non-H.C.

DENTAL Code: 1—Present, 2—Carious, 3—Missing, 4—Non-erupted.   17 Control

Right Lower					Left Lower					Right-Upper					Left-Upper				
42 MInc	1	2	3	4	34 MInc	1	2	3	4	26 MInc	1	2	3	4	18 MInc	1	2	3	4
43 LInc	1	2	3	4	35 LInc	1	2	3	4	27 LInc	1	2	3	4	19 LInc	1	2	3	4
44 Can	1	2	3	4	36 Can	1	2	3	4	28 Can	1	2	3	4	20 Can	1	2	3	4
45 PM1	1	2	3	4	37 PM1	1	2	3	4	29 PM1	1	2	3	4	21 PM1	1	2	3	4
46 PM2	1	2	3	4	38 PM2	1	2	3	4	30 PM2	1	2	3	4	22 PM2	1	2	3	4
47 M1	1	2	3	4	39 M1	1	2	3	4	31 M1	1	2	3	4	23 M1	1	2	3	4
48 M2	1	2	3	4	40 M2	1	2	3	4	32 M2	1	2	3	4	24 M2	1	2	3	4
49 M3	1	2	3	4	41 M3	1	2	3	4	33 M3	1	2	3	4	25 M3	1	2	3	4

50 Dent. Work   1   2
1—Yes   2—No

Remarks:

51-52 Total No. 1
53-54 Total No. 2
55-56 Total No. 1 & No. 2
57-58 Total No. 3
59 Total No. 4
60 Crowding
61 Shovel Shaped
62 Peg Teeth
63 Extra Incisors
64 Attrition

BLOOD SAMPLE ANALYSIS REPORT
U.P.R. BIOLOGICAL SURVEY

A

Serial Number......................

Name................................

Municipio..........................

Sex M   F

Other Cells:

35-36 White Cell Count....................
37-39 Red Cell Count......................
40-41 Lymphocytes %
42-43 Monocytes %
44-45 Polymorphonuclear neutrophils %
46-47 Eosinophils %
48 Basophils %

Fig. 2.   Field record blank for dental status.

A STUDY IN HUMAN BIOLOGY

UNIVERSITY OF PUERTO RICO BIOLOGICAL SURVEY
FIELD RECORD BLANK

1-4 Serial N⁰

Municipio.......................... Date..................
Name ....

5-6 Municipio No.
7-8 Age
9 Ethnic factor

10 Children Living		0 to 8, 9-Nine or over (——)		: 0 for males.	
11 Children Dead		0 to 8, 9-Uncertain		: 0 for males.	
12 Occupation	1—Female	2—Hard Labor	3—Light Labor	4—Sedentary	
13 Residence	1—Urban	2—Rural-Neighbors	3—Rural-Alone		
14 Residence Time	1—All life	2—Birth to 20	3—Over 20	4—10-20	5—0-10
15 Nutritional Class	1—Upper	2—Upper Middle	3—Lower Middle	4—Lower	
16 Subject	1—Chronic-Serious	2—Slight	3—Accident	4—Preg.	5—Non-H.C.

PHYSIOLOGY

17 Control Number

Samples taken: R W Count
                 2 Pipettes......

Blood for typing	—— (5 cc)	18-20 Pulse
Blood Analysis	—— (5 cc)	21-23 Pressure, Syst.
Thick Smear	——	24-26 Pressure, Diast.
Blood Chemistry	—— (10 cc)	27-29 Hemoglobin, Gms.
Feces	——	30-33 Temperature

34 Tuberculosis   0-No Report   1-Negative
                   2-Arrested   3-Active

Chest X-Ray   ——   35-36 White Cell Count...............
Urine   ——   37-39 Red Cell Count................

BLOOD TYPING REPORT
U.P.R. BIOLOGICAL SURVEY

Serial number.....................
Name.............................
Municipio............... Sex M F

	1	2	3	4
49 ABO Type	0	A	B	AB
50 Type of A	A-1	A-2	Not A	
51 Type MN	M	N	MN	

B

	Neg	Pos
52 Rh Type	0	1
53 rh'	0	1
54 rh"	0	1
55 rh'rh"	0	1
56 Rh₀	0	1
57 Rh₀'	0	1
58 Rh₀"	0	1
59 Rh₀'Rh₀"	0	1

FECES SAMPLE ANALYSIS REPORT
U.P.R. BIOLOGICAL SURVEY

Serial Number ....
Name.....................................
Municipio................................
Sex M F

Parasitology	Neg	Pos
60 Uncinaria	1	2
61 Ascaris	1	2
62 Trichuris	1	2
63 Schistosoma	1	2
64 Other............	1	2
....		

C

Fig. 3. Field record blank for physiology.

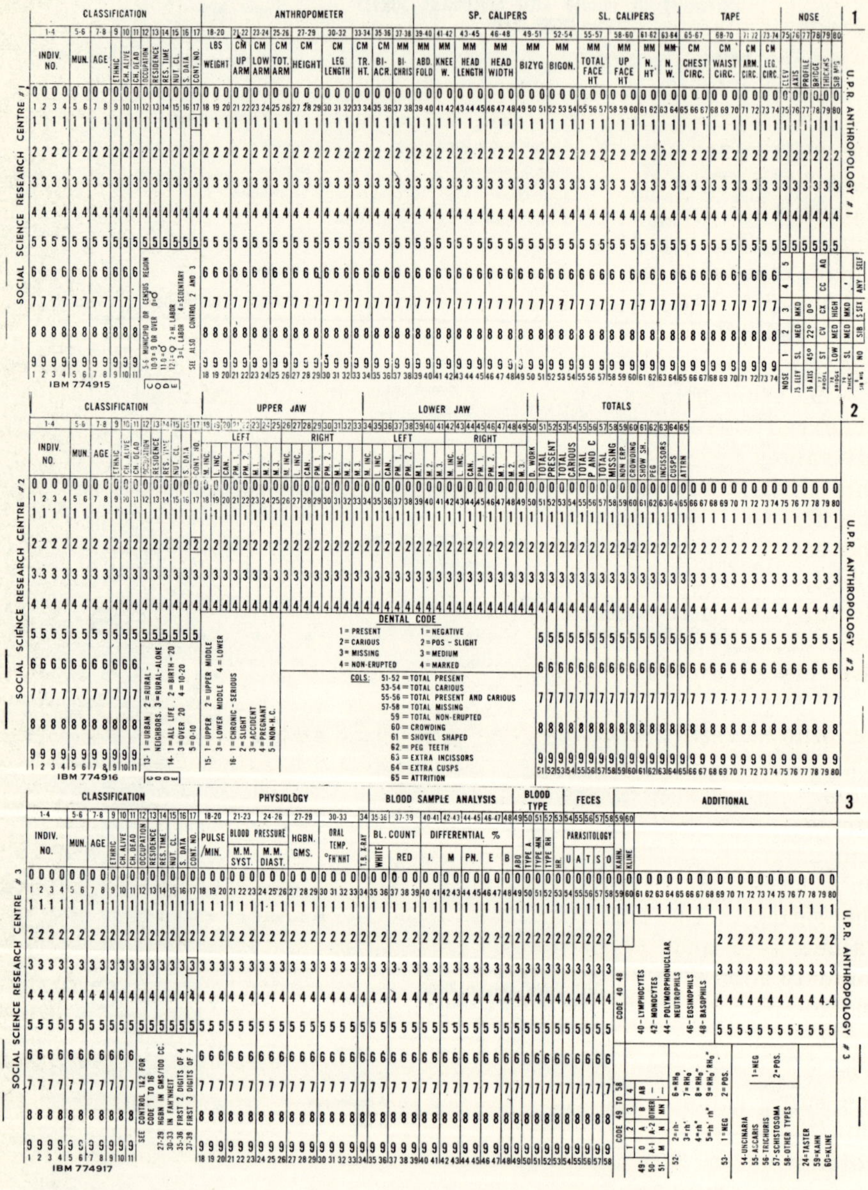

Fig. 4. IBM cards and codes.

geographic effect on body dimensions (Tables 25-61), only those persons coded as having been in a region "all their lives" or "over 20 years" were used.

7-8: Age. The subject's age in years to the last birthday.

9: Ethnic Factor. This factor is the racial indicator of the individual and is based upon values recorded for skin color, hair form, nose shape, and lip shape. The individual recorded values were entered in the space allotted on the form and then totaled. The highest values possible (32-16-8-8), a total of 64, would represent the most extreme Negroid phenotype; the lowest values (6-0-0-0), a total of 6, the most White. Actual value was scaled in the range listed in the ethnic factor space on record sheet 1, then the final value for the factor (ranging from 0 - 9) read off and recorded. For example, if the total of the observed values was 39, the ethnic factor would be 5, because all values from 36 to 41 inclusive were recorded as 5. It was this final factor value that was entered in space 9 at the top of the sheet. Those for each of the component parts making up the ethnic factor were recorded elsewhere on the final coded sheet, and each could be used separately in IBM sorting. Incidentally, with the exception of the comparison of the subject's inner-arm skin with the color scale, the subject was unaware that his racial phenotype was being evaluated.

The four values basic to the ethnic factor were obtained as follows: (1) Skin-color was read on a von Luschan ceramic chip color scale, and all values fell within a range of 6 to 32. This value was recorded in the blank in the fourth line of the ethnic factor space on sheet 1, and in columns 10-11 for males and columns 66-67 for females. (2) Hair form was measured on a five-point scale ranging from extreme White to Negro and the rating of the individual determined. Straight hair was valued as 0 and "pepper-corn" tight curls as 16, with intermediate forms intermediate. Value for hair form was recorded in column 58. (3) Nose shape was evaluated by the same system as for hair form except that the range was from 0 to 8. The value was recorded in column 65. (4) For lip thickness, the same value scale was used as for nose shape; extremely thin lips were recorded as 0. This value was recorded in column 68.

10: Children Living.

11: Children Dead. This number did not include still-births or miscarriages.

12: Occupation. For the males their stated occupation was rated and coded as either "hard," "light," or "sedentary."

All females were recorded as "♀" in this column. Agricultural work was classified as "hard;" all other occupations were evaluated individually in the light of information furnished by elaborating interview questions.

13: Residence. In Puerto Rico there are rural clusters or hamlets of houses which are neither urban or town concentrations nor dispersed and isolated as are rural dwellings. Biologically, residence class is possibly most important in terms of infectious disease transmission. Hence, our classification recognized three situations: "urban" (crowded city contact), "rural-neighbors" (clusters of houses but not urban crowding), and "rural-alone" (single houses). In the common demographic use of these terms, our classes "rural-neighbors" and "rural-alone" would be combined into "rural," but our "urban" would correspond to "urban." We made no restrictions on the size of the urban cluster. All municipio centers were considered urban.

14: Residence Time. Length of residence in years at the place of primary or biological residence. In determining variability by geographic regions, only persons in residence more than 20 years were included, that is, (1) all life; (2) birth to 20; and (3) over 20.

15: Nutritional Class. The nutritional background of the individual. This is fully discussed in Chapter VI. It is sufficient to say here that "1" represents the best and "4" the poorest class, with "2" and "3" the intermediate ratings. Which nutritional class was assigned depended on interview information, but the definition of each class was based on a schedule and outline derived from nutritional survey data.

16: Subject. The subject's sample source. It was recorded in this space and also double punched in column 17 of the IBM card in the unassigned digit spaces. See Chapter III for a description of the sample for the various sources contributing to it.

17: Card Number. The number used to distinguish between the three IBM cards for each sample subject.

Interview Summary. Between June, 1948, and January, 1949, the data in spaces 1-17 were gathered by Rupert I. Murrill. After that period, Carmen LaFontaine, who was trained by Murrill before he returned to the United States, completed the survey interviewing. Hence, there was essentially clear continuity and comparability in procedure throughout the survey. Occasional wire recordings of interviews were made to check the wording of questions and other details. The initial interview took about 5 minutes to complete; after that, the subject moved to the measuring station.

II. *Anthropometric Measurement* (Card No. 1). The spaces 18-70 on the record sheets represent these data. The number in parentheses following each measurement, or landmark, refers to one of the numbers used by Martin, which are standard anthropometric reference points.

18-20: Weight (A 71). Body weight in pounds without shoes but with indoor clothing. Individuals were weighed on a balance scale which was frequently checked for accuracy. Approximately 2 pounds for summer clothing should be subtracted to get the nude weight. All weights are fairly comparable, because the excess garments of the subjects were shed before weighing.

21-22: Upper Arm; 23-24: Lower Arm; and 25-26: Total Arm.

In the standard Martin technique, the one employed here, the body landmarks, Acromion (A 8), shoulder; Radiale (A 9) elbow; Stylion (A 10), wrist; and Dactylion (A 11) finger tip, are measured from the floor with the subject in a constant posture. Measure A 9 subtracted from A 8 gives the upper-arm length, A 10 from A 9 gives the lower-arm length, and A 11 from A 10 gives hand length; also, measure A 11 subtracted from A 8 gives total arm length. These body landmarks are so designed to give the dimension the skeletal segments.

27-29: Height or Stature (A 1): Standing height taken without shoes and giving the full, erect stature from floor to highest point on the head.

Sitting Height (A 23). This measure was taken directly for use in computing leg length but was not recorded on the IBM cards.

30-32: Leg Length. Standing height minus sitting height.

33-34: Trunk Height (A 25). Height of trunk from the sternal notch to the table on which the subject was seated. Care was taken that the feet were elevated sufficiently so that pressure of the thighs did not raise the trunk or lift the ischia above closest contact with the table.

35-36: Biacromial (A 35). Shoulder width.

37-38: Bicristal (A 40). Hip width.

39-40: Abdominal Fold (no Martin number). The diameter between surfaces of a skin fold picked up by the thumb and forefinger from the abdomen just superior to the right anterior superior iliac crest. Tissue was pulled out so that thickness of skin and subcutaneous fat was at a minimum. The purpose here was to get some measure of subcutaneous fat for use as a nutritional index. It has been successfully used in many studies for this purpose.

41-42: Knee Width (no Martin number). Maximum breadth across the knee while it is flexed (the subject sitting on table with foot on seat of a chair). This measurement represents the maximum bicondylar width of the femur and it was taken with spreading calipers. Care was used to select points lateral to the femur-condyle surfaces and not on the tibia or interarticular points.

43-45: Head Length (B 1).
46-47: Head Width (B 3).
Minimal Frontal (B 4). Diameter across the forehead, above the eyes and between the frontal crests. It was recorded but not punched on the IBM cards.

49-51: Bigonial (B 8). The maximum jaw width.
55-57: Total Face (B 18). Height of face from the lower projection of the chin to nasion (approximately the deepest depression above the bridge of the nose).

59-60: Upper Face (B 20). Height of face between nasion and the point between the middle upper incisors at the edge of the gums.

61-62: Nose Height (B 21). Length of nose from lowest tip, where it joins the upper lip, to nasion.

63-64: Nose Width (B 13). Width of nose between the flaring alae. This is usually the maximum nose breadth.

66-67: Chest Circumference (A 61). Circumference of chest when at rest, neither expanded or expired, at the height of the nipples. (It was not taken on females.)

69-70: Waist Circumference (B 62). Waist measurement at belt line or the minimum circumference between the chest and hips.

71-72: Biceps Circumference (B 65). Maximum circumference of the upper arm extended but relaxed.

73-74: Leg Circumference (B 69). Maximum circumference of calf of the leg while relaxed.

75-80: These spaces served to record various data such as migration status, time in prison, and individual characteristics.

After anthropometric measuring, the subject was examined with regard to the other items on record sheets 2 and 3, in the following order.

III. *Dental Information* (Card No. 2). The data obtained on condition and character of teeth are fully covered in Chapter IX, which see. Observations, according to the code below on each of the 32 teeth were recorded in columns 18-49.

By means of a dental mirror, probe, and adequate lighting, the condition of each tooth was noted. Tooth status was recorded in one of four coding categories: (1) Present and noncarious. (2) Carious. A filled tooth or one with one or more observable caries (the number of caries, if more than one per tooth, was not recorded). (3) Missing. (4) Nonerupted. This category applied mainly to third molars, but other teeth were recorded as such in persons who, for instance, lacked lateral incisors for which there was no space nor recollection, on the subject's part, of extractions.

IV. *Physiological Data and Blood and Fecal Reports* (Card No. 3). Following the dental examination the subject was examined for the following data, which is in blanks 18-33, recorded on field record sheet 3. In Chapters XI-XII these data are analyzed, see there for a full discussion of procedures.

18-20: Pulse.
21-23: Blood Pressure. Systolic.
24: Taster P. T. C. (Phenyl-thio-carbamide).
25-26: Blood Pressure. Diastolic.
27-29: Hemoglobin. In grams per 100 cc.
30-33: Oral Temperature. In degrees and tenths Fahrenheit.
34: Tuberculosis. This information, though recorded, was not used as we had serious doubts as to its accuracy.

V. *Sample Examinations* (Card No. 3). A: Blood-sample Analysis Report. From a slide taken by venipuncture and stained, differential cell counts of the blood sample were made by the regular, technical staff of the laboratories of the Puerto Rican Department of Health. These were entered on Form A and later coded.

B: Blood Typing Report. A sample of blood in a sterile, oxylated test tube was forwarded to the Blood Bank Laboratory of the School of Tropical Medicine, where it was typed under the direction of Señor N. Dobal. Reports of the typing for the ABO, MN, and Rh groups were then coded and recorded on Form B.

C: Feces-sample Analysis Report. A numbered container, marked also with the name of the subject, was given to each person to be returned with a sample of his feces. These samples were delivered to the School of Tropical Medicine for examination and the results were coded and recorded on Form C. The four entities listed on the original record sheet was expanded to include 17 of the significant helminths or protozoa found in Puerto Rico (see Chapter X).

OTHER ORIGINAL DATA

1. Photography. With funds supplied by the Viking Fund, Inc. (now the Wenner-Gren Foundation for Antrhopological Research), the author purchased photographic equipment to test the use of photoanthropometry on a large series of subjects. The equipment consisted of a 36-mm Bell and Howell turret movie camera which was equipped with both short and long focal-length lenses and a device for synchronizing a stroboscopic flash bulb with each exposure. Both the flash and the shutter were controlled by a single press button held by the operator. A stand on which the nude subject could be positioned and rotated for front, side, and rear views was used. The subjects were posed erect on the revolving stand at a given distance from the camera. The distance was calculated so that the tallest individuals filled the entire single frame. A telephoto lens on the turret enabled one to obtain a "close-up" of the head and neck without moving the subject. Later an Eastman 2 X 2 slide projector was so adjusted that the same lenses used in taking the films could project the negative image on a calibrated, beaded screen that was at the same distance from the lens as was the subject when the picture had been taken. In this way it was possible to project accurately the full-sized image of the individual for subsequent measuring.

Primarily, the purpose of this photography was to test the feasibility of obtaining a permanent record of a sample subject as a source of future measurement. For example, should data analysis indicate that the dimension of some part of the body not previously obtained by standard techniques was needed, the photographic record would make it available. We also put this equipment to intensive use to test whether or not it would be efficient for making rapid, large-sample anthropometric surveys, for detailed anthropometry is a time-consuming job and numbers of subjects are often hard to obtain in a sufficient flow to fit measuring speed. If one needs large samples to represent large populations and these are to be readily assembled, so that highly comparable records may be obtained, photoanthropometry seems to provide a solution. About 550 males in our sample were photographed in the nude, three views for each. A top rate per hour for 50 persons was attained. We feel, therefore, that this was a successful attempt to get: (1) photographs rapidly, with the subject in accurate pose which can be easily duplicated and from which measurements can be consistently taken, thus reducing error between individuals and phases of a lengthy survey. From our point of view the method was demonstrated to be feasible. Moreover, it should be pointed out that while this technique has optimum use for special problems or measurements, it would be of value for traditional studies.

    2. Mineral Content of Water. Analyses for the mineral content of the various municipal water supplies was provided by the Puerto Rican Department of Public Health. The Department collects samples at frequent intervals as a part of a regular program to test the quality of drinking water. Its data on mineral content was used by us in an analysis to test for causes of geographic difference in caries rates due to variation in amount of calcium or fluorine.

    3. Infant Mortality. Data on infant mortality was gathered through interviews of a select sample of upper-class women by Dr. Raymond Scheele. His data were used for comparative purposes and are reported on page 76 and in Table AR-2.

    4. Demographic and Vital Statistics. Current statistics from the Bureau of Vital Statistics of Puerto Rico, furnished by Dr. Jose Janer, were used together with births and death rates, in our calculations of the sample structure. Lists of causes of death and other on-going compilations were provided by other bureaus of the Department of Public Health.

    5. Prison Data. Although, for each prisoner examined, the Department of Prisons generously provided data on the length of time spent in prison, crime committed, and so forth, except for time in prison, they are not used in our present report.

    6. Nutritional Data. The nutrition specialists in the Department of Public Health made a detailed household study of the food habits of a selected sample of people. Results were used to assess the actual intakes of individuals. The data, which are reported in the chapter (VI) on nutrition, provided a reliable basis for evaluating our nutritional classification system.

III. THE SAMPLE

THE SAMPLE was made up of subjects selected to be representative of the adult population of the whole island, and was, in effect, a miniature Puerto Rico. To determine a sample structure of this nature the census data of 1935 and 1940 for Puerto Rico was extrapolated and adjusted to obtain the probable population breakdown for 1948. The Bureau of Vital Statistics of Puerto Rico, under the direction of Dr. Jose Janer, provided this for us and included a breakdown by sex, urban-rural residence, and age grouping for each municipio. Use of the official registry of births and migrations made this estimate more accurate than if it had been restricted merely to extrapolations. It took into account the changes of the war years and various internal developments that otherwise might have been excluded. From these data the number of males and females between 20 and 45 years of age which were needed from each municipio to give a total sample of 3,333 was calculated. This "calculated" sample is given, together with the "actual" sample achieved for each sex, in Table S-1.[1] These sample data are summarized in Table S-1A.

When the survey was first planned, a sample of 5000 was projected, but after the first few months of measuring, this goal was reduced by one-third or to 3333. As a result of this revision the numbers obtained in San Juan, Carolina, and Loiza (Regions 2 and 4), where we began our measuring, are above the final sample goals for these places. As San Juan is the urban "melting pot" of Puerto Rico, the excess there is probably not harmful, since many of its inhabitants originated in other parts of the island. Actually, the total sample amounted to 3562 (1649 females and 1913 males) because it included a prison sample of 395 males. The prison group was added, in part, to fill out the required number of males from some of the regions and, in part, to secure a sufficiently large sample of prisoners in order to test the hypothesis that they might form a selected group with, in consequence, distinct physical traits. By so doing, however, we ran 247 males over the 1666 of the calculated sample.

---

[1] For the detailed basis used in the calculation of the sample and the basic demographic data, see Table 1 of Murrill's (1955) report.

TABLE S-1
SAMPLE STRUCTURE

Total sample obtained compared to calculated sample by sex, municipio, and region. A = Census Region; B = Region number for this study.

REGION		MUNICIPIO	SAMPLE			
			Male		Female	
A	B		Calc.	Actual	Calc.	Actual
1	1	Aguadilla	34	37	34	42
	1	Camuy	15	14	15	16
	1	Hatillo	15	6	15	7
	1	Isabela	18	11	19	11
	1	Quebradillas	9	18	9	18
Total			91	86	92	94
2	2	Arecibo	64	108	64	71
	3	Barceloneta	15	14	15	7
	4	Bayamon	35	54	36	27
	5	Carolina	21	103	22	75
	4	Catano	10	8	10	2
	3	Dorado	8	16	8	--
	4	Guaynabo	18	27	19	3
	5	Loiza	17	73	18	37
	3	Manati	24	38	25	22
	5	Rio Grande	12	22	12	9
	2	Rio Piedras	85	32	86	54
	2	San Juan	212	201	215	188
	3	Toa Alta	9	16	10	10
	3	Toa Baja	10	21	10	7
	5	Trujillo Alto	9	2	9	4
	3	Vega Alta	10	35	10	28
	3	Vega Baja	17	36	17	25
Total			576	806	586	569
3	6	Ceiba	4	6	4	3
	6	Culebra	--	2	--	3
	6	Fajardo	19	35	19	35
	6	Humacao	26	35	26	30
	6	Luquillo	6	2	6	6
	6	Maunabo	9	5	9	8
	6	Naguabo	13	15	13	9
	6	Vieques	8	4	8	2
	6	Yabucoa	26	16	24	9
Total			111	120	109	105

TABLE S-1 (Cont'd)

REGION		MUNICIPIO	SAMPLE			
			Male		Female	
A	B		Calc.	Actual	Calc.	Actual
4	7	Arroyo	11	10	10	15
	10	Coamo	20	13	19	10
	9	Guanica	11	11	11	1
	7	Guayama	30	29	29	53
	9	Guayanilla	14	2	14	--
	7	Juana Diaz	23	18	23	23
	9	Lajas	13	13	12	5
	7	Patillas	15	16	15	28
	7	Penuelas	12	8	12	13
	8	Ponce	100	89	99	115
	9	Sabana Grande	13	14	12	4
	7	Salinas	18	13	18	12
	7	Santa Isabel	12	4	12	7
	10	Villalba	10	19	10	29
	9	Yauco	25	24	25	3
Total			327	283	321	318
5	11	Aguada	14	17	15	20
	11	Anasco	12	19	12	9
	11	Cabo Rojo	23	29	24	14
	11	Hormigueros	5	6	5	7
	12	Mayaguez	75	103	75	101
	11	Moca	14	7	14	9
	11	Rincon	7	3	8	3
	11	San German	21	21	22	11
Total			171	205	175	174
6	13	Adjuntas	22	13	21	14
	13	Ciales	15	23	15	20
	13	Jayuya	11	6	11	7
	13	Lares	22	25	22	30
	13	Las Marias	7	11	7	13
	13	Maricao	6	9	6	3
	13	San Sebastian	26	27	25	26
	13	Utuado	29	29	29	35
Total			138	143	136	148

TABLE S-1 (Cont'd)

REGION		MUNICIPIO	SAMPLE			
			Male		Female	
A	B		Calc.	Actual	Calc.	Actual
7	15	Aguas Buenas	10	12	10	10
	14	Aibonito	12	11	12	10
	14	Barranquitas	14	10	13	10
	15	Caguas	49	72	48	70
	14	Cayey	25	29	24	29
	14	Cidra	14	13	14	12
	14	Comerio	14	16	14	17
	14	Corozal	16	16	15	16
	15	Gurabo	11	4	11	3
	15	Juncos	16	5	16	3
	15	Las Piedras	11	9	11	3
	14	Morovis	13	20	13	12
	14	Naranjito	11	13	11	11
	14	Orocovis	16	15	16	8
	15	San Lorenzo	20	25	20	25
Total			252	270	248	241
TOTAL SAMPLE			1666	1913	1667	1649

TABLE S-1A
SUMMARY DISTRIBUTION OF SAMPLE BY REGION

Region	Male				Female			
	Calculated		Actual		Calculated		Actual	
	No.	%	No.	%	No.	%	No.	%
1	91	5.5	86	4.5	92	5.5	93	5.6
2	576	34.5	807	42.2	586	35.2	569	34.5
3	111	6.7	120	6.3	109	6.5	105	6.4
4	327	19.6	283	14.8	321	19.2	318	19.3
5	171	10.3	204	10.6	175	10.5	174	10.6
6	138	8.3	143	7.5	136	8.2	149	9.0
7	252	15.1	270	14.1	248	14.9	241	14.6
Total	1666	100.0	1913	100.0	1667	100.0	1649	100.0

The sample is composed largely (60 percent) of persons examined in Health Centers maintained by the Department of Public Health. The rest came from other sources (see Table S-15). People came to the Health Centers for several reasons; namely, to secure the health certificates required in certain categories of jobs, to have routine examinations done, such as tests for parasites or for venereal disease, or they came just to pass the time of day. To the Municipal Hospitals some came because of illness, most frequently colds and fevers, but for the most part the individuals taken from that source represent routine outpatients who were not involved in gross pathologies. In any event, we made special effort to select "average" people, typical of the general population. This does not mean, of course, that all were free of illness or in completely good health, for had this been a requirement we would have found very few to examine. Besides those from government health facilities, some persons were obtained from factories and others were government employees, workers on air bases and farms, or students at the University of Puerto Rico.

Selection of sample subjects to meet the calculated numbers was made on the basis of (1) residence and (2) age. Residence quotas were filled by going to certain municipios for a given number of each sex. We took at random anyone who was between 20 and 45 years old. But in some instances, younger or older persons would voluntarily get in line to be measured and, unless they were obviously immature, senile, or grossly pathological, they were not excluded. As a result, some 4 percent of the sample are younger, in the 17-19 age group, and 5 percent are older, and over 45. They too "represent" Puerto Rico, but they are outside our original sample calculations. A continuous tally by sex and municipio was all that we used to control our detailed sample structure. Although exact age, urban-rural residence, nutritional status, ethnic factor, occupation, and physical status were not in general selected for, since our sample is well composed, it is also representative of them (see Tables S-1A, S-2, S-3 and S-4). Urban-rural residence, age, and representativeness by regions are categories that can be compared with the census data. While there are census reports on frequency of "colored" in the population, they are not accurate, because the definition of who is or who is not "colored" varied, depending upon the personal opinion of the census taker. Comparisons between the rural-urban residence status in our sample and that in the census data are given in Table S-2. In spite of regional discrepancies in distribution, the percentage of urban

TABLE S-2

URBAN PERCENTAGE DISTRIBUTION OF SAMPLE COMPARED TO CENSUS DATA

Region	Sample		Census (1948)
	Males*	Females	Male + Female
1	23%	18%	24%
2	34	40	53
3	37	47	22
4	44	522	41
5	48	48	41
6	21	23	16
7	42	44	21
Total of Population...	34	44	38

*Including prisoners (classified by previous residence status). Only 26 percent of the prisoners were of urban origin.

residents in our total sample equals that in the 1948 census (both are 38 percent). Since many biological characteristics vary according to residence, this agreement is especially significant.

The sample-census comparisons in age distribution are given in Table S-3. Age comparisons between the sample and parental population are good, especially when the selection procedures we employed for age are kept in mind.

While the residence comparisons and concordance for age between sample and census data were good, those for regional representativeness were only rather good; these comparative data are given in Table S-4. Absence of complete agreement in the latter frequencies is largely due to the fact that an individual in our sample was classified according to the region of his longest residence. Since our purpose was to assign a subject to the regional scene which had exerted the greatest environmental influence upon him, the difficulty in reconciling our data of residence with the census regional distribution is apparent. For example, if we had already filled our sample requirements for Carolina and then later, while working in Caguas, measured some resident of the latter municipio who

TABLE S-3

DISTRIBUTION OF SAMPLE BY AGE GROUPS AND SEX COMPARED TO 1940 CENSUS

Age Group	Sample Frequencies		Census 1940	
	Male	Female	Male	Female
17-19	4.8	4.7	....	....
20-24	30.9	30.0	31.9	32.2
25-34	37.8	36.8	38.7	39.1
35-44	20.9	23.5	29.4	28.7
45+	5.6	4.9	....	....

TABLE S-4

REGIONAL PERCENTAGE DISTRIBUTIONS OF SAMPLE AND 1940 CENSUS POPULATIONS

Census Region	Sample					Census	
	Males		Females	Total		Age Group (20-45)	Total of Population
	1*	2†		1*	2†		
1	4.4%	5.2%	5.0%	5.6%	5.4%	5.6%	5.7%
2	42.2	43.1	34.5	38.6	38.6	34.8	33.1
3	6.3	3.7	6.4	6.3	5.1	6.6	6.8
4	14.9	14.2	19.3	16.9	16.9	19.4	18.8
5	10.6	10.1	10.6	10.6	10.3	10.4	10.5
6	7.5	8.7	9.0	8.2	8.9	8.2	9.0
7	14.1	15.0	14.6	14.4	14.8	15.0	16.1
Total	100.0	100.0	100.0	100.0	100.0	100.0	100.0

*Including prisoners (assigned to region of residence before incarceration).

† Excluding prisoners.

had actually spent 34 of his 35 years in the former, our Carolina sample thereby was augmented and in excess of the calculated need. In this way some 277 persons had their "biological" or longest residence in places other than where they were measured; that is, 118 of those examined in San Juan; 33, in Ponce; 20, in Mayaguez; 17, in Caguas; and 15, in Rio Piedras. No other place had as many as ten. It is, therefore, mainly because our method of residence classification differed that exact correspondence between sample and census numbers by region was not achieved. Lest our sample quality be underrated, it should be pointed out, however, that, comparing the female sample and the census for the 20-to 45-year-olds, there is no region in our sample in which the disagreement is over 0.8 of 1 percent. For the males all discrepancies are under 1 percent, except in regions 2 and 4 and the discrepancy in those regions does not introduce a significant sample error.

To sum up, comparison of our data with the census data indicate that, in terms of age, residence, and regional distribution for both sexes, our sample can be taken as highly representative of the Puerto Rican parental population. Furthermore, no discrepancy exists which would suggest that our sample is out of line for other factors and should not be used as a basis for evaluating the nature of the people of Puerto Rico. A complete breakdown by categories of sample is given in Tables S-5 to S-14.

TABLE S-5

MALE SAMPLE BREAKDOWN BY CENSUS REGION FOR OCCUPATION AND RESIDENCE CATEGORIES

Census Region	Sample Region	Sample Number	Sample Region Calculated Sample Number	Actual* Sample	Census Region Calculated	Census Region Actual	Occupation Hard Labor	Occupation Light Labor	Occupation Sedentary	Residence§ Urban	Residence§ Rural†	Residence§ Rural‡
1	1	79	91	85	91	85	44	16	19	19	5	55
2	2	314	361	341	...	...	112	133	69	134	29	151
	3	99	93	176	...	...	84	4	11	14	9	76
	4	58	63	89	...	...	55	1	2	6	3	49
3	5	183	59	201	576	807	158	11	14	25	33	125
	6	57	111	120	111	120	31	17	9	22	2	33
4	7	79	121	98	...	...	52	14	13	27	1	51
	8	88	100	90	...	...	40	32	16	49	0	39
	9	24	76	64	...	...	7	1	16	11	2	11
5	10	25	30	32	327	284	8	7	10	6	2	17
6	11	75	96	101	...	204	48	8	19	16	2	57
	12	78	75	103	171		49	16	13	54	1	23
	13	132	138	143	138	143	79	30	23	30	8	94
7	14	128	135	143	...	...	61	26	41	59	9	60
	15	99	117	127	252	270	53	32	14	39	1	59
		1518	1666	1913	1666	1913	881	348	289	511	107	900

*Males, plus prisoners.
†With neighbors.
‡Alone.
§Males, excluding prisoners.

TABLE S-6

MALE SAMPLE BREAKDOWN BY ETHNIC GROUP FOR
RESIDENCE AND OCCUPATION CATEGORIES

Ethnic Group	Number in Sample	Residence			Occupation		
		Urban	Rural*	Rural⁺	Hard Labor	Light Labor	Sedentary
0	4	3	0	1	1	1	2
1	46	23	3	20	11	19	16
2	343	104	30	209	163	91	89
3	677	242	32	403	380	162	135
4	188	72	8	108	119	44	25
5	54	20	5	29	36	11	7
6	62	32	7	23	37	15	10
7	76	12	12	52	66	5	5
8	68	3	10	55	68	0	0
9	0	0	0	0	0	0	0
Total	1518	511	107	900	881	348	289

*With neighbors.
†Alone.

TABLE S-7

FEMALE SAMPLE BREAKDOWN BY REGION FOR RESIDENCE AND RESIDENCE TIME CATEGORIES

Census Region	Region of Present Residence	Sample Region		Census Region		Residence			Residence Time				
	Region	Sample Number	Calculated Sample*	Calculated Sample	Actual	Urban	Rural†	Rural‡	All Life	Birth to 20	Over 20 yrs.	10-20	0-10
1	1	93	92	92	93	17	3	73	62	12	6	7	6
	2	312	365	...	...	154	35	123	92	88	2	119	11
	3	100	95	...	...	23	2	75	68	6	8	17	1
	4	32	65	...	...	15	0	17	10	6	7	3	6
2	5	125	61	586	569	35	25	65	76	25	0	22	2
3	6	105	109	109	105	49	8	48	44	17	2	27	15
	7	151	119	...	...	77	1	73	99	17	9	24	2
	8	115	99	...	...	65	0	50	65	16	9	25	2
	9	13	74	...	...	8	0	5	2	6	1	4	0
4	10	39	29	321	318	14	0	25	23	2	3	11	0
	11	73	100	...	...	16	2	55	39	6	7	21	0
5	12	101	75	175	174	67	0	34	56	4	5	35	1
6	13	149	136	136	149	34	7	108	93	18	6	20	12
	14	127	132	...	...	50	5	72	66	18	7	25	11
7	15	114	116	248	241	57	7	50	76	13	3	18	4
Total		1649	1667	1667	1649	681	95	873	871	254	75	378	71

*Calculated to represent each region proportionally correct in a total sample of 1667.
†With neighbors. ‡Alone.

TABLE S-8

PRISON SAMPLE BY REGION FOR NUTRITIONAL AND ETHNIC GROUP*

Region	Number	Nutritional Class			Ethnic Group							
		Upper Middle	Lower Middle	Lower	1	2	3	4	5	6	7	8
		2	3	4								
1	6	6	0	..	..	0	4	1	0	0	1	0
2	27	23	4	..	..	5	9	1	0	5	4	3
3	77	62	15	..	..	7	28	6	1	10	17	8
4	31	30	1	..	..	8	11	1	0	8	3	0
5	18	12	6	..	..	0	0	0	0	0	4	14
6	63	60	3	..	..	7	26	8	7	9	5	1
7	19	12	7	..	..	4	7	4	1	1	2	0
8	2	2	0	..	..	1	1	0	0	0	0	0
9	40	22	16	2	1	5	27	6	1	0	0	0
10	7	5	2	..	..	1	3	1	0	2	0	0
11	26	17	9	..	..	7	13	3	1	0	0	2
12	25	11	14	..	1	2	17	1	1	3	0	..
13	11	9	2	..	..	2	8	1	0	0	0	..
14	15	13	2	..	1	3	7	2	1	0	1	..
15	28	26	2	..	..	6	14	6	0	0	2	..
Total	395	310	83	2	3	58	175	41	13	38	39	28

*No prisoners in Ethnic Groups 0 or 9, nor in Nutritional Class 1 are included.

TABLE S-9

PRISON SAMPLE BREAKDOWN BY REGION AND OCCUPATION, RESIDENCE, AND RESIDENCE TIME CATEGORIES

Region	Number	Occupation				Residence			Residence Time			
		Hard Labor	Light Labor	Sedentary	Urban	Rural*	Rural†	All Life	Birth to 20	Over 20 yrs.	10-20	0-10
1	6	5	1	..	1	..	5	0	0	2	4	..
2	27	21	6	..	3	..	24	3	2	18	4	..
3	77	70	7	..	0	..	77	2	8	65	2	..
4	31	30	1	..	0	..	31	0	2	26	3	..
5	18	17	1	..	0	..	18	2	3	11	2	..
6	63	48	13	2	23	1	39	3	6	28	26	..
7	19	18	1	..	6	..	13	9	3	3	4	..
8	2	1	1	..	2	..	0	2	0	0	0	..
9	40	36	4	..	21	..	19	27	2	5	6	..
10	7	5	2	..	4	..	3	1	2	1	3	..
11	26	24	2	..	6	..	20	14	1	6	5	..
12	25	22	3	..	21	..	4	20	0	1	4	..
13	11	8	3	..	1	..	10	2	0	4	5	..
14	15	12	31	..	6	..	9	0	0	3	12	..
15	28	21	6	1	9	1	18	0	2	7	19	..
Total	395	338	54	3	103	2	290	85	31	180	99	0

*With neighbors. †Alone.

TABLE S-10

FEMALE SAMPLE BREAKDOWN BY REGION, AND NUTRITIONAL AND ETHNIC CATEGORIES

Region	Number	Nutritional Class					Ethnic Group									
		Upper	Upper Middle	Lower Middle	Lower	0	1	2	3	4	5	6	7	8	9
1	93	2	58	32	1	0	4	47	31	4	2	2	2	1	0
2	312	19	239	53	1	1	9	92	117	52	16	18	7	0	0
3	100	5	89	5	1	0	0	36	42	9	8	3	2	0	0
4	32	3	21	8	0	0	8	13	5	4	2	0	0	0	0
5	125	5	74	41	5	0	3	20	37	27	9	19	10	0	0
6	105	5	79	20	1	0	4	19	41	17	6	13	3	2	0
7	151	6	118	17	10	0	0	16	71	34	12	7	8	3	0
8	115	5	94	10	6	0	0	29	64	12	6	1	3	0	0
9	13	2	8	3	0	0	1	5	6	0	1	0	0	0	0
10	39	2	30	7	0	1	1	14	17	5	2	0	0	0	0
11	73	5	35	33	2	0	3	26	35	5	1	2	0	0	0
12	101	11	60	28	2	0	1	22	51	18	3	4	2	0	0
13	149	7	109	24	9	0	8	50	76	15	0	0	0	0	0
14	127	12	98	14	3	0	12	42	57	14	1	0	0	0	1
15	114	14	90	7	3	0	0	32	55	14	7	3	2	1	0
Total	1649	103	1202	302	42	2	54	463	705	230	76	72	39	7	1

TABLE S-11

MALE SAMPLE BREAKDOWN BY REGION AND NUTRITIONAL AND ETHNIC CATEGORIES

Census Region	Region	Nutritional Class				Ethnic Group									
		Upper	Upper Middle	Lower Middle	Lower	0	1	2	3	4	5	6	7	8	9
		1	2	3	4										
1	1	6	43	30	0	0	4	27	33	9	1	3	2	0	0
	2	23	229	58	4	2	19	90	126	41	13	16	5	2	0
2	3	3	91	5	0	0	1	20	39	9	3	4	15	8	0
	4	0	54	4	0	0	0	5	18	3	3	4	11	14	0
3	5	4	135	40	4	0	2	24	41	21	7	14	33	41	0
	6	3	32	20	2	0	3	12	17	11	7	5	2	0	0
	7	3	55	15	6	0	0	10	39	12	8	6	4	0	0
4	8	5	69	10	4	0	0	23	50	13	1	1	0	0	0
	9	10	11	3	0	0	0	5	15	3	1	0	0	0	0
	10	2	20	2	1	0	1	5	14	4	1	0	0	0	0
5	11	11	40	24	0	0	3	15	43	12	1	1	0	0	0
	12	8	43	25	2	0	1	9	41	13	4	5	3	2	0
6	13	4	108	17	3	1	8	41	72	9	1	0	0	0	0
	14	12	101	10	5	1	4	39	70	10	2	2	0	0	0
7	15	6	78	11	4	0	0	18	59	18	1	1	1	1	0
Total		100	1109	274	35	4	46	343	677	188	54	62	76	68	0

TABLE S-12

SAMPLE BREAKDOWN OF UNIVERSITY OF PUERTO RICO
FEMALES AND WORLD WAR II VETERANS BY REGION

Geographic Region	Females	Veterans
1	1	11
2	20	13
3	2	7
4	1	5
5	7	6
6	13	4
7	7	6
8	1	14
9	3	14
10	3	6
11	9	18
12	4	7
13	7	14
14	15	30
15	15	10
Total	108	165

34 THE PUERTO RICAN POPULATION

TABLE S-13
STRUCTURE OF NUTRITIONAL SUBSAMPLES

Sample	Nutritional Class	Number	Residence		Time in Residence						Occupation		
			Urban	Rural*	Rural†	All Life	Birth to 20	Over 20 yrs	10-20	0-10	Hard Labor	Light Labor	Sedentary
Male Prisoners	1	0	0	0	0	0	0	0	0	0	0	0	0
	2	310	70	2	238	44	24	160	82	0	262	45	3
	3	83	31	..	52	40	7	20	16	..	75	8	0
	4	2	2	0	0	1	0	0	1	0	1	1	0
	Total	395	103	2	290	85	31	180	99	..	338	54	3
Females	1	103	81	8	14	43	22	3	32	3	..	..	..
	2	1202	508	54	640	651	178	54	266	53	..	..	..
	3	302	87	32	183	149	50	17	71	15	..	..	..
	4	42	5	1	36	28	4	1	9	0	..	..	..
	Total	1649	681	95	873	871	254	75	378	71	..	..	..
Males	1	100	73	12	15	38	32	1	24	5	1	11	88
	2	1109	353	76	680	642	145	42	248	32	670	261	178
	3	274	77	18	179	141	37	17	74	5	182	70	22
	4	35	8	1	26	22	2	2	8	1	28	6	1
	Total	1518	511	107	900	843	216	62	354	43	881	348	289
World War II Veterans	1	63	43	8	12	28	21	0	13	1	0	1	0
	2	99	48	13	38	53	16	4	22	4	13	3	62
	3	2	1	0	1	0	1	0	1	0	0	0	83
	4	1	1	0	0	0	0	0	1	0	1	0	2
	Total	165	93	21	51	81	38	4	37	5	14	4	0
U. of P.R. Females	1	49	39	6	4	21	10	0	18	0	..	..	147
	2	54	38	10	6	34	8	0	11	1	..	..	..
	3	5	3	1	1	5	0	0	0	0	..	..	..
	4	0	..	..	..	..	..	..	..	..	..	..	..
	Total	108	80	17	11	60	18	0	29	1	..	..	..

*With neighbors. †Alone.

TABLE S-14

STRUCTURE OF NUTRITIONAL SUBSAMPLES BY ETHNIC GROUP

Sample	Nutritional Class	Number	ETHNIC GROUP									
			White					Negro				
			0	1	2	3	4	5	6	7	8	9
Male Prisoners	1	0	:	:	:	:	:	:	:	:	:	:
	2	310	0	1	51	136	31	10	30	31	20	0
	3	83	0	2	7	37	10	3	8	8	8	0
	4	2	:	:	:	2	:	:	:	:	:	:
	Total	395		3	58	175	41	13	38	39	28	0
Females	1	103	1	5	50	42	4	0	1	0	0	0
	2	1202	1	36	325	534	172	7	51	21	5	1
	3	302	0	12	84	106	49	15	18	16	1	0
	4	42	0	1	4	23	5	4	2	2	1	0
	Total	1649	2	54	463	705	230	76	72	39	7	1
World War II Veterans Males	1	100	1	5	39	47	5	0	2	1	0	0
	2	1109	2	34	237	500	139	35	46	60	56	0
	3	274	1	6	61	110	38	17	14	15	12	0
	4	35	0	1	6	20	6	2	0	0	0	0
	Total	1518	4	46	343	677	188	54	62	76	68	0
Females	1	63	0	1	23	34	4	0	1	0	0	0
	2	99	0	4	30	47	7	3	4	2	2	0
	3	2	0	0	0	0	1	0	1	0	0	0
	4	1	0	0	0	1	0	0	0	0	0	0
	Total	165	0	5	53	82	12	3	6	2	2	0
U. of P.R. Females	1	49	0	2	20	22	4	0	1	0	0	0
	2	54	0	5	13	25	5	2	3	1	0	0
	3	5	0	0	2	2	1	0	0	0	0	0
	4	0	:	:	:	:	:	:	:	:	:	:
	Total	108	0	7	35	49	10	2	4	1	0	0

TABLE S-15

SOURCE OF SAMPLE BY SEX

Source	Number of Individuals	
	Male	Female
University of Puerto Rico*	150	108
Municipal Hospitals	306	329
Health Centers of Department of Public Health	901	1212
Prisons	395	....
Other Sources†	161	....
Total	1913	1649

*Of the 150 males, 133 were Veterans of World War II and 17 nonveterans.

†Factories, farms, military-base civilian employees, and government employees.

TABLE S-16

DATE AND PLACE OF MEASUREMENT AND TOTALS MEASURED

Date	Place of Measuring	Number Measured
1948		
June 6-17	Health Center, Rio Puedras	97
June 23-July 30	Health Center, Santurce	455
Aug. 2-12	University of Puerto Rico	240
Aug. 16-23	Municipal Hospital, Carolina	128
Aug. 24-26	Municipal Hospital, Loiza	90
Aug. 30	Municipal Hospital, Vega Alta	62
Sept. 1-2	Municipal Hospital, Vega Baja	46
Sept. 7-12, 14-15	Municipal Hospital, Arecibo	168
Sept. 13	Municipal Hospital, Toa Alta	10
Oct. 6-18	Health Center, Aguadilla (including Aguada, San Sabastion, Isabela and Boriguen field samples)	181
Oct. 19-29	Health Center, Mayaguez	224
Nov. 4-5	Municipal Hospital, Humacao	120
Nov. 8-10	Health Center, Mayaguez (including Mayaguez Prison)	132

Date	Place of Measuring	Number Measured
1948		
Nov. 15	Health Center, Ponce (including Ponce Prison)	349
Dec. 6-7	Health Center, Guayama	77
Dec. 8	Health Center, Patillas	40
Dec. 9	Health Center, Arroyo	24
Dec. 9	Health Center, Guayama	19
Dec. 10	Health Center, Salinas	24
Dec. 13-14	Health Center, Utuado	61
Dec. 15	Health Center, Manata	28
Dec. 16	Health Center, Ciales	33
Dec. 17	Health Center, Morovis	23
Dec. 20	Health Center, Cayey	35
Dec. 21-23	Health Center, Caguas	101
Dec. 27	Health Center, Cayey	40
Dec. 29-30	Health Center, Caguas	71
1949		
Jan. 6-16	Penitentiary, Rio Piedras	262
Jan. 17	Health Center, Bayamon	44
Jan. 18	Health Center, Corozal	43
Jan. 18 & 21	Health Center, Comerio	26
Jan. 21	Health Center, Barranguitas	22
Jan. 24	Health Center, Fajardo	65
Jan. 26	Health Center, Quebradillas	26
Jan. 26	Health Center, Camuy	22
Jan. 27	Health Center, Lares	47
Jan. 28	Prisons, San Juan	20
Jan. 29	Prisons, Arecibo	20
	Miscellaneous (From Murrill's Project, etc.)*	87
Total		3562

PRISON SAMPLE

Rio Piedras 262
Mayaguez 54
Ponce 39
Arecibo 20
San Juan. 20

Total 395

*Measured mainly in the area surrounding San Juan, such as Boca de Congrejas, and outside Catano.

IV. GEOGRAPHIC REGIONS

ADAPTATION of biological organisms to their environment can significantly modify the adult phenotype, so that members of a single population, although all of the same genotype, may still vary considerably if resident in a diversity of geographical scenes. Puerto Rico provides such scenes despite its restricted area. Since, in the subsequent analysis of data the effects of geographic differences are frequently alluded to, a short description of Puerto Rican geography is in order. Reported body differences may then be more easily evaluated and the system of regional classification used here be better understood.

GEOGRAPHY OF PUERTO RICO

To understand the geography of Puerto Rico it is necessary to recognize, first of all, that the island is the top of a submerged mountain crest. The Atlantic Ocean reaches its greatest depth, 27,992 feet, in a chasm about 45 miles north of Puerto Rico, known as the Milwaukee Deep. To the south, the Caribbean Sea has a depth of about 12,000 feet a short distance from Puerto Rico's shore. There are three small satellite islands, Vieques, Culebra, and Mona, whose combined area when added to the main island, give Puerto Rico a territory of 3423 square miles, or approximately 2,000,000 acres. Almost three-fourths of the island of Puerto Rico itself is in the mountainous interior, which has elevations up to 4400 feet. The mountains slope down to a flat coastal plain which varies in width from 8 to 13 miles to the north and from 2 to 8 miles to the south. This plain is chiefly devoted to the raising of sugar, the central crop in the island's economy, and it is here that the majority of the population is concentrated. These topographical features are clearly shown on Map 1.

The coastal climate is semitropical, with a mean temperature of $73.4^о$ F. in the winter and $78.9^о$ F. in the summer. In San Juan the average number of annual hours of sunshine is 2845 (7.8 per day), which indicates a high level of solar radiation. The climate, however, is constantly moderated by the ocean breezes. Mountain temperatures average only $5^о$ to $10^о$ lower than coastal and variations from these mean temperatures are slight. The breeze blows from the sea during the day, but

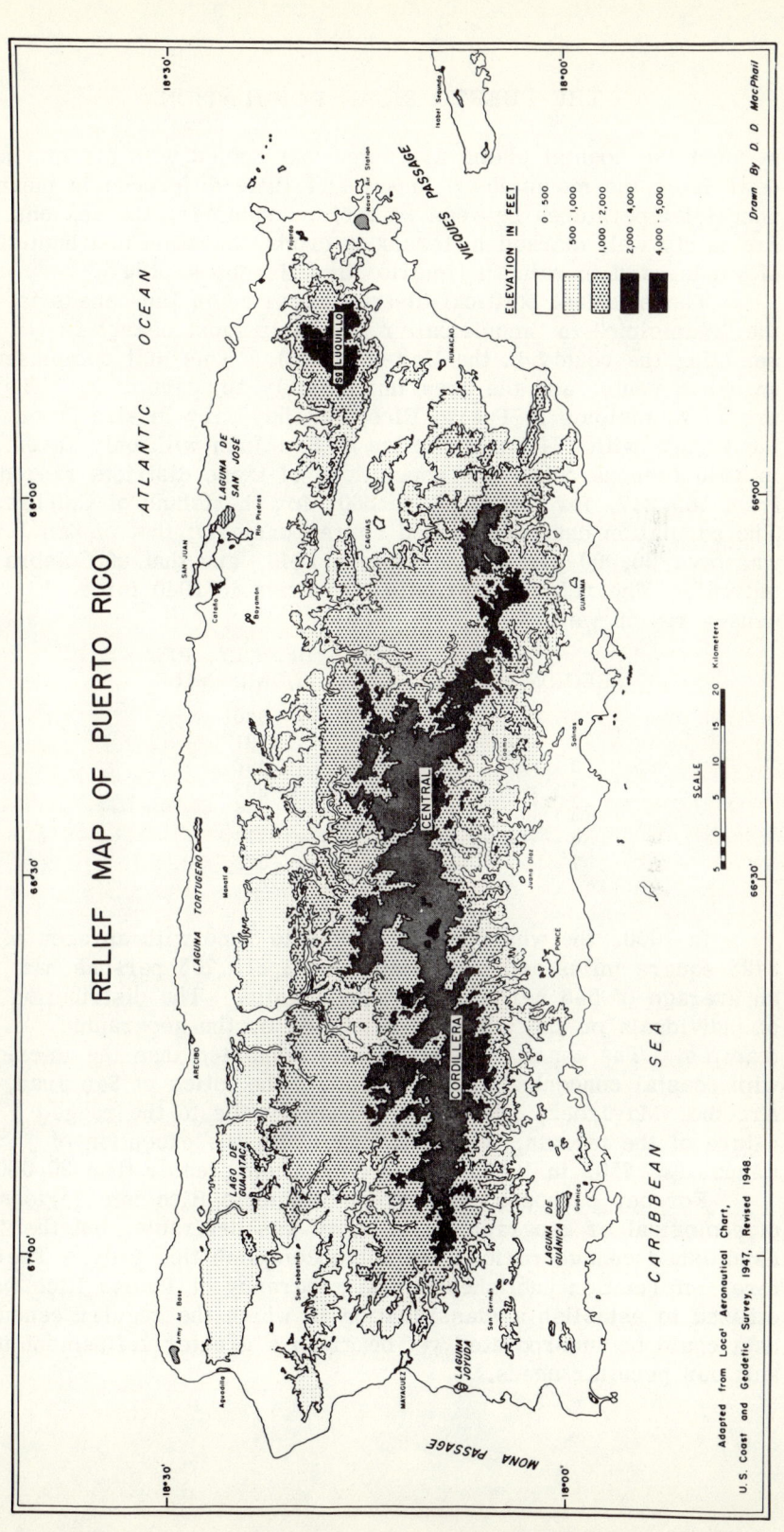

at night the coastal plains are somewhat cooled with air moving down from the mountains. In spite of little difference in mean annual temperatures between winter and summer, the seasons are fairly well marked in terms of crops, duration and humidity of winds, and in rainfall (Puerto Rico Handbook, 1947).

The smallest political district reported in the census is the "municipio" (a "municipality" probably most nearly resembling the county in the United States). This unit comprises an urban center and the area immediately adjacent to it. There are 77 municipios in Puerto Rico and they vary in size from the Utuado with 124 square miles to San Juan with only seven. In 1940 (census data), the populations of these districts ranged from 169,247, for San Juan, to 860, for the island of Culebra. The population densities varied correspondingly; that of San Juan was over 30,000 per square mile in 1940, and that of Culebra only 61. The relative population densities in 1940 for each census region were:

REGION	DENSITY, PER SQUARE MILE
1	630
2	1091
3	436
4	508
5	675
6	374
7	572
	627

In 1950, the whole island of Puerto Rico with an area of 3423 square miles and a population of 2,210,703 persons had an average of 646 persons per square mile. The distribution of individuals on the island is patterned by the geographic features. The coast is more heavily populated than the interior, with coastal concentrations surrounding the cities of San Juan, Arecibo, Mayaguez, and Ponce. Largely due to the rugged nature of the terrain, no island city, with the exception of Caguas (33,759, in 1950), has a population greater than 20,000.

For our purposes, a division of Puerto Rico into regions of ecological or geographic similarity was desirable, but the established census regions did not accomplish this fully. Therefore, information published on the geography of Puerto Rico was utilized to establish a classification in which the regular census data could be incorporated yet be given a greater refinement to suit our peculiar needs.

REGIONAL CLASSIFICATION SYSTEM

Official census data for Puerto Rico is divided according to seven census regions which were set up by the United States Bureau of the Census. Basis for the division is given in the United States census report, *Puerto Rico Population Bulletin No. 4, Migration Between Municipalities, 1940 (1946)*, p. 2, and is as follows:

> These regions represent the sub-divisions of the island into seven areas more homogeneous than the seven senatorial districts which have heretofore been used to a limited extent for a statistical summary. In these new regions, the coastal areas have been kept separate from the mountainous interior areas, the semi-humid areas from those with adequate or surplus rainfall, and those areas in which sugar-cane is the dominant crop from those devoted largely to coffee and tobacco.

Since the census divisions were excessively gross for our purposes, we undertook to make a more homogeneous grouping. Because of the adequacy of the census data, however, it was necessary only to subdivide the regions and not wholly revise them. Equivalence of the two systems, as well as a listing of the municipios in each and a descriptive characterization, is presented in Table G-1. See also Map 2.

The factors which were used to delimit a "region" include relative humidity, urban-rural character, economy, population density, racial origin, and the nature of the terrain. Within whatever freedom was allowed by the established original municipio and census-region units, contiguous areas of relative homogeneity, in terms of some (or even one) salient features, were clustered into 15 regions. In order to make this classification system work to advantage in the analyses of data and particularly in evaluating the possible effects of geographic factors on the individual, the length of time each subject had resided in a region and the place of longest residence was recorded. By this means the maximum biological effect of geographic background and response to environment could be analyzed.

TABLE G-1

DESCRIPTION OF CENSUS AND SAMPLE REGIONS

Census Region	Sample Region	Municipio	Description
1	1	Aguadilla, Camuy, Matillo, Isabela, Quebradillas	Northwest Coast, arid
2	2	Arecibo, Rio Piedras, San Juan	North Coast Urban (Arecibo and San Juan)
	3	Barceloneta, Dorado, Manati, Toa Alta, Toa Baja, Vega Alta, Vega Baja	North Central, low coastal plain, sugar economy
	4	Bayamon, Catano, Guaynabo	Contiguous to San Juan, urbanized
	5	Carolina, Loiza, Rio Grande, Trujillo Alto	Northeast Coastal Plain, sugar, high Negro frequency
3	6	Ceiba, Culebra, Fajardo, Humacao, Luquillo, Maunabo, Naguabo, Vieques, Yabucoa	East Coast
4	7	Arroyo, Guayama, Juana Diaz, Patillas, Penuelas, Salinas, Santa Isabel	South Coast, Eastern and Central, low plain, sugar economy
	8	Ponce	Urbanized region, including Ponce
	9	Guanica, Guayamilla, Lajas, Sabana Grande, Yauco	Southwest Coastal, arid in part, coastal plain, sugar
	10	Cormo, Villalba	Mountain foothill
5	11	Aguada, Anasco, Cabo Rojo, Hormiqueros, Moca, Rincon, San German	West Coastal, excluding Mayaguez
	12	Mayaguez	Urban Mayaguez
6	13	Adjuntas, Ciales, Jayuya, Lares, Las Marias, Maricao, San Sebastian, Utuado	West Central mountains
7	14	Aibonito, Barranquitas, Cayey, Cidra, Comerio, Corozal, Morovis, Naranjito, Orocovis	Central mountains
	15	Aguas Buenas, Caguas, Gurabo, Juncoas, Las Pidras, San Lorenzo	East Central, including Caguas Valley

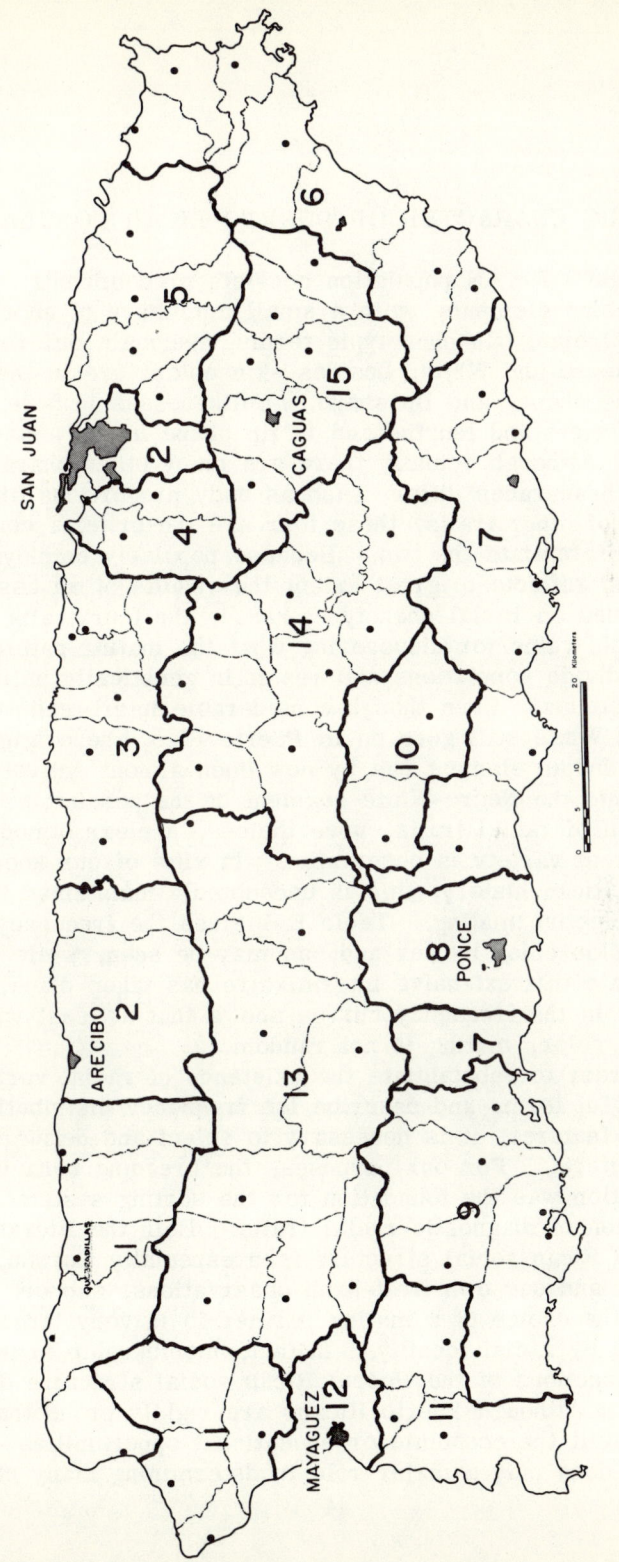

THE GEOGRAPHIC AND CENSUS REGIONS OF PUERTO RICO

V. ETHNIC CHARACTER OF PUERTO RICAN POPULATION

THE PUERTO RICAN population consists predominantly of Negro and Caucasian elements, with a small admixture of aboriginal American Indian. In phenotypic terms, the main differences between Negro and White, besides skin color, are in the hair form, nose shape, and lip shape. Unlikenesses in nose shape lie in the width and length, and in lip shape in the amount of eversion. Although actually there are many other characteristics in which these races differ, such as body proportions or the frequency of other traits, these four are the criteria commonly used to differentiate the two. Because popularly employed, their distribution reflects to great extent the results of an assortative mating based on racial phenotype; hence, the four traits are of considerable value for discovering what the mating patterns are which subdivide populations and result in genetically unlike breeding groups. Even though considerable interbreeding between Negro and White still goes on in Puerto Rico, the original American Indian element has by now been almost entirely hybridized into the Negro-White segment of the population. In the distribution of racial traits, nevertheless, a clear bimodality as well as great variety is observable. In view of our knowledge of Puerto Rican history, this is undoubtedly maintained by non-random selective mating. Table E-1 gives the frequency distribution of skin color by sex and, as may be seen, while these data indicate that extensive intermixture has taken place, yet bimodality in the frequency curves shows that at least with respect to color, mating is not random.

In order to substantiate the existence of racial variation in meaningful terms and describe the frequency distribution of diagnostic features, it is necessary to select and define useful sorting criteria. For our purposes, the breeding behavior of the population was the foundation for the sorting system and the selection of diagnostic racial traits. Both the literature on the Puerto Rican social structure (see especially Gordon, 1949 and 1950), and our own first-hand observations, support the view that the choice of a mating partner is in very large part determined by racial identity. In fact, membership in many important sections of the Puerto Rican social structure depends upon race. Although Puerto Ricans are rightly proud that race does not limit the economic or educational opportunities of their people, it does play a major role in determining many of the

TABLE E-1

FREQUENCY DISTRIBUTION BY SEX OF RECORDED SKIN COLOR

Skin Color (von Luschan color scale)	Number		
	Males*	Females	Prisoners
7	4	3	0
8	4	0	0
9	7	10	0
10	61	90	1
11	103	118	14
12	149	218	46
13	187	238	59
14	251	277	39
15	150	158	40
16	161	129	41
17	82	121	24
18	76	88	11
19	26	33	11
20	17	20	10
21	14	17	3
22	52	46	18
23	30	26	17
24	37	24	19
25	49	21	19
26	40	8	21
27	16	3	2
28	2	0	0
29	0	0	0
30	0	0	0
31	0	0	0
32	0	1	0
Total	1518	1649	395

*Excluding prisoners.

noneconomic groupings which establish social contact. The undoubted fact is that, as a pattern Negro most likely marries Negro and White marries White. Furthermore, the popular stereotype of what determines "Negro" and "White" is based (in descending order of importance) on skin color, hair form (its color plays little role in this brunette population), and either nose shape or lip form. Probably, there is failure in the popular eye to discriminate among these traits and an over-all evaluation is made of "Negro-ness" or "White-ness." However, no doubt whatever exists that skin color and hair form dominate the usual concept.

While various sociological data pointed to skin color as the most important factor in determining the racial status of individuals in Puerto Rico, a test of this was possible using our blood-type findings of this study. Since a complete discussion of these results is given elsewhere (Thieme, 1952) as well as being described in Chapter XII of this report, only the most pertinent are mentioned here. It was discovered that when the sample is grouped according to our categories of hair form, nose shape, and lip shape, by each of the 15 regions, the blood-type frequencies for each trait category are significantly non-homogeneous by the Chi square test. That is, the ABO and Rh blood types, which are significantly different for Negro and White (and for regions), do not sort into a homogeneous pattern. But this is not so for skin color, for with this trait it is homogeneous and the Chi square is not significant (For Rh the $\chi^2 = 88.77$; $d.f. = 70$; $t = 1.53$; $p = .126$). This means that for each skin-color category the Rh blood type frequencies for each region are not significantly different. One can assume then that each skin-color group is drawn from the same breeding population, membership in which is primarily dictated by skin color without regard to regional residence.

The system used in assigning ethnic factor (based on skin color, hair form, nose shape and lip form) is given on page 11; the results of analyses of racial variation are included in the sections devoted to the various groupings of measurements or observations, such as dental, physiological, and anthropometric. Since the interrelationship between these ethnic traits is of interest in itself, the mean values for each trait (in relation to the several categories for each other trait) are shown in Table E-2. Unfortunately, only the mean values can be given here, but despite this condensation, it is readily apparent that the traits are highly associated. Curiously, also indicated is the apparent less-Negroid character of the females compared to the males.

TABLE E-2

INTERRELATIONSHIP OF ETHNIC FACTOR TRAITS

Trait and Recorded Catagory	Mean Values Recorded									Ethnic Factor		Number in Catagory	
	Lip Shape		Nose Shape		Hair Form		Skin Color						
	Male*	Female	Male*	Female	Male*	Female	Male*	Female	Prisoners	Male*	Female	Male*	Female
Lip 1	...	...	1.9	1.8	2.6	2.5	13.2	13.6	13.2	2.2	2.1	147	143
Shape 2	...	...	2.1	2.1	2.7	2.6	14.2	13.9	14.5	2.8	2.7	1105	1046
3	...	...	2.4	2.4	3.2	3.1	16.9	16.4	17.7	4.0	3.9	420	392
4	...	...	3.9	3.6	4.5	3.9	23.3	21.0	23.5	6.8	6.0	176	63
5	...	...	4.7	4.1	4.9	4.3	25.0	19.4	24.7	7.8	7.1	65	5
Nose 1	1.6	1.3	...	...	2.3	2.4	12.2	13.1	...	1.6	2.0	32	33
Shape 2	2.1	2.1	...	...	2.7	2.7	14.3	14.0	14.4	2.8	2.8	1429	1307
3	2.8	2.6	...	...	3.5	3.2	18.5	17.3	20.6	4.6	4.3	214	230
4	3.8	3.5	...	...	4.6	4.2	23.2	21.9	23.8	6.7	6.2	148	73
5	4.5	4.1	...	...	4.9	4.3	24.5	21.0	24.8	7.8	6.6	90	6
Hair 1	2.0	2.0	2.0	2.0	...	...	13.3	13.2	...	1.7	1.6	51	61
Form 2	2.0	2.0	2.1	2.0	...	...	13.6	13.4	13.4	2.2	2.2	378	433
3	2.2	2.1	2.1	2.1	...	...	14.5	14.3	14.5	3.1	3.1	1104	949
4	3.1	2.8	3.1	3.0	...	...	20.0	19.9	20.8	5.5	5.2	168	156
5	4.1	3.3	4.2	3.5	...	...	24.1	20.9	24.1	7.3	6.5	212	50

*Including male prisoners.

A single observer (R. I. Murrill) evaluated and recorded values for each trait, hence, there is no accounting for this through internal inconsistency. Cosmetic practices, it is true, may be at work, but other studies report the same slight sex difference and there may, in fact, be a sex factor that is modifying the expression of the more extreme Negroid phenotypes in the females. The differences exhibited between the prison sample and the total male sample is due to our selection, in many instances, of prisoners by race. As a result this subsample alone is neither entirely representative of the total prison population nor of the parental island population.

Race distribution in Puerto Rico is not at random. Tabulation of data on skin color by region (Table 16) makes this clear, and the general pattern, as is also to be seen from the census data, is a relative concentration of Negroes in the coastal areas, with highest percentages on the northeastern coast. Inland regions are predominately White.

Finally, a word of evaluation concerning the ethnic factor used in this study. The results indicate this factor to be a highly efficient device for racial classification inasmuch as breeding behavior is closely associated with ethnic characteristics. The ethnic evaluation system was set up initially on the basis of our own preliminary observation and data from published reports. Now that our data have been analyzed we ask ourselves the question: Would we use the same system over again and, if not, how would we revise it? All through this study the real utility of skin color as a revealing sorting criterion was apparent. But, opposed to this, little seemed gained by adding lip- and nose-shape observations. Hair form was a useful adjunct to skin color and well worth the effort of noting. Possibly, our ethnic data would be just as good and, perhaps, better if only skin color and hair form had been recorded. Our final judgment, then, in answer to the postulated question, is that skin color, weighted over hair form by a factor of 2, as in this study, should be used, but that lip and nose shape can well be disregarded. Even here, however, a word of caution is needed for our system of ethnic notation was designed specifically for Puerto Rico and, perhaps, in different scenes the mating behavior and racial variation might not be fitted to it.

VI. NUTRITIONAL DATA AND CLASSIFICATION

THE IMPORTANCE of nutrition in determining a large share of the variability in body dimensions and in the health of the Puerto Rican population is clearly demonstrated from our survey. In fact most of the biological variation, except in certain racial or unit genetic traits can be largely attributed to it. Dental and physiological conditions are, likewise, affected. Because this is true, the nutritional classification system which was devised is fully explained. We established four nutritional classes, on criteria mainly based on work by Roberts (1949) but supplemented by data from a study of our own design (fully described below). The latter was performed by nutritionists of the Puerto Rican Department of Public Health, and the data served to check estimates of the dietary pattern.

Each sample subject was assigned to one of the four classes according to the diagnosic features of his daily diet. The classes were constituted as follows:

Class	Dietary Feature	Percentage*
1	Meat twice, Rice and Beans twice, Milk at least one pint per day	6.5%
2	Rice, Beans and Viandas.†	47.1%
	Plus:	
	$\underline{a}$ No protein, no milk. 7 2	
	$\underline{b}$ No protein, little milk 6.8	
	$\underline{c}$ Some protein, no milk 11.1	
	$\underline{d}$ Some protein, some milk 22.0	
3	Rice and Beans	33.6%
	Plus:	
	$\underline{a}$ No protein, no milk. 7.4	
	$\underline{b}$ No protein, little milk 7.9	
	$\underline{c}$ Some protein, no milk 4.7	
	$\underline{d}$ Some protein, some milk 13.6	
4	Starch and Viandas.‡	12.8%

*Percentage distribution according to Roberts' (1949) data. See Table N-1 for percentage distribution of our study compared to that of Roberts.

†Viandas are starchy vegetables such as yuca, malanga, plaintain, or breadfruit.

‡If this category were grouped with Class 2, as in many individual cases, the percentage distribution of our study and of Roberts' would match more closely.

The criteria listed, and used for placing the individual subject in a nutritional class, was based on data independently derived by Roberts (1949). While her study helped us establish the system, data from a supplementary study, of our design, by the nutritionists of the Department of Public Health, was used to confirm our estimate of the Puerto Rican dietary pattern.

Interviewing was used to elicit nutritional information and assignment of each subject to a nutritional class was based on his response. The questions used were developed in consultation with Professor Lydia Roberts of the University of Puerto Rico and conformed to the typology of her study (1949, Table 210), a study based on a selected representative sample of Puerto Ricans. Additional questions were formulated so that we might place the individual more accurately within a subgroup, but they accorded to the features given in her study chart 37 (see Roberts, 1949, pp. 188-90).

Before commenting on the supplementary study, a comparison of our classification results with those of Roberts is given. Tables S-8, S-10, S-11, S-13 and S-14, break down our sample by nutritional class and by further subgroupings of each nutritional class. Table N-1 relates our findings to Roberts' frequencies. Data in this table shows that our sample frequencies rank higher in Class 2 and below hers in Classes 3 and 4. Three reasons can account for this and probably all the forces

TABLE N-1

PERCENTAGE FREQUENCY IN EACH NUTRITIONAL CLASS
IN OUR STUDY COMPARED TO ROBERTS (1949)*

Nutritional Class	Percentage Frequency								Roberts' Study (Percent of Household)
	Our Study								
	Prisoners		Males		Females		Total		
	No.	%	No.	%	No.	%	No.	%	
1	0	0	100	6.6	103	6.2	203	5.7	6.6
2	310	78.5	1109	73.1	1202	72.9	2621	73.6	47.1
3	83	21.0	274	18.0	302	18.3	659	18.5	33.6
4	2	0.5	35	2.3	42	2.6	79	2.2	12.8
Total	395	100.0	1518	100.0	1649	100.0	3562	100.0	100.0

*Based on a study in 1946 of 1044 households, including 5670 persons.

they represent are operative to some extent. First, the general nutritional conditions in Puerto Rico are said to be improving; possibly, the results of our study, done three years after that of Roberts reflect this. Second, and much more likely, however, is that the subject exaggerated his status, for few people like to admit that they cannot afford life's necessities, especially if social status and prestige are involved. Combined with a tendency to exaggerate was the understandable failure of the subject to recall the "average" nutritional history of his past years. Third, the inclusion by us of persons of Class 3d, (as defined by Roberts) in Class 2 presumably contributes to the percentage differences between the two studies.

While our goal was to get a complete picture of each subject's nutritional history, it is unlikely that we ever attained it, and the probable bias is an overstatement of the level of diet. In consequence, our Class 2 includes some persons who should be in Class 3 and Class 3 some who properly belong in Class 4. Moreover, Class 1 was made up of persons whose economic status and educational background was distinctly superior to the Puerto Rican average. They were largely professional people and undoubtedly belonged in it, and here the agreement with Roberts' frequency is quite good.

Although our classification probably exaggerates the dietary status of the sample population, this does not greatly modify our results, for each class is significantly superior to the next lower. It will be seen from the discussion later that this is borne out by many of the comparisons where body dimensions relate to nutrition. Since primarily we were seeking to establish whether or not variation in nutritional level had an important effect on variability in body dimensions and health, lack of agreement between our sample frequencies and those of Roberts is of secondary interest. Only the most carefully controlled studies, made over extended periods of time, can show the detailed effect of specific elements of nutritional intake on body dimensions. Our study was not designed to give such information but rather to show the role of nutrition in causing phenotype variability and assess to some degree its importance in this respect.

Supplementary Study

This was a study designed and carried out (February 15- March 16, 1949) to give us more information for evluating the

Puerto Rican dietary levels. It was made by the Nutritional Section of the Puerto Rican Department of Public Health in response to our request for a detailed comparison of dietaries in and between rural areas, and between Negro and White groups in the same area. To the Misses Olga Martinez and Mates de Peiz, who performed the work we are indebted for its high quality and for the diligence with which it was carried out. They made a survey of 36 families in six rural areas (six families from each) which differed in racial and geographic composition. Locale and composition of the six groups of families were:

Groups I-II.   Campo Rico, Canovanillas; White; inland location.
Groups III-IV. San Isidro, Hoyo Mulas; Negro; inland location.
Groups V-VI.   Mediania Alta, Boca de Congrejos; Negro; coastal location.

Areas were so chosen that Negro and White comparisons could be made in essentially the same inland rural district, and so that inland versus coastal comparisons could be made between Negroes in these different districts. That is, Groups I, III, and V are from the municipio of Loiza, II, IV, and VI from that of Carolina. The inland families lived in the lowlands between the coast and the foothills, the coastal families on or close to the seashore. In each area 45 families were selected by interview to be typical of the agricultural workers, and of the 45, 36 were selected for study, 6 to each group. Most of the adult males were employed in the sugar-cane fields or refineries. All the families fall into the low-income group, less than $1,000 income per year, and in this respect were similar to about 75 percent of the total Puerto Rican population.

The study by Olga Martinez and Mates de Peiz is difficult to summarize, for the detailed data they gathered is truly impressive. However, salient features are obvious and their findings are in agreement with other studies, which have revealed the inadequacy of the Puerto Rican diet. A summary of the study follows:

Sample Group	Family Size		Race	Area
	Range of Family Size	Average		
I	4-18	9.6	W	Inland
II	4-13	8.1	W	
III	4-9	6.8	N	
IV	5-16	9.6	N	
V	5-12	8.5	N	Seashore
VI	4-10	6.8	N	

Procedure. Questionnaire forms were filled out on home visits and data taken on (1) individual food habits from birth to 21 years and (2) total food intake for the three days of the study on each family. The diet requirement of each individual, according to age, sex, and occupation, was calculated and compared to his actual daily intake. These requirements were established on the basis of standards set up for daily allowance by the National Research Council. Food values were calculated according to various well-established standards, as those proposed by the United States Department of Agriculture (Miscellaneous Publications 505 and 572), and on analyses made in recent years of various local Puerto Rican foods. The accuracy of the food values or the need for the allowances is not in serious doubt. In estimating total intake, each family was visited for three consecutive days and a complete record of food eaten was obtained. Food purchases were weighed and leftovers and peelings weighed and recorded.

Food Habits (Birth to Age 21). Food habits from birth to 21 years, for individuals of each family and group were stated in terms of duration of breast feeding of infants and of diet patterns for individuals of later years. Data for the infants are tabulated here.

Group	Months Breast Fed	
	Range	Average
I	6-36	16.5
II	0-14	6.1
III	6-24	17.0
IV	12-24	18.1
V	9-24	13.0
VI	4-24	12.6

The group patterns for the older subjects are in brief: (1) Groups III, IV, and VI ate rice and beans more often than viandas. (2) Groups I and II ate more fruits and vegetables, and Groups I, II, and III drank more milk than those from other groups. (3) Pork consumption was highest for Group IV. (4) During the time of the year when sea foods are abundant, Groups V and VI ate them more often than other groups, but when sea foods were scarce Group VI had the highest consumption.

Three-day Dietary Intake. The food consumed during the three-day home survey by each person was assessed against the standards and the dietary status of the family summarized in percent of daily requirements attained for each of 11 nutrients.

The status of the families in each group was then averaged and the results are given in Table N-2, actually a summary table prepared by us from the detailed family report sheets and analyses of each family nutrient intake, which were taken by the nutritionists. The range from the lowest to the highest families are also given so that the considerable variability can be appreciated.

Martinez and Mates de Peiz drew the following conclusions from their three-day survey:

> (1) The greatest deficiencies for all groups were in calcium, vitamin A, riboflavin, and vitamin C. This is due to the limited consumption of milk, fruits, and green and yellow vegetables. (2) Although the figures for protein are not as low as for other nutrients, an evaluation of the sources of protein should be made to determine the quality of the protein consumed. (3) In general, it may be said that Groups III and IV, as compared with the other four groups, give higher levels of intake of the following nutrients: Calories, protein, calcium, iron, thiamine, riboflavin, and niacin. The differences between the different groups of families in relation to the vitamin A intake were not significant, the intakes for Group I and II being slightly higher than those for the other groups. Those for vitamin C were more or less equal for the three types of families surveyed (I and II; III and IV; V and VI). (4) Taking into consideration the information gathered through the evaluation of food habits from birth to 21 years, families from Groups V and VI would probably give higher levels of intake of protein, if the study had been made at the time of the year when sea foods are abundant. It should also be noted that, although all the families fall into low income levels, the incomes of the families from Group V were slightly lower than those of all the other groups. This was due to the fact that a larger proportion of the men in this area did not work the full week and employed less than the men from the other areas surveyed.

The significance of this home study for the interpretation of the nutritional information in our survey is clear in several respects. First, it shows that the food intake in our Classes 2, 3, and 4, in which all these families would fall, is far short of the National Research Council standards. In many families the nutrient intake for most items is below the 50 percent level. Thus, when we interpret our data, we are probably correct in assuming that in our total sample gross dimensional variability is coupled with a truly wide variation in nutritional intake. Second, the fact that the Negro dietaries are superior to those of the White suggests that the greater body dimensions of the

TABLE N-2

AVERAGE PERCENTAGE OF DAILY REQUIREMENT FOR EACH OF NINE NUTRIENTS IN THE SELECTED SAMPLE GROUPS STUDIED BY MARTINEZ AND MATES DE PEIZ

GROUP	NUTRIENTS									Total Average
	Calories	Protein	Calcium	Iron	Vit. A	Vit. B$_1$	Vit. B$_2$	Niacin	Vit. C	
Inland (Loiza)										
Group I (White)	69.3	78.6	39.5	91.1	71.5	82.8	56.5	51.8	68.1	67.7
Group III (Negro)	88.5	109.5	63.1	122.3	33.1	98.5	55.6	67.5	57.5	77.4
Inland (Carolina)										
Group II (White)	69.6	77.3	29.3	70.6	39.0	82.8	45.1	73.6	68.1	61.7
Group IV (Negro)	104.6	110.3	50.3	122.0	41.0	117.0	64.6	87.5	61.8	84.3
Coast (Loiza)										
Group V (Negro)	65.5	69.1	20.3	67.3	37.3	63.0	40.6	56.5	38.3	50.9
Coast (Carolina)										
Group VI (Negro)	73.1	74.5	58.1	77.5	57.6	100.8	52.3	65.0	115.3	74.9
Summary										
Groups I & II (White-Inland)	69.5	78.0	34.4	80.6	55.3	82.8	50.8	62.7	68.1	64.7
Groups III & IV (Negro-Inland)	96.5	109.9	56.7	122.2	37.1	107.8	60.1	77.5	59.7	80.9
Groups V & VI (Negro-Coastal)	69.3	71.8	39.2	72.4	47.5	81.9	46.5	60.8	76.8	62.9
Minimum-Maximum Negro: III, IV, V, VI	34-136	21-150	8-168	33-183	7-138	36-183	13-87	29-113	5-265	....
White: I, II	37-99	42-121	15-57	31-172	18-148	46-108	30-87	40-109	17-224	....

Negroes (see Chapter VIII) may result from a superior diet. Although such a conclusion, based on these limited data, is risky, the greater average height and weight and the larger size in most other dimensions of the Negroes in Puerto Rico is probably not alone due to genetic factors. The home-study data indicate, moreover, that there may be food-habit differences which play some role in bringing about the anthropometric racial distinctions which are so noticeable in Puerto Rico. Whatever conclusions the comparisons of Groups I and II (White) with III and IV (Negroes), all from the same region and occupationally and economically equated show that the Negro has an appreciably higher average intake (basic and caloric) for six of nine essential nutrients, including calories and proteins.

The question of how persistent food habits were (a question in which we were quite interested) was not well answered by this type of short-term household study. It does not disprove that life-long nutritional history can be elicited by interview, but it does nothing to substantiate it. We were left with no greater assurance than before, when we accepted as reasonable the assumption that a person can be placed with some validity in a nutritional class that reflects his whole dietary history. Other data of our study, however, do more to support this assumption and are reported in Chapter VIII, which gives the analysis of the anthropometric data. But to anticipate those results, we may say that average body weight, which is highly correlated with nutritional intake, is highest for our Nutritional Class 1 and decreasingly less so for each lower class as would be expected if our classes were appreciably different in nutritional status. Average stature in a sample of the same racial background is likewise highest for Class 1 and decreasingly less for each lower class. These results suggest that class status probably is of long standing and well represents the nutritional history of the individual.

In conclusion, our nutritional classification system is probably quite suitable for such purposes as we used it. The interview technique proved well designed and, in accordance with information independently established, to be meaningful. There is another factor that adds to the reliability of our system and is especially important in balancing the errors potentially inherent in any nutritional survey depending on interview technique. This is the fact that Puerto Rico has an unusually simple and consistent national food-habit pattern, (see Blanco, 1946; Roberts, 1949; and others). As a result, certain key questions can reveal at once the status of each individual with reference to the main outlines of the national pattern. Furthermore, the high general correlation between economic status and food intake is useful in establishing dietary level. All these elements were skillfully incorporated into our interview questions by Professor Roberts and her advice and co-operation in this is greatefully acknowledged.

VII. ANTHROPOMETRIC DATA

CHIEF INTEREST of the study centered in ascertaining the body dimensions of the Puerto Ricans and the variability among these in relation to environmental and genetic factors. Hence, while some emphasis has been put on dental and physiological observations and measurements, the bulk of the tabular and graphic matter deals with the anthropometric findings. In the analysis of the data weight is given in particular to the variability in terms of regional (or geographic) residence, nutritional status, and racial origin. A description of the total island population may be achieved by massing the data of our representative sample. Males (nonprison), females, and male prisoners are reported separately, since nothing was to be gained, except occasionally in the case of the males, by combining the subsamples. Before taking up the anthropometric results (see Chapter VIII), some background information which will assist in evaluating our results is necessary. Our method of handling the data, testing for its internal consistency, and the correction procedures and statistical methods used are, therefore, discussed first.

TREATMENT OF DATA

Data from each subject was coded and then punched on IBM cards for machine analysis. Coding, punching, and verifying were done in Puerto Rico and three sets of data cards made. One card remained at the Social Science Research Center of the University of Puerto Rico; one was deposited at the American Museum of Natural History, and one was used by the author for his analysis. Preliminary sorting and tabulating were done in Puerto Rico at the School of Tropical Medicine, but most of the analytic work was carried out later at the Watson Scientific Computing Laboratory at Columbia University, the Computing Laboratory of the Horace H. Rackham School of Graduate Studies, and in the computing room of the School of Public Health, at the University of Michigan.

Extensive use of electronic computers at the Watson Laboratory made it possible to treat the data in many combinations, many of which are not reported here. For example, correlation coefficients for all the measurements in all the sample combinations were made; these aided in planning further analysis and also contributed to an understanding of the corpus of data. Since the calculations number in the thousands they are not included as a part of this report, but are on file in the Laboratory of Physical Anthropology at the University of Michigan. Standard machine procedures were used to check the accuracy of the computations; each mean and derived statistic has been calculated at least twice. The tables were printed by IBM tabulators directly from the cards, thus eliminating transcription error, so accuracy should be high. Simple seriated distributions of the whole sample for each measurement were taken to discover abnormal recorded card values and to check for normality of distribution. While no measures of skewness were made, all the distributions, except for abdominal fold, weight, and waist circumference, were approximately normal. Therefore, the range within which 66%, 95%, or 99% of the sample will fall can be quite reliably secured by adding to and subtracting from the mean value given 1, 2, or 3 times the standard deviation, respectively.

Although machines are a great boon, when such a large body of data needs analysis, they can tempt one to derive more answers than are useful. While one enjoys the advantage of knowing that little of value has not been extracted from the data, which to choose among thousands of tabulations that deserve reporting becomes a major problem. With regret, the correlations, most of the indices (except those in tables Nos. 126-127 and some in graphs Nos. 54 to 66), and many of the side excursions have been omitted. All of them, however, are on file in the Laboratory of Physical Anthropology at the University of Michigan and are available to interested persons.

INTERNAL CONSISTENCY OF DATA

In spite of systematic attempts at standardization, differences continue to exist in the techniques practiced by anthropometrists. For this reason, trial sessions aimed at achieving uniformity were held in New York and in Puerto Rico prior to the start of field work. Once the sampling began the two anthropometrists (Thieme and Finkle) made every attempt to hold their landmarks and practices constant throughout the study. After results were punched and verified and all the seriated data were tabulated and checked for errors in the record blanks, a test was made to determine whether significant differences existed in the values recorded by the two workers. The statistics for two pairs of matched samples of males and of females, one of each pair which had been measured by each anthropometrist, were compared. The two pairs of samples (400 males and 350 females) were matched for sex, age, ethnic origin, skin color, nutritional status, and region of residence. Since it is these factors that account for most physical variability, we assumed that, if differences did occur between the matched samples, they most probably would be attributable to differences in measuring technique.

Statistical values for all measurements from each of these samples were compared and tested for significance of difference. At the 5% confidence level, 14 measurements were significantly different, and 12 of these at the 1% level. The measurements and the differences between the means are given in Table A-1. No independent judgment was available to decide which anthropometrist was the more accurate. But, as Miss Finkle had measured the most individuals (1166 males, 222 prisoners, and 1175 females, or 2563 of the 3562 in the sample), the decision was made to correct Thieme's measurements to conform with hers.

A simple correction procedure was used. A correction factor (Table A-1), determined by the difference between the means in those measurements which were significantly different, was multiplied by the number of individuals in the sample who had been measured by Thieme. This product was added or subtracted, according to its sign, to the sum of the values of that measurement in the sample. When this value was divided by the number in the sample, the corrected mean resulted. An alternate procedure could have been used in which all the recorded values for the 14 measurements would have been corrected on the cards by the amounts of the correction factor. This tedious procedure could have had one advantage, namely, that the sums of the detailed values squared would then have also included the corrected values. Thus, the calculation of the distribution of the sample array would perhaps have been more accurate. However, since this procedure was much more laborious and only a very little more efficient, it was rejected. Because the corrections are relatively small, in terms of range especially, the measures of sample variability (variance, standard deviation, and standard error) are only very slightly in error using the simpler procedure. If this relatively small statistical inaccuracy has any bearing on the interpretation of our data, it enters only when tests of difference are at the

TABLE A-1

COMPARISONS BETWEEN THE MEANS OF MEASUREMENTS ON MATCHED MALE AND FEMALE SAMPLES MEASURED BY TWO DIFFERENT ANTHROPOMETRISTS*

Measurement	Females	Males
Upper Arm Length (cm)	-.65	-.54
Lower Arm Length (cm)	-.66	-.99
Total Arm Length (cm)	-.98	-1.24
Trunk Height (cm)	-1.26	-1.61
Biacromial Diameter (cm)	-.58	-.37
Bicristal Diameter (cm)	-2.09	-1.97
Abdominal Fold (mm)	+2.55	+2.55
Knee Width (mm)	-.95	....
Bigonial Diameter (mm)	-3.90	-3.42
Total Face Height (mm)	+5.18	+4.21
Upper Face Height (mm)	+3.55	+3.29
Nose Height (mm)	+4.31	+3.54
Waist Circumference (cm)	-2.14	-2.07
Arm Circumference (cm)	-.63	-.89

*The negative corrections are for measures where the mean values of subjects measured by Thieme were larger than those measured by Finkle at the 5% level or below, and the positive values when this was reversed. Only significantly different measurements are shown.

5% level. Certainly, they do not affect the value of p over one or two-tenths. Therefore, at the 2% or 1% level of significance, this source of slight error can be disregarded.

The necessity of adopting corrective procedures is mentioned with reluctance, but the consistency of our data is so improved by their use that to have omitted it would be inexcusable. Any study which employs more than one anthropometrist runs the risk of such error. By correction we achieved internal comparability of measurements--our goal in any event. What the "true" dimensions are, when standard instruments and "soft" landmarks are used, is always somewhat subject to a personal equation.

The pattern of differences between measures indicates that two factors account for most of them; namely, the location of nasion and pressure differences in taking circumferences, diameters, and skin fold. In fact, these accounted for 10 of the 14 measurement differences; differences in posturing of the body explained the remaining 4. The measurements that have more stable landmarks, such as head dimensions and stature, showed no differences.

STATISTICAL PROCEDURES

All statistical procedures were adjusted to fit machine operations and no corrections in any case were made for small sample numbers by using N minus 1. The sum of the values and squared values were secured from a machine run of the sample deck. As the machine capacity allowed two measures to be run simultaneously, the sum of the cross products was also taken and thus was used in the calculation of correlation coefficients. The sum of values divided by the number (N) gave the mean (M). The variance (σ^2) is simply the sum of the squared values divided by the number (N) less the mean squared. The standard deviation (S.D.) is the square root of the variance. The standard error squared (S.E.^{2}) is obtained by dividing the variance by N and the standard error is the square root of this value.

A simple test for significance of difference can be used. In this the difference between the two means of the measurements under test is squared and divided by the sum of the two S.E.^{2}'s of these. This gives t^2. The square root of this can be referred to standard t tables for determining the value of p. As this form of the t test using the S.E.^{2} is so easy to use, the values of S.E.^{2} are provided in most of the anthropometric tables. The square roots used in this study to obtain the S.D. and S.E. were all computed by a pair of relay calculators at the Watson Center; one machine performed the calculation and the other repeated and compared it as a check for accuracy. As the S.D. and S.E. were never used in running t tests, nor checked in any other way except by the relay machines, the values of variance and S.E.^{2} should preferably be used if a discrepancy in the square roots is found. All values were carried in the machines at least one place more than shown on the tables, but rounding was not done in reading them out on the tabulation.

VIII. ANTHROPOMETRIC RESULTS

ONE of the main purposes of this study was to describe the Puerto Rican population anthropometrically. The findings that resulted are chiefly given in tabular form. There are 139 basic tables, which are coordinated with 76 graphs. Both this set of tables and the graphs are grouped in Part 2. An index to them is furnished there, but their arrangement is outlined and discussed below. The tables and graphs are combined into five groups and in each group the anthropometric measurements, whenever possible, are ordered numerically.

ORGANIZATION OF DATA

The Tables

1. *General* (Tables 1-17). — These tables concern the various aspects and subgroupings of the total sample. Wherever mentioned, "Total Sample" refers to the full complement of males exclusive of prisoners (M), females (F), and prisoners (P) which constituted the actual sample.
2. *Selected Subsamples* (Tables 18-24). — Tables dealing with characteristics of subgroups selected from the total sample because of certain distinctive features. University of Puerto Rico students, World War II Veterans, and the measurements of migrants and *Sedentes* are also included.
3. *Measurements by Geographic Region* (Tables 25-95). — A further subdivision of these measurements yields three categories which comprise:

   a) Mean values and associated statistics for all regional samples of M, F, and P for each measurement taken (Tables 25-61). Only statistics derived from individuals of permanent residence in a region are included.

   b) Values for each regional sample by nutritional class for all measurements (Tables 62-70).

   c) Values for each regional sample by ethnic group for all measurements (Tables 71-95).
4. *Variability by Region, Race, and Nutrition* (Tables 96-125). — These analyses are further subdivided for:

   a) Regional Variability (Tables 96-111). Statistics for 16 measurements of a selected sample (Sample A) of persons, all of Ethnic Group 3 and Nutritional Class 2, from each of the 15 geographic regions. This is an analysis designed to test the effects of geographical differences.

    b) Ethnic Variability (Tables 112-119). Statistics for 16 measurements of a selected sample (Sample B) of persons, all of Nutritional Class 2, from each of 8 ethnic groups. In these tables the few persons in Ethnic Group O (M = 4; F = 2) are combined with Group 1 and the single one (a female) in Group 9, is combined Group 8.

    c) Nutritional Variability (Tables 120-125). Statistics for 16 measurements of a selected sample (Sample C) of persons, all of Ethnic Group 3, for each of the 4 nutritional classes.

5. Anthropometric Indices (Tables 126-127). — Values for 4 selected indices for each of the 4 nutritional classes.

6. Dental Status (Tables 128-129). — The content of these tables is described and discussed in Chapter IX.

The Graphs

    The graphs that portray the tabular data are divided into 5 groups according to measurements covered, samples used, or data reported. These groups are briefly characterized below:

    1. *Selected Subsamples* (Graphs 1-45). — These graphs combine and give visual expression to the analyses of anthropometric data listed in Tables 96-125. Sample numbers for each group that appears on the graphs can be ascertained by referring to the appropriate table. The values of 2 S.E. above and below the mean are also shown so that rough tests of significance of difference by the "overlap test" can be made. These graphs cover samples A, B, and C (described above) and thus show the variability between regions shown by persons of the same racial and nutritional background, that by race for persons of the same nutritional class, and that for those of the same racial background by nutritional class.

    2. *Dental Status* (Graphs 46-53). — These graphs which are discussed in Chapter IX, give various data by age, region, sex, ethnic group, nutritional class and tooth site.

    3. *Anthropometric Indices* (Graphs 54-66). — The index values for 9 selected indices for the total sample of males (including prisoners) and of females arrayed according to ethnic and nutritional groupings.

    4. *Physiological Measurements* (Graphs 67-76). — Give the mean values for pulse, hemoglobin, blood counts and

pressure are recorded for each ethnic and nutritional class in these (see Chapter XI, for a full discussion).

5. *Measurements by Occupational Group* (Graph 76). — This is a summary of 6 measures for males who were grouped according to their occupational status.

DISCUSSION OF DATA

General Results

1. *Characteristics of Total Samples.* — Table 1 gives the mean, standard deviation (S. D.), and range for each measurement on the total samples of males, females, and prisoners. Unless otherwise noted "males" excludes the prison males who are treated separately. The S. D. is not given for skin color, age, and ethnic factor. For each other measurement the value of 1 S. D. above and below the mean should include about two-thirds of the sample; 2 S. D. should include about 95%; and 3 S. D. all but about 1% of the total. For persons who wish to estimate the ranges within which a certain proportion of Puerto Ricans are expected to fall, these values can be used with considerable security as the sample is distributed normally and is quite representative of the total parental Puerto Rican population. In regard to this, however, it should be noted that weight, abdominal fold, and to a lesser degree, waist circumference are all skewed distribution curves with the mean closest to the low values of the range. No other curves are significantly skewed.

From these data on measurements it is apparent that Puerto Ricans are small-dimensioned compared to the population of the United States. This is best seen in the average weight and stature of the males, with mean values of less than 130 pounds and 5 feet 5 inches; these values are approximately 25 pounds and 4 inches under those for United States male "separatees" measured following World War II. In their other dimensions the Puerto Ricans, like most Latin Americans, are small and gracile. The "smallness" typical of this population is partly owing to undernourishment and partly to the public health affecting island life, plus a heritage derived from Caucasians who are typically small.

2. *Weight and Height by Age and Weight by Height.* — The height-weight-age tables are of limited use in establishing size standards. In Tables 2-9 the weights and heights of males, females, and prisoners are given for each age and for ages

combined by three-year intervals. While the weight does increase by age very slightly for each sample, the increment is much less than in the United States population. Middle- and late-aged adults in Puerto Rico are not overweight and expected or normal weight increases (according to U. S. standards) were not observed. In Table AR-1 mean weight is given for each inch of height for males and females. Although these are average figures for Puerto Ricans, in view of age and racial difference in body proportions,

TABLE AR-1

MEAN BODY WEIGHT PER INCH OF STATURE

Sample measured consisted of 1913 males (including prisoners) and 1518 females. Body weight was to the nearest half pound.

Stature (inches)	Weight		Stature (inches)	Weight	
	Males	Females		Males	Females
56	.....	94.0	65	130.5	132.0
57	.....	98.0	66	134.5	136.0
58	.....	102.0	67	139.0	.....
59	.....	106.0	68	143.0	.....
60	109.0	110.5	69	147.5	.....
61	113.5	115.0	70	152.5	.....
62	117.5	119.0	71	159.0	.....
63	121.5	123.0	72	166.0	.....
64	126.0	128.0	..	.....	.....

some caution should be used before they are rigidly applied in setting up standards of normal weight for each height group. As standards, they are comparable to the values in tables currently used by insurance companies for other populations. Because stature was taken in centimeters, this table is derived from a smoothed curve and extrapolated into even inches. Variations of plus or minus 5 pounds from these values should be within the expected range and any more rigid use of these data for establishing normal values should be avoided.

   3. *Weight-Height by Residence Status.* — Urban-rural comparisons for height and weight are given in Tables 10 and 11. The "rural" category has been further subdivided into "rural-alone," those living in isolated households, and "rural with neighbors." The latter division involves a cluster of a few houses, but it is distinctly nonurban. No significant difference in these measures exists according to residence

category, except, in the "rural with neighbors," for male stature. As these groups are not equated for nutritional or ethnic status, these factors may be held accountable.

4. *Seasonal Variations in Weight.* — Because employment in sugar production is seasonal, a great number of people, and their families, suffer economically especially during the fall and early winter months. Furthermore, general yearly levels of unemployment lead to underemployment of many individuals as part time work may prevail even during seasonal peaks. Since such conditions bring about yearly average nutritional inadequacy, the marked effects should be expressed in seasonally changing body weight and in thickness of subcutaneous fat, a major site of body-fat deposit. Abdominal fold was measured expressly for this, because it is highly correlated with total body-fat content. Fall and early winter months are the periods of greatest seasonal work layoff and, as can be seen from Tables 12 and 13 the mean weight and fold thickness decrease from summer to early winter months. Data on males only are shown in these tables, but the females and children are presumed to follow the same pattern. Certainly, this is another reflection of the marginal nutritional state which characterizes the seasonal and probably the yearly diet of most Puerto Ricans. Seasonal variations in weight and fat deposit are not uncommon in other populations, but the pattern is quite different when exercise and activity rather than undernutrition cause the seasonal declines.

5. *Weight and Height Variation by Number of Living Children.* — Even though differences are not great, the pattern shown in Tables 14 and 15 indicates that it is the taller and heavier women who have the greatest number of living children. Better nourishment seems to account for this, because the mean number of deceased children (stillbirths plus childhood deaths) increases as nutritional status declines (Table 16). However, the mean number of deceased children, except for Group 1, does not vary significantly by ethnic background (Table 17). Since biological fitness, especially in a marginal environment, is individually revealed by an above-average size and body weight, it is no surprise to find that effective fertility is correlated with this. Increased infant mortality in Puerto Rico is not due solely to nutritional inadequacy, but it is probably an important item in a complex which contributes to poor health in mother and child.

Selected Subsamples

1. *University of Puerto Rico Students and World War II Veterans.* — These two groups can be considered together because most of the male students were also veterans. All these individuals represent selected populations, either by reason of superior economic and social status or because of superior health status. Because of this, these groups are more fully discussed in another section, the one describing the characteristics of Puerto Ricans in "good health" (Chapter XIII). Even though the differences shown are minimal because the total samples used in the comparisons include these persons, the statistics for these selected groups compared with the general island averages shows that university students or veterans are significantly larger than the general average. Male veterans and students are about 10 pounds heavier and 1 inch taller than the average male. The female students are not so different in weight (3 pounds heavier) from the average, but they also are about an inch taller. Comparisons of the other measurements follow the same pattern. Both the males and females have a lower ethnic rating (2 to 3 units lighter in skin color) than the island average and are better nourished. Since the Negro in Puerto Rico is significantly taller and heavier than the White, the differences noted above are even less than actually exist between these students and racially comparable persons. If a sample racially comparable to the university students and veterans were drawn from the total sample, the differences noted would probably be nearly doubled. Table 114 shows, for instance, the ethnic differences in stature to be in the order of 5 cm, between extremes in the ethnic range, when nutrition is the same.

2. *Migrant Sedentes Comparisons.* — Comparisons between migrants and *"sedentes,"* those who stay in the homeland, are given in Tables 22-24. Only selected measurements are included. The comparisons are of special interest on at least two counts. First, if migrants are a selected segment of the parental population, what is the net effect of their loss to Puerto Rico? Second, is phenotypic selection operative in the choice of migrants from Puerto Rico? An answer to the first question is of practical administrative interest and the second is of general interest in the study of human evolution and population dynamics. As these question are of special interest Chapter XIV, is devoted to the migration problem (also see Thieme, 1957).

Anthropometric Measurements by Geographic Region

The people examined from each region are described for each measurement taken in Tables 25-95. The tables, however, are broken down into three groups: the first for the total samples for each region; the second, for these same regional samples but breaking them down into the 4 nutritional classes; and the third, for values for each of the ethnic groups. The reason for this was to make both comparisons between regions possible and to enable subsequent students to evaluate the degree of change in body dimensions that might occur in Puerto Rico through time. The anthropometic tables then are purely descriptive and are in no way designed to discover the causes of variability or the degree to which such causes interact and participate in bringing about the development of the individual and his phenotype. Evaluation of our data in this respect is discussed in the next section, but the three groups referred to above are briefly discussed below.

1. *Regional Total Samples*. — Statistics for males, females, and prisoners that relate to each anthropometric measurement are given in Tables 25-61 for subsamples the members of which are permanent residents in one of the 15 geographic regions (see Chapter IV, for the geographic features of Puerto Rico). In these tables no account has been taken of the ethnic or nutritional status of these regional samples; hence, the variations noted between regions cannot be assumed to be due to geographic factors alone. The tables do, however, describe the adult permanent residents of each region as they are.

The individuals included in the basic regional samples are those who were recorded as having resided: (1) for their whole life, (2) from birth to 20 years of age, or (3) for over 20 years in a particular region. Persons of less than 20 years residence are excluded, but some not presently resident may be included in a region. For example, quite a few of our total San Juan sample had recently migrated from the municipio where they had lived all their previous life, and these were coded for the municipio of prior residence. Although these data exclude persons of less than 20 years in a region, nevertheless, they picture the regional samples quite well because permanent residents account for about 70% of the total number measured in each region (Table S-13). It is impossible to characterize or summarize these tables satisfactorily, but one may say that, while variability of a limited amount does occur between regions, no particular pattern is apparent.

2. *Regional Total Samples by Nutritional Class.* — The statistical values of each measurement for each nutritional class (abbreviated here as N. C.) are given in Tables 62-70. Four hundred subjects were randomly selected from the total N. C. 2 sample for males and for females to ease the handling of cards in the machine operation. This reduction in sample size was justifiable, because it introduces little inaccuracy. Although the descriptive tabulations were primarily made to display the dimensions of each nutritional class in each region and not to reveal the effects of varying diets on body dimensions, they suggest (and later Tables 120-125 verify) that major variation does result from nutritional differences. Such differences are most often highly significant, for the best nourished persons were absolutely largest in all dimensions except for lower arm length, total face height in females, and nose width. The size of the differences between nutritional classes and the number in each class, however, is not the same for each region for the various measurements. But this cannot be interpreted as a consequence of varying regional conditions, as the ethnic composition of the nutritional classes was not alike. Tables 96-111, showing the regional differences between samples composed of the same nutritional and ethnic background, can be used to discover the effects of the regional variations.

In Table 70 the mean number of children for each class is recorded. There are fewer children in N. C. 1; that is to be expected since the members are slightly younger (1-4 years) and more favorably situated educationally and economically, facts which frequently have the effect of delaying marriage and may be associated with controlled family planning. The net effect is to give a higher per person level of family nutrition and the individual share of total income which characterizes this group.

3. *Regional Total Samples by Ethnic Group.* — Body dimension descriptions are given for each regional ethnic group in Tables 71-95. The subjects in Ethnic Groups 1 and 2 are White by all standards, the ones in 7 and 8 are clearly Negro, and those in 3 to 6 are more or less a mixture. A fairly constant gradient is noted as one goes from the first to the last ethnic category with the smallest persons being the least Negroid. Of course, strictly racial features, as nose length, do not follow this pattern, but it is clear that in Puerto Rico Negroes are larger than Whites. While the South European extraction of the majority of Whites may be held accountable, an alternate theory, that the Negroes are better adapted to the Puerto Rican environment and as a result biologically most fit, cannot be

rejected out of hand. Also, better food habits may contribute to this dimensional superiority of the Negro.

Variability between ethnic groups in each region and between similar groups in different regions cannot be taken as due to regional effects alone as the nutritional status of these are not equated. Tables 112-119, in which the analysis for the effect of ethnic variation is more precisely given, are discussed below. It is clear, however, that he ethnic composition of the regions varies and it appears also that there may possibly be a small difference between the dimensions of persons of the same ethnic group who come from different regions.

Variability by Region, Race, and Nutrition

In respect to causes of variability, the analysis of the data has been organized to show the effects of three fundamental factors; namely, the geographic, the racial or ethnic, and the nutritional. But under these broad headings a multitude of operative factors are probably acting to produce the physical variation observed. For example, under the heading "geographic," one may list the influence of temperature, humidity, soil, water, topographic irregularity, atmospheric pressure, cyclical features of the weather, actinic radiation, faunal or floral associations, and culturally created environmental features, and many more. All these may work individually or in combination to cause physical differences when race and nutritional status are equated. Nutrition, likewise, is multifactored and race the summation of a genetic complex.

The classification system set up here, however, cannot exceed in complexity that which is warranted by our data. We have no information, for instance, which would allow a breakdown of the given political and census regions into subclasses which would recognize all the features of geography which might vary, and the same is true of nutrition and race. For this reason the analysis follows the simple three-part classification which is carried out. In the first part, persons of the same ethnic and nutritional class (Sample A) are subdivided into 15 regional samples and only those persons of permanent residence in these regions included. In the second, only persons of the same nutritional class (Sample B) are used and they are subdivided into various ethnic groups in order to observe the effects of racial or ethnic variation. In the third and last, all persons of Ethnic Group 3 (Sample C) are subdivided according to the nutritional classes, a procedure which permits seeking out the physical effects of differing diets. Since initial work had established that geographic variations were not large or systematic in pattern, it was decided to ignore geographic residence in the ethnic and nutritional analysis. The results attained in this three-part arrangement are discussed below.

    1. *Regional Variability (Sample A).* — Tables 96-111 give the statistical values for 16 selected anthropometric measurements for each of 15 regional subsamples, the subjects all of Nutritional Class 2 and Ethnic Group 3 and permanent residents in one or other of the various 15 geographic regions. Our 15 regions can be grouped to give the seven of the United States Census and, if mean anthropometric values are desired for residents of these, data for our regions can be combined (see Table S-1) and the proportional weight of each in the combined mean calculated by considering the relative sample number from each of our regions in each census region. The tabulated regional variability shown in Tables 96-111 is also graphically arrayed (Graphs 1-15). In these graphs the mean plus and minus 2 S.E. is plotted for each of 14 measures for each regional sample by sex.

    In body weight and stature, Region 10 females differ significantly from those in Regions 8 and 13, and there are regional differences for several other measurements. Between the sexes differences occur in the variability found in each region; for example, the amount is different in head length, head breath, and nose length in the females compared to the males. Similar sex differences are present in many of the other measurements.

    Despite the frequent occurrence of differences between regions in many measurements, no consistency is apparent. Mountain people are like coastal people, east coastal like west coastal. The deviant group is only occasional; hence, one must assume either that some underlying factor related to geography, whatever it might be, has an unlike effect on the size of each body dimension or, as is more probable, that the variability is due to several causes or is comparatively random with the net effect of "geography" not discernable. Possibly, the ethnic and nutritional classification is sufficiently gross to allow for some degree of difference, or the small size of the regional samples introduces random errors that might disappear if their size were greater. Whatever may be the cause, it does seem correct to conclude that the effect of geographic influence is small. In contrast, if Graph 1 is compared with 16 and 17 and Graph 3 with 20 and 21, it will be seen that nutrition and ethnic factors cause much greater differences and that these are clearly patterned.

Even though geographic influence appears negligible, the fact that some regional differences are at significant levels suggests the desirability of further tests on larger samples. A more refined geographic classification which was not dependent upon political or traditional census units might show that some features of the physical environment do modify body dimensions. It is our belief, however, that the heterogeneity of the distribution of intestinal infestation, economic activities, and urban-rural proportions by region, as well as other culturally modified features of the environment, are more important.

2. *Ethnic Variability (Sample B).* — Tables 112-119 and Graphs 16-45 supply data that show the variation in ethnic background of a sample of persons belonging to Nutritional Class 2. The population of Puerto Rico is composed predominately of people with either White (South European) or Negro backgrounds, and these ethnic comparisons exhibit variation along a scale from practically unmixed White to unmixed Negro. Intermediate groups are mixed to various degrees. Since the effect of racial differences in body dimensions in Puerto Rico is surprisingly constant and shows the Negro to be larger than the White in most measurements, the results can be quite simply summarized. In all except four dimensions the Negro is larger, and usually significantly so, than the White. Of the four exceptions, two (trunk height and bigonial diameter) show no differences to speak of and in two (head width and nose height) the Negro is significantly smaller. These latter are, of course, characteristic differences between Negro and White. Age in these samples is quite comparable.

The fact that, except for four dimensions, the Negro is larger than the White while not predictable is not unexplainable. The South European populations from whom the Puerto Rican White is mainly derived are relatively short among peoples of Caucasian extraction. The Puerto Rican Negro is not small or unrepresentative of his parental race. Even so, the impression persists that in the same Puerto Rican scene the Caucasian element continues to be small-sized, as compared to its parental populations, while the Negro is seemingly unaffected or even benefited by it. It would be interesting to know if original differences have been enhanced or not, but whether the Negro is more capable of adapting to the conditions of life there or whether selective conditions in the original migrations made the Puerto Rican population unrepresentative of the parental populations is not clear. Either or both might account for many of the present differences. In addition, it is apparent and should be emphasized that, while the differences in body dimensions shown here are often highly significant statistically, they may not amount to much in the practical terms of daily living.

Assuming geographical factors to be insignificant and nutritional background to be a constant, the ethnic differences shown here are attributable to genetic causes and are of the "nature" of these subsample groups. But, the genetic differences between these groups controlling body dimensions in a racial sorting of this nature do not necessarily mean very much in terms of capacity or efficiency. These "natures" may be different but it is well to point out that many careful studies of racially distinct populations have failed to show any correlated differences in capacities which are fundamental either at the psychological or biological level. Yet, the question of whether there are differences in the efficiency of adaptation between races is enticing. On the face of it, the Puerto Rican Negro seems to be superior in his adaptation and a better biological specimen than the White. This is in relation to their relative anthropometry as well as to their ancestral stocks. The White in Puerto Rico seems to be small compared to Southern Europeans, whereas the Negro is either quite comparable or even larger than the West Africans thought to represent the slave populations. If this is truly real evidence of adaptive superiority, collaborative evidence should exist and be expressed most markedly in the body features which are more responsive to environment and are indications of health. However, a test of this shows it not to be the case. We find, for instance, no racial differences in hemoglobin, blood pressure, intestinal infestation, or blood counts. Such would be a likely expectation if racial fitness to the Puerto Rican scene was involved.

3. *Nutritional Variability (Sample C)*. — In Tables 120-125 and Graphs 16-45 persons all of Ethnic Group 3 are subdivided according to nutritional background. The mean values of the 16 measurements included in the tables are graphically displayed plus and minus 2 S.E. These tables and graphs are strikingly uniform and dramatic in their presentation of the uncontestable fact that better nourished persons are larger than those less well fed. Significant differences, and very highly so, occur between N.C. 1 and 3 or 4, for example, in 14 of the 16 measurements shown. Some exceptions, however, do occur. For female head width and male nose width there are no differences.

This is also true for cephalic index (C. I.), shown in Graphs 28 and 29. Head length and breadth are related to nutritional effects with the exception of female head length in which the N. C. 1 mean is less than for Classes 2 and 3. In addition to head length, female nose width for N. C. 1 is under that of Classes 3 and 4. Also, while the general pattern of nutritional effect is fairly uniform, there are differences in the degree of response for each body dimension, a fact more fully discussed below.

The possible effects of age differences between the nutritional classes should be mentioned. In these samples and comparisons, the age differences present tend to minimize the apparent size of the nutritional effects. Older persons are usually larger than younger ones, especially in the early adult years. In our sample the N. C. 1 persons are the youngest yet the largest. If age were corrected the differences between classes would be larger than shown. For males, N. C. 1 is significantly younger than Classes 2, 3, and 4. For the females, while N. C. 1 is the youngest, the differences between any class are not siginificant. The existence of age differences, then, tends to minimize the nutritional effects.

In order to understand the role of nutrition in controlling certain features of Puerto Rican anthropometric variability a general discussion of this factor is in order. First, it seems appropriate to describe the general nature of the nutritional classes by contrasting the nature of N. C. 1 with the rest of the sample. The persons of the best nutritional background belong to this class and are mainly White. By examining Tables S-14 and S-50, it becomes apparent that for males and females the ethnic-group distribution in the nutritional classes is not random. Skin color is appreciably lighter and the mean ethnic value lower. Positively correlated with this is the high frequency of sedentary occupation in N. C. 1 contrasted with the other groups. For the males 88% of N. C. 1 are sedentary, whereas for N. C. 2, 3, and 4 the values are 16%, 8% and 3%, respectively. Professional persons, public officials, and businessmen largely make up this male N. C. 1 group. Such persons are, for the most part, of superior economic and educational status, and White.

The women in our sample were not classified occupationally, but they were probably of similar status. The N. C. 1 females were chiefly nurses, government employees, and wives of N. C. 1 males. The number of living children of these females increases as nutritional status declines (Table 70), with 1.52 the mean value for N. C. 1 and 4.55 for Class 4. The 1.52 value is somewhat expected as the N. C. 1 females are slightly younger and come from a class in which marriage is frequently delayed. In Table 16 we see the same pattern repeated although in this case the measure is of deceased rather than living children. N.C. 1 has appreciably lower mean values than the other classes with a steady increase in number of dead children as nutritional level declines. While probably related to the higher fertility of the lower classes, it may also be a direct response to poor nutrition and such economic factors as housing. Comparative data from a selected sample of upper-class women were provided by Dr. Raymond Scheele (Table AR-2). Of 448 children born to 200 women, only 14 children died, a rate of 3.13%; 96% of the women had lost none; the mean number of deceased children dead per woman was 0,07. In our total sample, 1649, 1041 of the women had none dead (only 63%); the remaining 608 women lost 1248, which were distributed as follows:

Number of Children Died (per Woman)	Number of Women	Total Number of Children
1	306	306
2	146	292
3	76	228
4	34	136
5	13	65
6	20	120
7	7	49
8	4	32
9	1	9
11	1	11
Totals	608	1248

TABLE AR-2

INFANT MORTALITY IN 200 SELECTED UPPER-CLASS MARRIAGES*

Children Died	Marriages (Percent)	Total Cases
0	96.0	192
1	2.0	4
2	1.5	3
3	0.0	0
4	0.5	1
Total	100.0	200

*From data provided by Dr. Raymond Scheele and based on interview during October, 1948, of 200 selected upper-class women. The total number of children born to these women was 448.

The mean number of children dead in our total sample is .76± .003. Thus, the mean for Scheele's sample, probably all upper nutritional class, is one-tenth that of the island average. Also these women, although their exact age is unknown, were presumably older on the average than those in our sample group and thus with more completed fertility cases represented, factors which would accentuate the differences in frequency.

As would be expected the N.C. 1 sample is largely urban (79% of females and 73% of the males), a much higher rate than the urban frequencies for the other classes (see Table S-13).

In general the data points to the close relationship between nutritional status and economic status. Also, undernutrition for the majority of families whose adult heads are in Classes 2, 3, and 4 is complicated by their higher fertility rate. Since, in 1948, over 75% of the Puerto Rican families had a living standard based on an income of less than $1,000 a year, a fertility difference becomes crucial in deciding individual nutritional status.

An interesting question of both theoretical and practical interest, that can be tested with our data, is whether or not there are long-term effects on the skeletal system from pre-adult malnutrition at the levels observed in Puerto Rico. Some Puerto Ricans contend that the small size and gracility of that people is due to their nature and is in no way connected to the undernourishment that prevails, that, despite the standards of living, the individual finally achieves his naturally potential dimensions even though the yearly rate of growth may be less. The same view was expressed by Morant (1949) in an attempt to disprove that changing environmental conditions are the cause of secular changes, as in stature, that are observable in successive generations in one country or between migrants and *sedentes*. In effect, it is argued that comparisons have usually been made between early adults, those 18-21 years of age, and thus any later growth which might occur in the unfavorable environment was disregarded. But our data support no such contention. They show that long-term poor nutrition does have a lasting effect and comparisons between full adults whose racial origin is matched are significantly smaller in most body dimensions at all ages than in well-nourished persons. Furthermore, the delayed growth said to occur in the 20-30 age span does not exist (see Tables 6-9) at a level comparable to that between nutritional classes. Hence, it seems clear that an individual's genetic potential for growth is never achieved when he lives under the depressing effect of malnutrition.

Another observation of general interest is the disproportionality of effects that skeletal components show as a result of malnutrition. Not all parts are equally affected and strangely enough some may even show enhanced size under such conditions. This pattern of disproportionality is well known, but the degree of which the smaller undernourished person is not an exactly proportioned miniature of the larger well-nourished one has seldom been quantified. Because our data, however, are ideal for such an analysis, it is discussed in some detail. The analysis used was the "difference of log" method of Simpson (1941) which is designed to compare the relative proportions of different samples. That is, if the size ratio between samples is constant for each measurement, one being merely a miniature of the other, the samples will be represented by parallel lines in the graph of difference of log. Any disproportionality will disturb this pattern.

In this analysis the mean values of N.C. 2 and 3 males are compared to the means of N.C. 1, which was arbitrarily used as the reference group. N.C. 4 was excluded because the sample size is small (N = 35) and, consequently, errors are large. The logarithm of the mean for each measurement in N.C. 2 and in N.C. 3 are subtracted from those of N.C. 1, giving the difference of log. The resultant differences are then plotted for each class and are shown in Graph AR-1 for 8 selected measurements. The measurements used and difference in log between means are shown for the three nutritional classes. The calculations are not included but the corresponding statistics shown in Tables 62-70 for each measurement and nutritional sample were the basic data.

In Graph AR-1 the pattern of differences is emphasized by collecting the 8 measurement values for each nutritional class. N.C. 1, the reference group, is a vertical line and N.C. 2 and 3 would also be vertical if they were proportionally the same and, if smaller, their curves placed on the negative side of N.C. 1 on the difference scale. However, the fact that the line for each class is not parallel to any other shows the disproportionate effect of different nutrition levels on the various body dimensions.

The significance of difference between the means of measurements representing each nutritional class could be estimated using this graphic method, but as other graphs and tables serve this purpose, the standard errors are not shown here (see Graphs 16-45 and Tables 120-125). It should also be pointed out that in this method, graphic comparisons between the same measure

A STUDY OF HUMAN BIOLOGY

GRAPH AR - 1

DIFFERENCE OF LOGARITHM BETWEEN NUTRITIONAL CLASS 1 AND 2 OR 3 FOR 8 MEASUREMENTS

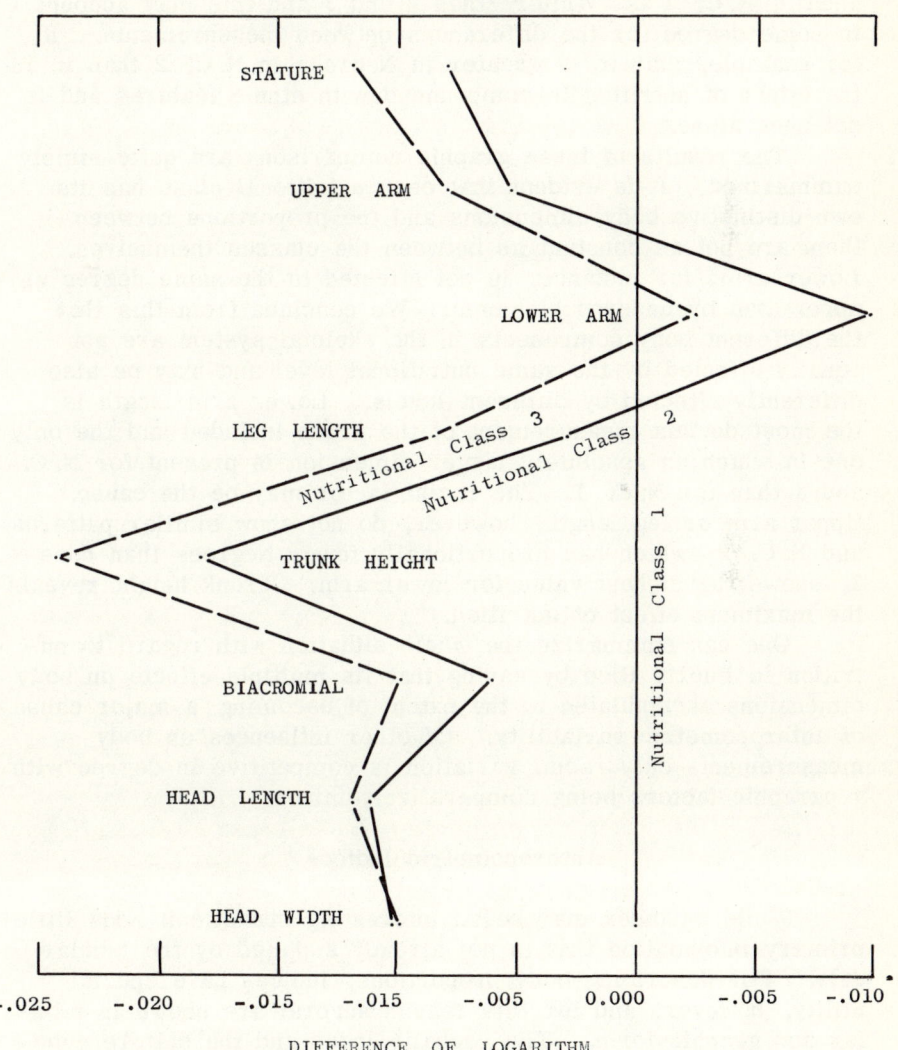

for different classes are valid and may be meaningful but those between different measures in the same class are not. The log method does not make the latter comparisons possible.

Before mentioning some of the individual measurements and general conclusions, it is necessary to point out that the ethnic constitution of the three nutritional classes used here are not equal. N.C. 1 is "Whiter" than 2 and 3 and this may account to some degree for the differences between measurements. If, for example, stature is greater in Negroes in N.C. 2 than in 1, the effect of nutrition is compounded with ethnic features and is not seen alone.

The results of these graphic comparisons are quite simply summarized. It is evident that each nutritional class has its own distinctive body dimensions and the proportions between them are not as constant as between the classes themselves. Lower arm, for instance, is not affected to the same degree as upper arm by undernourishment. We conclude from this that the different bony components in the skeletal system are not equally affected by the same nutritional level and may be also differently affected by different levels. Lower arm length is the most deviant measurement of the group included and the only one in which an absolutely larger dimension is present for N.C. 2 and 3 than for N.C. 1. The racial factor may be the cause. Upper arm or leg length, however, do not show similar patterns and N.C. 2, which has proportionally fewer Negroes than does 3, shows the highest value for lower arm. Trunk height reveals the maximum effect of nutrition.

One can summarize the whole situation with regard to nutrition in Puerto Rico by saying that its multiple effects on body dimensions accumulated to the extent of becoming a major cause of anthropometric variability. Of other influences on body measurements only racial variation is competitive in degree with geographic factors being comparatively minor.

Anthropometric Indices

While an index may be an interesting statistic it adds little primary information that is not already supplied by the tabular data. For describing body proportions, indices have special utility, however, and for this reason several are shown in tabular and graphic form. The cephalic index and the stature/cube-root-of-weight, leg-length/stature, and trunk height/stature indices for the total samples of males and females and for each nutritional group are given in Tables 126-127. Thirteen indices are presented graphically (see Index to Graphs, Part 2 or Graphs 54-66), but these were not all that were calculated. Eighteen were calculated from the measurements on each individual's record and the total sample was used of males, including prisoners, and of females.

In addition to the ones shown in the tables and graphs, the statistics for the following are on record and available in the Laboratory of Physical Anthropology at the University of Michigan. They are: Upper Arm/Total Arm; Lower Arm/Total Arm; Trunk Height/Leg Length; Biacromial/Stature; Nose Height/Upper Face Height; Upper Face Height/Total Face Height; and Bizygomatic/Head Length. Mean index values were also calculated for every recorded skin-color category, but as the ethnic analysis' shown in the graphs, parallels each one of them closely, they are omitted in this report.

In the tables (126-127) the indices are arrayed by nutritional class in order to see what the effects of dietary difference were on four body proportions, noted above. Of these, only height/cube-root-of-weight showed a consistent response to nutritional differences. The head shape of males, surprisingly, becomes slightly more brachycephalic (or round-headed) with poorer nutrition, but this was not so of females. Although this difference for males is not highly significant, increased brachycephaly is contrary to expectation especially as the Negro has, on the average, a lower C.I. and is represented more frequently in the N.C. 2, 3, and 4 groups (see Graphs 28 and 29 which give the relative C.I. decrease in Negroes).

In graphs portraying the indices, the four nutritional classes (curve "E") and the ethnic groups (curve "D") include all persons in the total sample. These curves, therefore, are descriptive values for the classes and are not completely efficient for detecting the cause of the variability. Ethnic composition of each nutritional class is not the same, it may be recalled, and vice versa.

Significant variation occurs for many of the indices, as would be expected, and inspection of the graphs gives a visual summary which no lengthy description can replace. Of special interest, due to the widespread use of cephalic index in racial studies, is the finding that in addition to being longer headed than the Whites, as is well known, the head shape of the Puerto Rican Negro is relatively broader in those from the more poorly nourished groups. The fact that the relative proportion of Negroes in each nutritional subsample increases from the first to the third and fourth makes this pattern even more difficult to understand. None of our data explains this observed phenomenon. In Graphs 28-29, in which the mean cephalic index of persons all from Ethnic Group 3 are shown for each nutritional group, these values confirm that the mean C.I. increases, with N.C. 1 having the lowest value for each sex. The differences are not significant and are somewhat less than found in Table 126.

The analysis of index values for each subsample listed adds to the supplementary data already given on the anthropometric variability encountered. In contrast to other analyses, however, the indices usually have the effect of minimizing differences--at least the ones in gross size. Because of this, the comparison of indices is a mere elaboration and adds nothing to our previous methods of analysis in which the major causes of variability are sought. While they have some value for ascertaining such causes, they are really included for another reason, and that is their descriptive and comparative value. Their inclusion allows our data on Puerto Ricans to be compared with any other populations for which such data are given.

The height/cube-root-of-weight index (Table 126) deserves some comment. In most studies of constitutional type it is claimed that this is the value most diagnostic of the hereditary body build of individuals and that it is relatively unaffected by nutrition. Our data show a steady increase in this value by nutritional class and many of the differences between classes are highly significant (for instance, N.C. 1 campared to N.C. 3 for both sexes). Hence, the effect of nutrition on this index is real and body weight relative to stature does decrease as malnourishment increases.

OTHER DATA

1. *Dental Status.* — Tables 128-139 and Graphs 46-53 deal with dental data (see Chapter IX).
2. *Physiological.* — The data bearing on physiology are given in Graphs 67-76 and discussed in Chapter XI.
3. *"Good Health"*. — Chapter XIII deals with a subsample selected for superior health status. These data are selected because of value for those concerned with clinical standards for evaluating individual health.
4. *Prisoners.* — Throughout this report the anthropometric values for the special prison sample have usually been kept separate in the tables (see Index to Tables, Part 2) from those of

the male civilian group. Reference to these tables (no prisoner data are shown in the graphs) will give the description of this group. This prison sample was included for three reasons: (1) To answer, if possible, the question of whether prisoners are an anthropometrically distinct and selected group or whether they merely represent a biologically random sample of the parent population; (2) because of the ease of getting a fairly large number of subjects and, particularly, because persons could be selected according to their region of previous residence, which would fill out gaps in our sample; and (3) because it permitted testing of the feasibility of photographic anthropometry, which required that pictures be taken of subjects in the nude. Of the civilians, only the University of Puerto Rico males could be persuaded to disrobe so our efforts were mainly confined to prison males. The results of this measuring method are reported in Chapter II. We obtained 395 males in the prison sample. Even though selected to some extent in order to fill out our regional representation, we do not know how well our sample represents the total prisoner population. But assuming it is representative, as can be seen from Table 1, the prisoners are slightly heavier but shorter than the free males and their ethnic-factor average is higher. Their ages are comparable to the free males and the few other anthropometric differences are as might be expected.

Our data do not support a conclusion that prisoners are a nonrandom, or selected, sample of the parental population. Some differences do occur, between them and nonprisoners, but they are probably not very meaningful as far as indicating selection is concerned. For example, although the prisoners are 0.5 cm shorter than free males, no one can seriously contend that such slight difference could characterize criminals, as compared to ordinary civilians, or predispose them to a life of crime. Possibly, their economic and nutritional background is less adequate and it is this which makes them smaller, but our data do not warrant this generalization either. The prisoners are heavier than the men outside, and higher values for waist and other circumferences indicate they are better nourished. Their nutritional background before prison is listed in Table S-13 and can be compared to that of free males. In prison, since the diet of all is the same, perhaps prisoners are better fed than free men, or perhaps the inactivity of prison life makes prisoners tend to gain weight.

Data on the type of crime, length of time in prison, number of offenses and other pertinent sociological data were gathered on each prisoner. These have not been used in this report nor have they yet been analyzed, but, in any event, we are indebted to the prison authorities in Puerto Rico both for their help in gathering the sample and for their co-operation in making data available to us.

IX. DENTAL STATUS

THE DENTAL HEALTH of the people in Puerto Rico is unusually poor. Shourie, *et al.* (1949, Table 6), reported that dental disease is present in 99,400 out of every 100,000 Puerto Ricans. In other words, only six of each 1,000 Puerto Ricans have teeth free from caries, peridontal disease, oral calculus, missing teeth, or dental work. The rate of decayed, missing, and filled teeth (the DMF rate) per individual is, of course, also high and Shourie, using visual and X-ray examination, found that in a group of 622 male, 14-year-old children the DMF rate was 8.6 per child. His data confirm our own findings that the dental conditions of all age groups in Puerto Rico is indeed deplorable.

METHODS OF EXAMINATION

Examination was by means of a mouth mirror and probe explorer.[1] Adequate natural or artificial light was available and examinations were conducted under favorable conditions. Each tooth was examined and its condition coded as follows: (1) present and noncarious; (2) present and carious; (3) missing, that is, extracted or lost; and (4) nonerupted. Teeth that were filled, regardless of whether there were additional decayed areas or not, were classified as carious. The number of caries on a single tooth were not distinguished, nor whether there was a slight or massive amount of decay. When an adult said that a missing tooth had not been extracted, it was usually recorded as nonerupted, rather than missing, especially when there was lateral symmetry. In adults absence of third molars

---

[1] In Shourie's (1949) study of Puerto Ricans, the DMF rate by visual examination, when X-ray was not used, was 7.9 per mouth. The use of X-ray examination increases the average score by about 17%. Studies using visual examination alone give minimum DMF rates and cleaning and drying the teeth before examination may result in the disclosure of 20% more lesions. Accurate diagnosis in any event is difficult in the posterior teeth but easier and more accurate in the anterior; consequently, using about 20% as a correction factor would probably exaggerate the total underenumeration of actual caries resulting from visual examination under field conditions. In any event, our data are a minimum of actual caries rates.

was likewise coded as nonerupted. Lack of X-ray equipment made an accurate estimate of nonerupted teeth and their locations impossible. Since, in the analysis of dentitions, the attention is not centered on DMF rates but on the number of teeth present and noncarious, the study is structured to show the levels of dental health as well as the frequencies of healthy teeth in subsamples with different backgrounds.

GENERAL CONSIDERATIONS

Each adult normally has 32 permanent teeth and any variation is extremely rare. How many of these teeth remain at death, except those traumatically lost, depends on a variety of biological and environmental circumstances. Primarily tooth loss is a consequence of caries and or peridontal disease. The hereditary nature of the individual is believed to determine, to some extent, his resistance to dental loss from caries; considerable evidence indicates similarity in dental-loss pattern in families or other genetically related groups. No one knows, however, whether resistance to caries is caused by differences in tooth structure or is owed to inherited immunity, or results from innate qualities inherent in the physiological or biochemical nature of the individual. In any event, it is certain that the way of life or habits of a person affects his dental health. The physical and oral environment, including nutritional factors, also affects the resistance to tooth decay, and there obviously are significant differences in this respect between populations. The causes are undoubtedly numerous but the presence of fluorine and calcium in the water, or food, have marked effect. It is possible, too, that some yet unknown factors in the external environment may affect caries frequencies.

Nutrition is possibly the most important factor influencing dental health. Large amounts of carbohydrates or refined sugars, for instance, frequently characterize the diets of those with high caries rates. To understand, however, the relation of food to caries production is not simple, for the changes in caries rates are often delayed long after dietary shifts occur. But, since nutrition affects the well-being of the individual, caries frequencies and general health may be basically correlated. Although this correlation is difficult to state in terms of cause, it is almost certain that the condition of the teeth is not independent of the biological status of the person involved. Pathological conditions, variation in food intake, and other factors which act on the body processes, may either do harm or benefit to dentition, especially if tooth development is under way or incomplete. An unfavorable oral environment as expressed by a high lactobacillus count, has been claimed to have a marked effect on caries frequencies. Some individuals may possess inherited or acquired relative immunities to lactobacillus, or the lactobacillus count may be otherwise controlled, and thus have favorable oral conditions. However, the relatively low correlations between caries rates and bacillus counts, at least in Puerto Rico,[2] showed that caries immunity was not alone dependent on this feature of the oral environment.

Keeping these general considerations in mind, the report of dental conditions in Puerto Rico is organized in a variety of ways so that the maximum value can be realized. First, the variation in number of sound teeth in relation to the important biological variables of age, sex, and site of tooth is analyzed. Second, regions of residence, in view of man's dependence on soil and climate for his health, are analyzed. (Fluorine availability is noted in this section.) Third, the effect of nutritional background, racial origin, urban-rural residence, and occupation are discussed. Last, the amount of dental work and the frequency of anomalous conditions, such as crowding, shovel-shaped incisors, peg teeth, extra incisors and attrition are reported.

Frequency of Noncarious Teeth

1. *Differences by Age and Sex.* — A significant difference between males and females in the rate of loss of sound teeth is evidenced. At age 20, males and females have about the same number of sound teeth (approximately 25); at 40, the females have only 10 left as compared to 18 for the males. Table D-1 shows the changes by age groups for each sex. Sample A was used in this analysis (Nutrition Group 2, Ethnic Group 3) and, consequently, gross differences in heredity and nutritional status have been eliminated. From the data it follows that the rate of loss of noncarious teeth is 0.29 teeth per year for males and 0.58 teeth per year for females. It will be seen that for males, on the average, one tooth is lost or becomes

---

[2]Shourie (1949) reported low correlations of approximately $r=0.3$ between lactobacillus counts and DMF measurements in several test combinations. No correlations were higher than 0.33.

TABLE D-1

MEAN NUMBER OF NONCARIOUS TEETH IN MALES AND FEMALES OF SAMPLE A* BY AGE

Age Group	Males			Females		
	Mean No. Noncarious	Mean Age	No. in Sample	Mean No. Noncarious	Mean Age	No. in Sample
18-19	25.00	18.55	34	25.14	18.32	37
20-29	23.78	23.90	337	22.16	23.95	389
30-39	21.25	33.96	168	16.13	34.35	220
40-49	18.08	42.97	91	10.18	42.57	51
50+	15.40	50.40	5	12.50	52.12	8

*Subjects of both Nutritional Class 2 and Ethnic Class 3.

Carious every four years and for females, one every two years. Graph 46 gives the plotted data and the rate of loss by age for each sex.

Sex differences in rate of loss have been reported in other populations. It has been suggested that part of the reason for this is that eruption of teeth in females is more precocious and their teeth, in consequence, are longer exposed to carious attack. But our study, in which the number of sound teeth at age 20 is the same for each sex, does not support this view. Rather, it seems, there must be something which varies resistance by sex after this age. Demands of pregnancy and lactation, especially in women of marginal nutritional background, appear to be the most probable cause of these sex differences in Puerto Ricans. Yet, innate differences in tooth structure between the sexes or other factors must not be discounted.

From Table D-2, comparisons can be made between individuals of Sample A in rate of decayed, missing, and filled teeth (DMF rate) by sex and by age groups. Starting from approximately the same level, the DMF rate for the females especially up to age 40, is higher than for the males. Higher rates for noncarious teeth, lower DMF rates, slightly higher averages for nonerupted, and lower averages for missing teeth characterize the males when they are compared to the females. When the two groups are effectively equated for heredity and nutrition (as in Table D-1) the differences are highly significant. Mean number and standard error of noncarious teeth for the total male (including prisoners) and total female samples is: Male, $21.456 \pm .178$; Female, $18.988 \pm .217$. The differences are highly significant with $p = .0001$. If one assumes that the rate of tooth loss is a function of sex, then an age correction to make the two sexes age comparable can be made and the

TABLE D-2

AVERAGE RATE OF DMF* TEETH
FOR TOTAL SAMPLE BY AGE AND SEX

	Females		Males	
Age Group	Number Examined	DMF* Rate Per Person	Number Examined	DMF* Rate Per Person
17-19	81	4.79	92	5.58
20-22	293	6.31	381	5.94
23-25	302	9.26	316	8.28
26-28	200	12.10	240	9.87
29-31	174	14.01	196	10.82
32-34	148	14.46	171	12.37
35-37	167	17.13	133	10.94
38-40	152	18.82	164	12.21
41-43	40	17.42	73	14.23
44-46	54	22.17	80	16.04
47-49	17	19.94	30	19.83
50-58	21	20.57	32	19.09
Total	1649	....	1908	....

*Number of decayed, missing or filled teeth per person.

differences in mean number of noncarious teeth calculated. From these various comparisons it is obvious that some basic biological difference that affects caries rates exist between males and females.

2. *Differences by Site of Tooth*. — The different teeth in the mouth are quite variable in their resistance to carious attack (see Graph 49)[3]. In each sex, differences in this respect occur between anterior and posterior teeth: for example, between molars and incisors and between canines and premolars. Upper

---

[3]Differences by site may be affected by the fact that teeth erupt at different times. The third molar, which is very late and varies most in time of eruption, cannot be easily compared to the other teeth as they may be either "missing" or not yet erupted. For calculation of rates, therefore, only the teeth present and noncarious are considered. For most teeth the assumption is that all not included in the "present, noncarious" category are probably defective. For the third molar, this is less probable. Thus, the date for the third molar are minimum estimates.

and lower teeth also differ in vulnerability, but not right and left. It is apparently random whether a corresponding right and/or left tooth will be decayed or lost. Differences between upper and lower and between anterior and posterior teeth are highly significant; in males, that between upper first incisors and lower first incisors is approximately 25 percent. Between lower incisors and molars it exceeds 50 percent. Interestingly, the anterior-posterior differences are not the same for upper and lower jaws; the anterior lower teeth and the posterior upper are those most resistant to caries. All three upper molars are much less attacked than are the three lower. Of the anterior teeth, the lower first and second incisor, the canine, and the first premolar are less liable than are their corresponding upper teeth. Only in the second premolar is there no significant difference between rates for the upper and lower jaw.

As with rate loss of sound teeth, there is a consistent sex difference at every site. For each tooth, males proved to be more resistant and have a higher percentage of noncarious (5 to 10 percent more) than the females. The sex differences in decay, therefore, do not arise in a single dental region of the mouth, but rather are due to some basic systemic cause (or causes) that acts on all teeth equally. What makes the anterior teeth more resistant to carious invasion than the posterior teeth and the upper more so than the lower jaws is not clear from our data. Probably, the molars are more prone to attack than either the incisors or canines because of their form and larger exposed surface. But size and morphology do not explain the differences between the upper and lower teeth. It may be that the histological structure of the teeth makes for differential resistance. Yet, it could also be that the external surrounding of the teeth varies between upper and lower jaw and anterior and posterior regions. Whether the lactobacillus counts are high or low cannot be a factor, for these organisms are present in the saliva, and the lower anterior teeth, which are most resistant to caries, are those teeth constantly bathed by saliva. If lactobacillus count fails to explain this, another explanation seems plausible and that is calculus frequency. Shourie, *et al.* (1949), after examining the incidence of supragingival oral calculus in different regions of the mouth on 617 subjects in Puerto Rico, noted that the heaviest and most frequent positions are on the lower anterior teeth and upper posterior teeth. Only 7 (1.1%) of the 617 had calculus on the upper anterior teeth (6 with one tooth affected and 1 with three). In contrast, 140 (23%) had calculus deposits on the lower anterior teeth with 107 having four or more teeth affected. That is, 304 (49.3%) had calculus on one or more of their upper posterior teeth, whereas only 83 (13.4%) had deposits on their lower posterior teeth. For subgingival calculus, the differences between the two areas were not so marked; however, lower anterior teeth and upper posterior teeth again showed the highest frequency of calculus.

Calculus frequency undoubtedly does not completely account for caries freedom at different sites in the mouth, but the agreement between a high calculus rate and a low caries rate is probably important. Caries rates decrease where calculus rates are high. It seems logical that a tooth surface protected by calculus should have increased resistance to caries. Lest it be concluded that calculae are wholly beneficial, one must point out that by causing gingival disease they increase the rate of tooth loss. Since our study did not record gingival disease — except to note that it is very frequent — no comment on this relationship can be made.

3. *Difference by Ethnic Group and Caries by Tooth Site.* — The graphs (50) for the upper left and (51) for the lower left dental arches show what percentage of teeth were noncarious for each of the different ethnic groups. In this analysis, ethnic groups 1 and 2 are combined, as are 3 with 4, 5 and 6, and 7 with 8, so that four comparison groups are obtained. It was done to simplify the graph and to show that relatively large samples could be so used. From Graph 50 it is seen that the persons in groups 7 and 8 (Negro ancestry) have, in general, the greatest resistance to caries for all sites of the upper left mouth, with the exception of the second premolar, of any of the groups. For the lower left, groups 7 and 8 are most resistant for all the teeth anterior to the molars. For the molars, groups 3 and 4 have the highest percentage. Since these comparison groups are not equated for nutritional background, food habits could partially account for this pattern, as could racial differences.

4. *Differences by Nutrition and Caries by Site.* — In Graph 52 the percentages of noncarious teeth present by site in the lower left half of the mouths for the four nutritional classes (right-left differences are not significant, see Graph 49) are shown. Superior nutrition (Group 1) increased caries resistance significantly in the anterior teeth but decreased it in the posterior; the poorest nutrition (Group 4) resulted in the greatest number of carious teeth in the anterior sites and the least among the molars. One can only suggest that the increased caloric intake characteristic of the superior nutritional group, because it

involves a much larger total intake of carbohydrates, may account for this differential resistance.

Graph 53 presents the same kind of data as Graph 52, but for the upper left jaw for each nutritional class. In this case, the difference between the best and the poorest nourished individuals is not nearly as clear as for the lower jaw comparisons. Yet, again, the first nutritional group shows the lowest number of caries-free first and second molar teeth of any of the nutritional groups. Subjects in this group are slightly younger than in any of the other groups, so the third molar has been less exposed to attack. As this tooth is rarely caries-free, exposure time is an important factor. In the anterior teeth the difference between the first, second, and third nutritional groups does not appear to be significant, but the fourth nutritional and poorest nourished group shows a marked decrease in caries resistance in the second incisor. This is probably not meaningful and may be due to small sample size.

5. *Summary of Tooth-site Differences*. — Differences in caries-resistance pattern between the upper and lower jaws and the anterior and posterior segments of either jaw should be of great interest in the study of caries control and caries frequency. They are either related to some element of the external (mouth) environment of the tooth or to its hereditary nature. Evolutionary studies of primate teeth, including man, indicate, that in general, the canine is the tooth most resistant to morphological change and is the pivotal tooth in the dentition. In our study, in both the upper and lower jaws, the canine was the tooth most resistant to caries. Its smooth surface may contribute to this, but if this were the only consideration, the lateral incisors, which are smaller and have less area for invasion, should be more resistant than the canines. But this is not the case. Evolutionary studies show that there have been area patterns in the changes that have taken place in the human dentition through time. The incisors as a group have a pattern of similarity; the canine is self-distinct and does not group with any other teeth; the premolars form a group as do the molars. In general, the most posterior tooth in each of these morphological areas seems to be, from an evolutionary point of view, the one that is most rapidly changing and most variable. The most stable teeth, in evolutionary terms, are possibly also the most resistant to caries. Such a pattern is suggested but is not completely borne out by our data. While it is not contradicted in the lower jaw, it is in the upper jaw where the lateral incisor and the second premolar show greater resistance to caries than do the

more anterior teeth in their group. No matter how the data are arranged, the third molar shows startling susceptibility to caries. This tooth, the last one erupted, is the most carious and the least successful of man's teeth.

Dental Condition by Geographical, Ethnic, and Nutritional Groupings

1. *Differences Related to Geographic Region.* — Although Puerto Rico is a small island only 30 miles wide and 100 miles long, it is nevertheless geographically diverse. This diversity is reflected in its soil constitution and water-mineral content. When the subjects in our sample were undergoing primary dental development, some 20 to 50 years ago, their main source of drinking water was surface runoff and rain water. For this period, then, there would be relatively little geographic difference in water-mineral content. In 1948, however, there was considerable variation in the mineral content of other water supplied in the public water systems. Nutritional intake varies in kind by regions; for example, fishing in some of the coastal areas and subsistance gardening in others provide local variety. The proportions of regional populations of various racial extraction are also variable.

Given such regional variability, we expected, and in fact found, that dental characteristics varied as well. In Tables 128-133 the frequencies of carious, noncarious and missing teeth are given for males, females, and prisoners, for each of the 15 regions. Even when our regional samples are made comparable for age, nutrition, and race, significant differences still occur, differences that are probably related to geographic factors that are operative.

In carrying out the regional comparisons corrections for mean age differences were introduced. The mean age for the total female sample used was 28.28 years. The females from Region 4 had a mean of only 23 years, while from Region 5 it was 25.46 years. These two regions are the only ones in which the mean age for the region was more than one year different from the total sample mean. The mean age of the total male sample was 29.4 years. Region 7, with a mean age of 32.74, and Region 5, with one of 33.35, were the only regions with a deviation of over three years. Three other regions (8, 10, and 12) had a deviation between two and three years, three more had a deviation of less than two years, and seven more less than one year.

As females lose teeth at the rate of approximately 0.58 and males at 0.29 teeth per year (see Graph 46, which demonstrates the importance of age), the mean caries rate of the female and male samples of each region was corrected according to the deviation in mean age for each region from the mean age of the total sample.

The final regional comparison, corrected for age, for persons of the same ethnic and nutritional background (Ethnic 3 and Nutritional 2) is shown on Graph 47. On the graph, twice the standard error is indicated by a bar above and one below the mean for males. In this sample, the age corrected mean for noncarious teeth in males was 22.31; in the females, 20.07. The difference between the two means is highly significant ($p = .001$). Regional differences in the male sample, by the "overlap test,"[4] were numerous. For example, Region 3 is significantly different from six other regions. As an example of the statistical meaning of the overlap test, t values for the difference between Regions 1 to 14 were calculated. The test showed a value of 3.414, which gives a probability equal to .00068.) On the basis of the data that is presented in Graph 47, it seems conclusive that regional differences in resistance to caries do occur in Puerto Rico.

Because recent work had begun to relate freedom from caries to levels of fluorine in drinking water, in our study the fluorine content of the water was correlated with the dental findings. The data for this were furnished by the Department of Public Health of Puerto Rico, but two facts qualify its usefulness. (1) Most of the drnking water is either surface runoff or rain water, both of which would be fluorine free and not subject to Health Department analysis, and (2) the aqueduct system in Puerto Rico was relatively new in many areas and many people did not drink water from this source, even if available. In addition, the maximum content of fluorine recorded for aqueduct water was only 0.6 parts per million. This is far below the level thought to be necessary to prevent caries. The maximum level was obtained at Corozal in Region 14. Interestingly, the mean number of noncarious teeth listed for individuals

---

[4]In this test if the top of the 2 SE bar of one subsample is below the horizontal level of the bottom of another subsample bar, they are significantly different. The level is slightly more than one percent but not as great as 5 percent.

from this region was well above the island average for both males and females. In contrast, however, the four municipalities showing fluorine contents of .4 ppm, the next highest rate, are not in regions which show high percentage of noncarious teeth. They are Toa Baja, Dorado, Carolina, and Toa Alta. Three of them (Dorado, Toa Alta, and Toa Baja) are in Region 3 and the fourth in Region 5. Although Region 5 exhibited a higher than average resistance to caries, Region 3 does not. It is worth mentioning that the former, with its many Negroes, has a greater dependence upon home gardening and fishing than is true for most regions. But since the Region 5 sample used for this comparison had been roughly equated for nutritional intake and ethnic background, this fact cannot be considered very important, whereas the fluorine content may still be. In general, therefore, although there are regional and municipio differences, the generally low concordance with caries frequencies makes fluorine content alone a poor explanation for such differences as exist.

To sum up the geographic effects on dental conditions, it is clear that when the people of Puerto Rico are equated as to sex, age, ethnic background, and nutritional intake, the fact that significant differences are present as between regions becomes apparent. The cause or causes of these are not readily discoverable as the caries frequencies by regions are not the same for males and females. For instance, Region 5, which shows the highest caries resistance of all the regions for the males, shows one of the lowest for females. Region 10, in contrast, is high for both sexes. Even though the way of life for males and females is quite different in Puerto Rico, the regional differences for sex should roughly parallel each other, if caries frequency differences between the regions were dependent on variations in a single factor, such as fluorine content of the water. Hence, it seems that more than one, perhaps several, causes must be responsible for the regional differences found.

2. *Differences Related to Ethnic Group.* — Dental differences between ethnic groups are illustrated in Graph 48. In this case (Sample B) individuals of Nutritional Group 2 are compared on the basis of differences in their ethnic origin. Corrections were made for age so that each group would be comparable. The clearest pattern shown, true for both males and females, was the higher resistance to caries (based on count of noncarious teeth) in the more extreme Negroid groups. Even so, there is no consistent trend in the curve. Ethnic Groups

3, 4, and 5 had a greater resistance to caries than either Groups 1 and 2 or 6 and 7. Only in Group 8, particularly for the females, do the extreme differences occur and, in view of the fact that the sample number in this last group is relatively small, this perhaps should be suspect.

Again (Graph 48), the difference between the sexes shows a consistent pattern, but one less clear than between the ethnic groups. The intermediate individuals, who might be said to be White-Negro hybrids, show a caries resistance superior to the more predominantly White or the predominantly Negroid groups. It is doubtful whether this should be taken as evidence of hybrid vigor, because racial mixtures in Puerto Rico are of long standing. It is also impossible to state whether nutrition or heredity (here, ethnic group) plays the more important role. Each appears approximately equal in causing variability in resistance to caries. Since sex, region, and tooth site in the mouth also may contribute to such variability, we are again forced to conclude that there is no single cause of caries, nor is it assignable, in a dominant proportion, to either heredity or environment. In Tables 134-137 the frequencies of carious, noncarious, and missing teeth are given for each ethnic group of males, females, and prisoners. These tables give the basic description of total group characteristics by ethnic group and do support the contention that the ethnic group is a major basis for dental-condition variability.

3. *Differences Related to Nutritional Status.* — Tables 138 and 139 give the tooth counts in the total sample by nutritional classes for the males, females, and prisoners. Comparisons suggest that improvement in nutritional status guarantees no improvement in caries resistance. In the first section of Table 138, in which the number of carious teeth is given, the mean for the Nutritional Class 1 males is 5.58 per mouth, whereas in the other three groups (2, 3, and 4) it is not above 4. Again, for the females, Class 1 shows the highest number of carious teeth. However, when carious and missing teeth are combined, differences are not as sharp. Yet, it is certainly true that improvement in nutrition does not result in a low count of carious and missing teeth. Actually, when the data of Table 139, which shows the total number of teeth noncarious, are used, a t test for significance of difference among the four nutrition classes did not give any basis for concluding that nutrition had any appreciable effect on resistance to caries. It should be noted, however, that the samples within the nutritional classes, which are compared in Tables 138 and 139, do not have the same

ethnic background. But samples of similar ethnic background are compared on the basis of differences in nutritional status in Graph 48. Since age plays an important role in determining the number of noncarious teeth, all data in this graph was corrected for age differences. The comparisons in the C samples in Graph 48 indicate, after such correction, that the males and females in Nutritional Class 1 had the most carious teeth of any group. The next highest rate in caries, or lowest rate of noncarious teeth, is for Nutritional Class 3; then, Nutritional Class 2; and finally, Class 4 has the highest rate of noncarious teeth. Since Class 4 is the group which has a submarginal level of nutritional adequacy, the conclusion is unescapable that, while the differences are not marked, improvement in nutritional status is associated in Puerto Rico with a decline in dental status.

4. *Differences Between Other Sample Groupings*. —

   a) Residence. - Groups classified as "urban," "rural with neighbors," or "rural, alone," failed to show any significant differences in frequency of carious plus missing teeth. Urban individuals had a higher carious and missing-tooth rate than did the rural. Although consistent, the difference was relatively slight and corrections for age reduced them still further. The mean age, ethnic and nutritional composition of the residence groups are given in Table D-3.

   b) Occupation. - Rates of decayed or lost teeth by occupation among the males; that is, grouped according to background of hard labor, light labor, or sedentary, were not significantly different in any analysis.

TABLE D-3

MEANS OF AGE, ETHNIC, AND NUTRITION VALUES
FOR TOTAL SAMPLE BY RESIDENCE

Residence	Mean Age		Mean Ethnic Group		Mean Nutrition Class	
	Male	Female	Male	Female	Male	Female
Urban	27.97	28.70	3.28	3.22	2.095	2.036
Rural, with Neighbors	27.18	27.73	3.95	3.53	2.083	2.273
Rural alone	30.46	30.46	3.69	3.02	2.225	2.276

c) Dental Work. - All facilities that attend to dental needs, it is agreed, are inadequate. Our reports on dental conditions certainly supports the view. Signs of dental work were looked for in each mouth. Tooth fillings were regarded as proof of professional attention. It was also assumed that the wearing of total dentures was evidence of dental attention, but the frequently poor fit between dentures and gums made one wonder whether this was a gratuitous assumption.

Of the females, 548 (33.23%) had received dental work; of the males, 428 (28.21%); and of the prisoners, 40 (10.12%). Differences were present between the nutritional classes. As nutritional status is highly correlated with economic status, this is as would be expected. Table D-4 shows the percentage frequencies for each nutritional group and Table D-5 for each ethnic group.

TABLE D-4

PERCENTAGE OF TOTAL SAMPLE SHOWING
EVIDENCE OF DENTAL ATTENTION

Nutritional Class	Females	Males	Prisoners
1	72.81%	82.00%	(None in class)
2	32.52	27.16	10.96%
3	25.16	15.70	7.23
4	14.28	5.71	Insignificant

TABLE D-5

PERCENTAGES OF TOTAL SAMPLE HAVING
HAD DENTAL WORK DONE BY ETHNIC GROUPS

Ethnic Group	Males	Females	Prisoners
1	43.47%	38.88%	(None in group)
2	32.36	35.85	17.24%
3	29.39	34.18	8.57
4	18.18	28.26	9.75
5	33.33	25.00	7.69
6	25.80	34.72	7.89
7	27.63	23.07	2.56
8	10.29	14.28	21.42

To determine the relationship between dental condition and dental work, an analysis of males and of females who were in both Nutritional Class 2 and Ethnic Group 3 (Sample A) was made and the results are given in Table D-6. Subjects with dental work had approximately six less noncarious teeth than those with none. Apparently, those with the greatest need visit the dentist more often, yet we were impressed by the frequency of unfilled caries. People who had visited the dentist usually needed still more work, and less than one-third of the sample examined had ever been treated. One percent of the males and 21.8% of the females had complete dentures; 9.89% of the males and 15.03% of the females had less than 10 teeth left out of the complement of 32 that is man's inheritance.

In summary: First, females go to dentists more frequently than males. Second, economic background of the individual is highly correlated with presence or absence of dental work. Third, individuals of the lighter colored ethnic groups more frequently have had dental work. The difference by race, however, is not nearly as striking as it is by nutritional class or by sex; ethnic status is coupled partly to economic status. Another indication of the importance of economic background is the 18.1% difference that exists between the prison and nonprison males. Inevitably, all the data leads to the conclusion that professional dentistry is greatly needed in Puerto Rico, and especially for the poorest groups.

TABLE D-6

RATES OF NONCARIOUS TEETH AND MEAN AGE
IN SAMPLE A* ACCORDING TO
DENTAL-WORK STATUS

Dental-work Status	Males		Females	
	Teeth Noncarious	Mean Age	Teeth Noncarious	Mean Age
With.......	17.45	29.27	15.12	29.69
Without....	23.82	29.23	21.71	27.98

*Subjects of both Nutritional Class 2 and Ethnic Group 3.

Dental Observations

Condition of each individual was recorded for the presence or absence of: (1) Shovel-shaped incisors (including the degree of shoveling); (2) crowding of teeth; (3) peg teeth; (4) extra incisors; and (5) attrition or wear. Because many teeth were absent, the number of observations for the calculation of frequencies varies.

1. *Shovel-Shaped Incisors.* — Shovel-shaped teeth, usually incisors, are a heritable trait and are found in varying degree and frequency among all races of living man. Such teeth are readily recognizable by the extraordinary development of the lateral borders and congulum of the lingual surfaces of the incisor crowns, which results in a depression in the center and incisal part of the surface that give the impression of a shovel. As a rule, when present, all four upper incisors are so marked, with the mesials, because of their larger size, having the deepest depressions. The shovel shape is sometimes in modified form or is only a trace or suggestion and may occur in the canines as well as in the incisors.

Shoveling of incisors was recorded as "absent," "slight," "medium," or "marked." Only the medium or marked were considered to be clearly shovel-shaped in the calculation of frequencies. Of the total female sample, 225 out of 1205 (18.68%) had medium and marked shoveling in the upper incisors. Twenty-seven percent of the female sample lacked incisors as did 19.3% of the males, and 28% of the prisoners. Samples of 1224 males and 292 prisoners were observed; 18.30% of the nonprison males and 25.34% of the prisoners showed medium and marked shoveling. In the combined samples, 523 of the 2721 observed, giving a frequency of 19.22%, showed medium and marked shoveling. No analysis was done which would indicate that tooth loss was related to the shoveling trait, either positively or negatively. Our impression was, however, that shovel-shaped teeth were more rugged and resistant to loss.

Data for the males and females in the general civilian samples were almost identical with regard to frequency of shoveling. The higher frequency for male prisoners (some 7% higher than for free males or females), is difficult to explain. Nothing else suggests a different genetic background for the prison group; rather, it appears to be representative of the general population.

As a world pattern, the highest concentration of shoveling occurs in Mongoloid populations, with related peoples showing high levels. The American Indian, for instance, has a high frequency, 67% for the markedly shoveled median incisors and 76% for lateral incisors.[5] When Hrdlicka's "semi-shovel-shaped" and "shovel-shaped" for this race are combined, the frequency is slightly over 90% for both mesial and lateral incisors. The male American Negro, in contrast, shows a percentage for median incisors of 4.9% and for lateral incisors of 4.5%. The figures for the White male in the United States, are 1.4% for the mesial and 1.4% for the lateral; for the White female they are 2.6% and 1.0%. When Hrdlicka's "semi-shoveled" are added to the "shoveled," the frequency for the American Negro is about 15% and for the American White about 10% or less.

Valid comparisons between reported frequencies for shovel-shaped incisors are difficult to make, because the bases of observation vary. But in spite of this, it seems true that the Puerto Rican is intermediate between the American Negro and White on the one hand and the American Indian on the other. The most ready explanation for this appears to be that it resulted from an admixture at an early date of American Indian stock to the mixed Negro and White stocks, which predominate in the present island population. This theory is borne out by a comparison by regions of the shovel-shaped incisor frequencies. In general, the regions of Puerto Rico which lie in the central mountain area, the populations of which represent the oldest Puerto Rican migrants have a definitely higher shovel-shaped incisor frequency than do the coastal regions. In contrast to the mountain areas, Region 5, which lies in the northeast coastal area and has the highest concentration of Negroes (who came to the island relatively late) of any region in Puerto Rico, has a frequency, of medium and marked categories, of only 7.9%. The region which includes San Juan and Arecibo, both north coastal urban centers, has one of 9.01%. Regions 13, 14, and 15, the central mountain regions show percentage frequencies well above the coast regions and above the island average. Table D-7 shows the frequency distribution of shovel-shaped incisors by region.

---

[5]Hrdlicka (1921) gave a table of shovel-shaped incisor frequencies. His classification is "shovel-shaped," "semi-shovel-shaped," and "none." Although it is difficult to know whether his "semi-shovel-shaped" is equivalent to what we classify as "medium" or "slight," if it does represent the "slight" shoveling in our classification, then only his "shovel-shaped" category is equivalent to ours. If his "semi-shovel-shaped" parallels our "medium" and his "shovel-shaped" our "marked," these should be combined in comparisons with our data.

TABLE D-7

FREQUENCY OF SHOVEL-SHAPED INCISORS*
OBSERVED BY REGION

Region	Females			Males		
	Number Observed	Frequency of Shoveling	Percentage	Number Observed	Frequency of Shoveling	Percentage
1	60	7	11.7	68	10	14.7
2	152	15	9.9	172	27	15.7
3	63	12	19.0	154	36	23.4
4	25	4	16.0	59	3	5.1
5	105	8	7.6	183	16	8.7
6	95	17	17.9	104	19	18.3
7	110	23	20.9	80	17	21.3
8	60	12	20.0	42	14	33.3
9	11	3	27.3	60	8	13.3
10	32	7	21.9	28	5	17.9
11	51	11	21.6	78	18	23.1
12	57	12	21.1	65	20	30.8
13	155	46	29.7	146	43	29.5
14	125	32	25.6	163	35	21.5
15	104	16	15.4	114	27	23.7
Island Total	1205	225	18.67	1516	298	19.65

*Only those classifiable as "medium" or "marked" in degree of expression were recorded.

In the course of the analysis of blood-group frequencies, a test was run to see whether the total group of those with shovel-shaped incisors showed also unique blood-group frequency distributions—unique in the sense that the Puerto Rican might be much closer to the Mongolian or American Indian type frequencies than to the total island sample. It was assumed that if an Indian admixture did account for the high Puerto Rican shoveling frequency, then blood-type distribution would confirm it. But the results shown by the shovel-shaped incisor sample were not significantly different in blood-type distribution from that of the general population. For instance, in the Rh groupings, "Rh negative" frequency for the shovel-shaped incisor sample is 6.8% compared to 8.78% for the total population. This is not a significant difference but is in the expected direction. Although it might also be expected that the sample with shoveled incisors would show higher type O frequencies, since American Indians show extremely high frequencies of this type blood, this is not the case. The type O frequency for the shovel-shaped incisor sample is 50.74% compared to 53.99% for the general sample. Unfortunately, the blood-group frequencies of the aboriginal Carib Indians who mixed with the colonial Spanish and later with the imported Negro slaves are unknown. The presumption is that they had the characteristics of the modern American Indians of this general area.

Despite the inconclusive blood-group data, the fact that the Puerto Rican population exhibits shoveling frequencies which are intermediate between those of the Indian and Negro-White, a definite influence, undoubtedly Indian, is indicated. The central mountain regions of Puerto Rico, from all historical accounts, were the last holdout of the aboriginal Indians in the island. Admixture of races there was, undoubtedly, higher and continued later than on the coast. Support for this belief comes from the fact that Region 13, an isolated and mountainous region, has a shoveling frequently of about 30% for males and females, significantly higher than the island over-all frequency of 19.22% ($t \pm 2.5$, $p \pm .01$). Regions 13, 14 and 15 have a combined frequency of 24.6% which is well above the island average.

2. *Crowding of Teeth.* — Crowding was only recorded when there was an overlap between adjacent teeth, indicative of insufficient space for those present. Our criteria of crowding was probably extremely critical and rendered only minimum estimate of frequencies. Tooth loss being frequent added to the underenumeration. Of the 3250 persons observed 18.12% showed tooth crowding (589 individuals). Of those positive, 16.19% were females; 21.49%, males; and 12.92%, prisoners. Results of the analysis by nutritional class are shown in Table D-8.

3. *Peg Teeth.* — Among human beings reduced size of teeth and absence (not loss) of teeth are, in general, closely interrelated. The absence of a lateral incisor or a third molar on one side, for example, is frequency associated with the presence of a peg tooth on the other. Fully developed teeth may, consequently, be absent on one or both sides. Of all teeth, third molars and lateral incisors are most frequently under-developed, or congenitally absent. In our survey, the only peg teeth we noted were at the lateral-incisor and of third-molar

TABLE D-8

PERCENTAGE FREQUENCY OF TOOTH CROWDING OBSERVED BY NUTRITIONAL CLASS

Nutritional Class	Males	Females
1	16.66%	17.2%
2	20.57	15.6
3	27.16	18.4
4	22.58	14.2

positions. Peg teeth were found in 157 (5.22%) of 3002 persons examined; the majority of them lateral incisors.

4. *Extra Incisors*. — Supernumerary teeth are infrequent in man. Stafne (1932) found 500 supernumerary teeth in 441 individuals, out of 48,550 patients studied with the aid of dental roetgenograms. Pederson (1949) in reviewing the literature on various racial groups also finds them to be rare. In all events, the question of whether or not they represent retained deciduous teeth cannot be settled. Extra teeth may very infrequently occur at any position in the mouth, but only extra upper lateral incisors were noted in our sample survey. Six (.43%) of 1397 females, 7 (.51%) of 1384 males, and 2 (.57%) of 353 prisoners displayed extra incisors; that is, only 15 (.48%) of the total sample of 3134 showed the trait.

5. *Attrition or Wear*. — In Puerto Rico, attrition is most directly related to the practice of chewing sugar cane. Since the cane has a high mineral content, incidentally a cause of serious wear of sugar-mill equipment, it is only natural that human teeth show wear when it is frequently chewed. In some individuals, attrition is so severe that the teeth were worn down to the alveolar border. In many others, wear was more than half the total height of the tooth. Only when the total crown surface of the tooth had been worn smooth and the cusp eminences obliterated was attrition judged to be present. Anterior as well as posterior teeth participate in this war. Of 2465 individuals, 353 (14.32%) were affected to a marked degree (10.44% of the females, 19.90% of the males, and 10.22% of the prisoners). In view of the fact that indivduals of lower economic status were also most frequently sugar-cane workers, it was felt that there should be some correlation between the amount of attrition and nutritional status. Table D-9 give these data.

TABLE D-9

PERCENTAGE FREQUENCY OF TOOTH ATTRITION
OBSERVED BY NUTRITIONAL CLASS

Nutritional Class	Males	Females	Prisoners
1	4.5%	7.6%	....
2	18.6	10.1	9.2%
3	28.7	9.72	13.2
4	14.8	25.7	....

In many American Indian skeletal series, in which attrition had progressed to the alveolar border, there is no evidence of carious invasion of the exposed pulp and enamel edge. In Puerto Ricans suffering extensive attrition, the same absence of caries in the worn teeth was observed. Shourie (1949), in their dental survey of Puerto Rican children made no notation of attrition in relation to caries, nor have we carried it out systematically. It is certainly our impression, however, that caries and attrition are not positively correlated.

X. INTESTINAL INFESTATION

INTESTINAL PARASITES are, it is well known, a major cause of morbidity in Puerto Rico. That our study presented an opportunity to gather data on rates of intestinal infestation and to investigate subgroup variability in relation to environmental and innate causes was recognized at the outset and made one of the primary objectives. While the presence or absence of infestation is basically correlated with the nature and abundance of the particular organism, it is important to know why some persons or clearly definable groups in an infectious environment are comparatively free of infection while others show high levels. Even though demonstration of significant differences between groups may not reveal their causes, it is helpful in understanding the connection between environment and infection and of value in practical public health administration. The analysis of data is designed, therefore, to show the differences in infestation rate by organism according to age, sex, race, occupation, and residence status (urban or rural), and also by island geographic region. In addition, the nutritional and ethnic differences are tested.

ORGANIZATION OF ANALYSIS OF DATA RESULTS

Samples of fecal matter taken from 961 subjects were examined. These individuals had been selected because 83.6% were positive for at least one of the more important helminths and protozoa which infest Puerto Ricans. No attempt was made to obtain specimens from all subjects in the total island sample for two reasons: (1) submission was voluntary and involved a return trip to the clinic, and (2) arrangements had to be completed so that the specimens could be examined by the laboratory of the School of Tropical Medicine.[1] Prior to this, reports were furnished by another laboratory but for only four species; 17 later were included. The earlier data are not given; they lack comparability with the later more complete findings.

In addition to being a report on only a partial sample from the total study, the data have other limitations. In the first

---

[1] Dr. Morales Otero, Director of the School of Tropical Medicine kindly arranged for the analysis, which was carried out under the direction of Dr. Gonzales. We are much indebted to them for this service.

place, we could not be certain that the fecal specimen was that of the person who submitted it. Although the subject was given a numbered container with his name on it and told that the findings would be reported to him, the specimen could have come from another person. Such substitution would not appreciably qualify the frequency data nor probably modify the group comparisons significantly, yet it is a possible source of error. In the second place, a single fecal specimen may not accurately represent an individual's infestation. Chandler (1944), for instance, considered that a single sample underestimates the true frequency of *Endamoeba histolytica* by a factor of 2. Our report, therefore, gives minimum frequencies. In the last place, our data, while they report whether or not the subject is infected by each species, overlook the degree of infection. Although this does not render the conclusions regarding frequencies for the total island or for subgroups inaccurate, it does influence adversely the findings that relate to individual health and infestation and hemoglobin level, it is important to know whether 10 or 1000 worms are present before it can be said that the presence of some species causes variations in hemoglobin content. The plan of analysis of data is as follows:

1. Total island and subgroup frequencies for all species combined.

Total-sample frequencies (Tables I-1 and I-2).

Urban or Rural residence, Nutritional and Occupation subgroup samples (Table I-3).

Age subsamples by decades (Table I-4).

Ethnic subgroups (Table I-5).

Regional subsamples (Table I-6).

2. Subgroup frequencies for the three most frequent species of both helminths and protozoa:

Nutritional, Urban or Rural, and Regional Subgroups (Table I-7).

3. Test for significance of departure from random distribution in the pattern of infestation comparing subgroups (Chi-square test):

Test results for total helminths and for protozoa by categories of sex, residence, occupation, nutrition, ethnic, age, regional and rainfall subgroups (Table I-8).

Test results for six individual species of parasites by sex and residence subgroups (Table I-9).

4. Sex Differences for individual parasite species (Table I-10).

5. Comparison of mean hemoglobin values of sample groups with and without helminths (Tables I-11 and I-12).

6. Comparison of red cell counts, eosinophil levels, and mean ethnic and nutritional values for various combinations of infestation by *Necator americanus* (Table I-13).

7. Data on blood pressure related to infestation. The sex and regional distribution of *Schistosomiasis mansoni* are mentioned at the end of the chapter.

TABLE I-1

INTESTINAL INFESTATION IN MALES, FEMALES, AND TOTAL SAMPLE FOR EACH SPECIES OF PARASITE TESTED

Species	Males		Females		Total Sample	
	No.	%	No.	%	No.	%
Schistosoma mansoni	25	4.4	1	0.25	...	2.7
Fasciola hepatica	0	0	0	0	...	0
Taenia sp.	0	0	0	0	...	0
Hymenolepis nana	1	0.18	1	0.25	...	0.21
Necator americanus	249	44.1	89	22.5	...	35.2
Ascaris lumbricoides	27	4.8	33	8.3	...	6.2
Trichuris trichiura	338	59.8	256	64.6	...	61.8
Enterobius vermicularis	0	0	0	0	...	0
Strongyloides stercoralis	16	2.8	8	2.0	...	2.5
Endamoeba histolytica	49	8.7	53	13.4	...	10.6
Endamoeba coli	150	26.5	156	39.4	...	31.8
Endolimax nana	65	11.5	55	13.9	...	12.5
Iodamoeba williamsi	10	1.8	10	2.5	...	2.1
Giardia lamblia	14	2.5	7	1.8	...	2.2
Chilomastix mesnili	2	0.35	2	0.51	...	0.42
Trichomonas hominis	0	0	0	0	...	0
Balantidium coli	0	0	1	0.25	...	0.21
Total	565	....	396	....	961	....

TABLE I-2

COMBINATIONS OF PERSONS POSITIVE AND NEGATIVE FOR PARASITES IN THE TOTAL SAMPLE TESTED

Subjects	Helminths	Protozoa	Number	% Frequency of Total Sample
Females	Negative	Positive	52	5.41%
	Positive	Positive	144	14.98
	Positive	Negative	138	14.36
	Negative	Negative	62	6.45
Total			396	41.21
Males Civilians ..	Negative	Positive	25	2.60%
	Positive	Positive	90	9.37
	Positive	Negative	117	12.17
	Negative	Negative	47	4.89
			279	29.03
Males Prisoners ..	Negative	Positive	20	2.08%
	Positive	Positive	59	6.14
	Positive	Negative	159	16.55
	Negative	Negative	48	4.99
			286	29.76
Total Sample .	Positive	Positive	804	83.66%
	Negative	Negative	157	16.34
			961	100.00

		Negative	Positive
Females			
Helminths	......	114	282
Protozoa	......	200	196
Males			
Helminths	......	140	425
Protozoa	......	371	194

TABLE I-3
POSITIVE INFESTATION FREQUENCY FOR EACH SEX BY VARIOUS SUBGROUPS

Subgroups	Male Positive				Total Sample	Female Positive				Total Sample
	Helminths		Protozoa			Helminths		Protozoa		
	No.	%	No.	%		No.	%	No.	%	
Residence										
Urban	128	74.0	65	37.6	173	115	68.5	69	41.1	168
Rural	297	75.8	129	32.9	392	167	73.2	127	55.7	228
Nutritional Class										
1	1	16.6	4	66.7	6	8	57.1	6	42.9	14
2	338	76.1	149	33.6	444	195	68.7	143	50.4	284
3	72	73.5	32	32.7	98	69	81.2	39	45.9	85
4	14	82.4	9	52.9	17	10	76.9	8	61.5	13
Occupation										
Hard	335	77.7	140	32.5	431	...	...	...	...	...
Light	72	69.2	44	42.3	104	...	...	...	...	...
Sedentary	18	60.0	10	33.3	30	...	...	...	...	...
Total	425		194		565	282		196		396

TABLE I-4

POSITIVE INFESTATION FREQUENCY BY AGE GROUP

Age Group	Male				Total Sample	Female				Total Sample
	Helminths		Protozoa			Helminths		Protozoa		
	No.	%	No.	%		No.	%	No.	%	
-19	20	80.0	13	52.0	25	15	83.3	11	61.1	18
20-29	186	76.2	76	31.1	244	117	74.5	75	47.8	157
30-39	139	75.5	61	33.2	184	100	67.1	79	53.0	149
40-49	74	72.5	39	38.2	102	42	67.7	26	41.9	62
50-59	5	55.6	5	56.0	9	8	80.0	5	50.0	10
60+	1	100.0	0	0.0	1	..	..	..	..	..

TABLE I-5

POSITIVE INFESTATION FREQUENCY BY ETHNIC GROUP

Ethnic Group	Male				Total Sample	Female				Total Sample
	Helminths		Protozoa			Helminths		Protozoa		
	No.	%	No.	%		No.	%	No.	%	
0	1	100.0	1	100.0	1	8	50.0	10	62.5	16
1	3	37.5	1	12.5	8	82	71.9	52	45.6	114
2	75	76.5	36	36.7	98	113	72.9	82	71.3	155
3	205	76.5	94	35.1	268	39	72.2	27	50.0	54
4	50	73.5	21	30.9	68	13	65.0	6	30.0	20
5	17	70.8	8	33.3	24	15	75.0	7	35.0	20
6	26	70.3	14	37.8	37	8	66.7	9	75.0	12
7	33	84.6	12	30.8	39	3	75.0	2	50.0	4
8	15	68.2	7	31.8	22	1	100.0	1	100.0	1

TABLE I-6

POSITIVE INFESTATION FREQUENCY BY GEOGRAPHIC REGION OF RESIDENCE

Census Region	Geographic Region	Male						Female					
		Helminths		Protozoa		Total Sample		Helminths		Protozoa		Total Sample	
		No.	%	No.	%			No.	%	No.	%		
1	1	28	90.3	8	25.8	31		32	78.0	17	41.5	41	
2	2	15	75.0	5	25.0	20		0		0		0	
	3	47	72.3	16	24.6	65		4	36.4	6	54.5	11	
	4	15	62.5	4	20.0	24		11	73.3	9	60.0	15	
	5	11	78.6	5	35.7	14		0		0		0	
3	6	55	68.7	24	30.0	80		30	73.2	22	53.7	41	
4	7	39	79.6	24	49.0	49		48	65.7	33	45.2	73	
	8	13	68.4	6	31.6	19		12	63.2	12	63.2	19	
	9	23	76.7	12	40.0	30		2	100.0	1	50.0	2	
	10	2	50.0	1	25.0	4		3	75.0	2	50.0	4	
5	11	31	81.6	14	36.8	38		26	86.7	12	40.0	30	
	12	35	77.8	21	46.7	45		36	81.8	14	21.8	44	
6	13	33	78.7	16	38.1	42		44	78.5	31	55.4	56	
7	14	49	77.6	27	42.2	64		29	59.2	34	69.4	49	
	15	29	72.5	11	27.5	40		5	45.5	7	36.4	11	
Total						565						396	

TABLE I-7

INCIDENCE OF POSITIVE INFESTATION IN VARIOUS SUBGROUPS OF THE PUERTO RICAN POPULATION FOR THREE HELMINTHS AND THREE PROTOZOA

Subgroup		Male Helminths			Male Protozoa			Total Males	Female Helminths			Female Protozoa			Total Females
		1*	2	3	4	5	6		1	2	3	4	5	6	
Nutritional Class	1	0	0	1	1	4	0	6	0	0	8	0	4	4	14
	2	198	22	264	40	111	51	444	63	22	176	40	110	37	284
	3	43	3	61	5	27	10	98	21	11	63	11	35	12	85
	4	8	2	12	3	8	4	17	5	0	9	2	7	2	13
Total		249	27	338	49	150	65	565	89	33	256	53	156	55	396
Residence Urban		64	8	105	15	54	17	173	18	17	107	17	50	23	168
Rural		185	19	233	34	96	48	392	71	16	149	36	106	32	228
Geographic Region	1	17	3	23	0	8	3	31	11	4	29	3	15	3	41
	2	6	1	11	1	3	2	20	0	0	0	0	0	0	0
	3	19	1	41	3	13	2	65	2	0	4	1	6	2	11
	4	10	0	9	0	3	1	24	6	0	9	3	9	2	15
	5	4	0	11	1	1	3	14	0	0	0	0	0	0	0
	6	37	0	44	4	14	8	80	6	2	27	5	18	6	41
	7	15	6	28	9	19	11	49	7	9	43	10	27	14	73
	8	7	0	11	2	5	4	19	5	0	11	3	7	5	19
	9	18	0	17	5	10	2	30	0	0	2	0	1	1	2
	10	1	0	1	0	1	0	4	0	0	3	0	0	1	4
	11	26	1	26	2	10	3	38	11	1	24	4	11	1	30
	12	19	5	34	4	18	5	45	6	5	34	1	10	7	44
	13	19	5	29	7	11	6	42	25	8	38	10	22	7	56
	14	27	3	33	9	24	12	64	9	4	27	12	27	6	49
	15	24	2	20	2	10	3	40	1	0	5	1	3	0	11

*1 = *Necator americanus*; 2 = *Ascaris lumbricoides*; 3 = *Trichuris trichiura*; 4 = *Endamoeba histolytica*; 5 = *Endamoeba coli*; and 5 = *Endolimax nanal*

TABLE I-8

CHI-SQUARE TESTS FOR TOTAL HELMINTHS AND PROTOZOA BETWEEN POSITIVE AND NEGATIVE INDIVIDUALS FOR VARIOUS SUBSAMPLE CATEGORIES

Chi-square values between 95% and 99% confidence limit are underlined; values above 99% are double underlined.

Subsample Category	Degrees of Freedom	Helminths		Protozoa	
		Chi-Square Value	Confidence‡	Chi-Square Value	Confidence‡
Residence					
Urban Males; Rural Males	1	.17	ND	1.34	ND
Urban Females; Rural Females	1	1.25	ND	__8.10__	99.5
Urban Males; Urban Females	1	1.43	ND	.45	ND
Rural Males; Rural Females	1	.58	ND	__31.17__	99.9
Occupation					
Hard; Light; Sedentary	2	8.00	98	3.38	ND
Nutrition, Males: (1,2) X 3 X 4	2	.56	ND	2.51	ND
Nutrition, Females: 1-4	3	6.27	ND	2.0	ND
Ethnic, Males: 2-8 (omit 1 and 9)	6	3.36	ND	3.36	ND
Ethnic, Females: 1-6 (omit 7-9)	5	3.27	ND	7.65	ND
Age, Males: 1 X 2 X 3 X 4 X (5,6)*	4	3.43	ND	6.63	ND
Age, Females: 1 X 2 X 3 X 4 X 5*	4	3.85	ND	2.81	ND
Census Region, Males: 1-7	6	9.83	ND	__13.93__	95
Census Region, Females: 1-7	6	__18.25__	99	__12.58__	95
Rainfall, Males: (1,2,3,4) X (5,6, 15) X (7,8,9) X (11,12,13,14)†	3	2.67	ND	__15.17__	99.5
Rainfall, Females: (1,3,4) X (6,15) X (7,8) X (11,12,13,14)†	3	3.49	ND	.18	ND
Sex: Female; Male	1	1.96	ND	__21.82__	99.9

*First digit of age decade.
†No females from Regions 2 and 5 were included, because fecal study began after these regions were sampled. Region 10 was excluded because it does not fall readily into a rainfall or group category.
‡ ND = No Difference

TABLE I-9

CHI-SQUARE TESTS FOR SELECTED SPECIES OF PARASITES
BETWEEN POSITIVE AND NEGATIVE INDIVIDUALS FOR VARIOUS
SUBSAMPLE CATEGORIES

Species	Subsample Category*		
	Urban Males by Rural Males	Urban Females by Rural Females	Urban Males by Urban Females	Rural Males by Rural Females
Necator americanus	4.86	23.68	31.09	15.24
Ascaris lumbricoides	0.00	1.21	4.32	1.16
Trichuris trichiura	0.03	0.19	0.44	2.37
Endamoeba histolytica	0.00	17.34	0.14	6.90
Endamoeba coli	2.53	11.09	0.06	32.37
Endolimax nana	0.74	0.00	1.02	0.57

*One degree of freedom was recorded for each Chi-Square value; 95% to 99% confidence levels are single underlined; values over 99% are double underlined.

TABLE I-10

WILCOXON SUMS TEST FOR SEX DIFFERENCES FOR EACH SPECIES OF PARASITE TESTED, AND CONFIDENCE LEVEL

Species	Wilcoxon Sum	Confidence Level*
Necator americanus	1	99
Ascaris lumbricoides	14	ND
Trichuris trichiura	21.5	ND
Endamoeba histolytica	10	95
Endamoeba coli	8	95
Endolimax nana	29.5	ND

*ND = No difference.

TABLE I-11

MEAN HEMOGLOBIN VALUES OF SAMPLE GROUPS NEGATIVE FOR ALL INTESTINAL PARASITES AND OF THOSE POSITIVE FOR HELMINTHS ONLY

Hemoglobin in grams per 100 c.c.

Group	Sample Size	Mean	Standard Error	95% Confidence Limits
Males:				
All Negative	45	12.754	0.181	12.392 - 13.116
Helminth+ Protozoa -	117	12.565	0.012	12.541 - 12.589
Females				
All Negative	61	11.347	0.019	11.309 - 11.385
Helminth + Protozoa -	138	11.251	0.119	11.013 - 11.489
Prisoners				
All Negative	47	12.354	0.210	11.934 - 12.774
Helminth + Protozoa -	140	12.339	0.093	12.153 - 12.525

TABLE I-12

MALE AND FEMALE RED CELL COUNTS BY INFESTATION FOR *Necator americanus*

Category	Number	Red Cell Count $\pm$ S.E.^{2}
Males		
Negative	65	4.099 $\pm$ .67
Positive	84	4.037 $\pm$ .58
Females		
Negative	43	3.664 $\pm$ .80
Positive	157	3.744 $\pm$ .39

TABLE I-13

EOSINOPHIL COUNT FOR PERSONS WITH AND WITHOUT *Necator americanus* INFESTATION

Category	Mean Eosinophil (in per cent)	Number	Mean Nutritional Class	Mean Ethnic Factor*
Males				
No Infection	8.06	33	2.33	3.15
Other +, *Necator* -	7.92	100	2.34	3.40
Other +, *Necator* +	10.69	98	2.38	3.17
Females				
No Infection	4.82	39	2.15	3.33
Other +, *Necator* -	6.31	162	2.30	3.31
Other +, *Necator* +	10.11	55	2.43	3.13

*Sample number for nutrition class and ethnic group is total tested in category.

RESULTS

Total Island Frequencies. — The total frequencies by each of the 17 disease entities are given in Tables I-1 and I-2, and in Table I-2 they are grouped according to the subsample structure and show the numbers of the various combinations of helminths and protozoa infections. Several of the entities were rather abundant, while others were quite rare. Certain combinations of them occurred frequently in the same individual, and only 16.34% of those tested were negative for any parasite. It should be emphasized that while these are minimum-frequency estimates, the problem of parasitic infestation is island-wide. How these total frequencies are distributed among the various subgroups is shown below.

Infestation Related to Sex. — For only one of the common helminths, *Necator americanus*, was there a highly significant difference in intestinal infestation between the sexes (99% level), with males being the higher; for all helminths taken together there was no significant difference. For protozoans, when persons entirely negative were tested against those positive for any protozoan entity, we got a highly significant difference between the sexes (99% level), with females having the higher frequencies (Table I-8). When analyzed by specific entities (Table I-10), both *Endamoeba histolytica* and *Endamoeba coli* showed significant differences (95% level). In contrast to the helminths, the grouping of all the protozoan entities enhanced the frequency differences. Our data do not point to causes for these differences, but they may well be ecological rather than biological (see the urban-rural comparisons (Tables I-8 and I-13). Schistosomiasis is almost entirely confined to males.

Intestinal Infestation Related to Urban-Rural Residence. — For total helminths no urban versus rural differences in infestation frequencies exist for either sex. This is not true for total protozoans (see Table I-8). Urban females were significantly less infected by protozoans than their rural counterparts (99.5% level), and rural males significantly less than rural females (99.9% level). No differences were shown between urban males and urban females, and between urban males and rural males. Thus the rural female is set off as a highly infested group as compared to other females or to males wherever located. This is not surprising for the rural scene is less healthy than the urban due to an almost complete absence of effective sanitation facilities. What is surprising is the fact that helminths as well are not more frequent in rural females. Rural laundry practices expose the women to these parasites during the infective stages.

Of the helminths, only for *Necator americanus* were there sex frequency differences in infection. Males were more often infested than females; and this was likewise true for this species in and between urban and rural groups (see Table I-9). The results of analyses by nutritional groups are excluded from this table, but in every case such values were not significant. Apparently, the nutritional status of the individual does not affect the occurrence of infestation.

Infestation Related to Occupation. — Only males were analyzed for differences of infestation by occupation. They existed (98.0% level) for total helminths but not for total protozoans (Tables I-3, I-8, and I-9). The group contributing most to the Chi-square value were sedentary males. These, being largely urban and economically superior to the general island average, enjoyed a more healthy environment. Also, their work less often brought them in contact with the infectious organisms.

Infestation Related to Geographic Region. — For total helminths, only the females showed non-homogeneous geographic patterning of infestation; but both sexes did show it for total protozoans. For the former, Regions 5 and 6 had frequencies above average; for the latter, the males were high in Region 4 and the females in Regions 2 and 7. For the helminths, Region 7 had the lowest frequency for males and females; for protozoans Region 2 for both males and females. Since rainfall is presumed to be the climatic factor of geography that chiefly affects the vegetation and general ecology, it was suspect for parasites as well. On the basis of amount of precipitation per annum our 15 coded geographic regions fall into the following 4 groups: (1) North Coast (Regions 1, 2, 3, 4), less than 70"; (2) Eastern Area (Regions 5, 6, 15), 70" to 80"; (3) Southern Area (Regions 7, 8, 9), less than 70"; (4) Central Area (Regions 11, 12, 13, 14), over 80".

Admittedly these groupings are gross, but they cannot be further refined because of the geographical coding and the requirements of sample size. In the distribution of total protozoa infections in the male, a highly significant heterogeneity was observed (99.5% level). However, the failure to find a similar pattern for helminths in males or for either in females suggests that rainfall levels alone do not account for regional differences. They may, of course, be basic to the scene which promotes infection.

Infestation Related to Nutrition. — Nutritional background did not seem to be involved in any differences, whether of total helminth or protozoan infections. The categories of nutrition used in this study are associated with very real differences in anthropometric and other characteristics and there is no doubt that they are valid. Yet, contrary to a widespread belief that they are influences, they failed to affect infection rates for any group or individual species of parasite tested here. Very possibly levels or degrees of infection differ between nutritional classes, but if so it is not known to us. Thus, immunity to infection is not conferred by adequate diet and associated good health, though a lowering of resistance might be shown in quantitative infestation. A related finding (Table I-11) is that no hemoglobin differences are found between various groups when positive infested are compared to negative. In Chapter XI we report a positive association between nutrition and hemoglobin level and the failure to find a hemoglobin-infestation association here supports our contention that nutrition plays no role in infestation.

Infestation Related to Age. — Age appeared to have no real effect on infection rates. Subjects under 20 and those of each older decade group were compared, but no significant differences were found to occur (see Table I-8; the categories used there are decade groups).

Infestation Related to Ethnic Status. — It has been frequently said in the literature that race ("ethnic factor") as an innate cause, affects relative immunity to infection. In these accounts Negroes are said to have a greater innate immunity than do Whites. Puerto Rico, with its high rates of infection and clear-cut Negro-White differences, should provide an ideal scene for testing this hypothesis. Chandler (1944) remarked that "racial differences in susceptibility exist without reference to habit." Yet no close observer of any culture can state unequivocally that where Negro and White co-inhabit the same area they lead the same daily lives. Opportunities, habits, and a host of other things vary by race and employment; education and leisure activity and unlikenesses in cultural conditioning exist and are expressed in group role and status. If we agree that differences in infection between the sexes is owing to differences in life roles, then we should reasonably expect race differences to act similarly. In most locales, it is unlikely that "racial" heredity gives immunity; but, rather that any observed differences are caused by the extent of freedom from the job, the kind of housing, health conditions, and so on, that make for infectious contacts. All these factors are usually not equal for different races even in the same society or locale.

In Puerto Rico, White and Negro work in agriculture side by side and the majority of the male population is thus employed. The agricultural laborer, whether Negro or White, is equally exposed to infection. Although there is no racial equality at upper class levels, the general freedom from racial discrimination in agricultural work well accounts for the failure of the usual "racial" patterns in immunity to prevail. We do not contend that inherited immunity at the physiological or biochemical level does not exist, but that cultural explanations of immunity differences are the more important and should be considered to prevail until evidence of innate immunity is demonstrated, and not assumed. Our data (Tables I-5 and I-8) support the belief that there is no significant racial difference between Negro and White in their immunity to intestinal infestation whether by helminths or protozoa. While levels of infection and, presumably, the individual's reaction to it, for which we have no data, may differ—the broad outline seems to show no evidence of racial difference.

Hemoglobin Values Related to Infestation. — Certain helminths specifically attack the blood cells. To test for the consequences of such infestation, individuals who were negative for both helminths and protozoa were compared with those positive for helminths but negative for protozoa, (see Table I-11). Contrary to expectations, there is no significant difference between these two groups (males $p = .62$, females $p = .57$, prisoners $p = .10$). Infestation by helminths alone seemed to have no effect on hemoglobin levels.

Necator americanus and its Effect on Other Characteristics. — Because this much-studied helminth has been reported in the literature to have marked effects on the blood, a careful analysis of its effects was carried out. There are significant sex and urban-rural differences in frequency of infestation by this parasite. Males more than females and rural more than urban individuals are affected. The factors of age and race are not involved. Since way of life controls the likelihood of contact with any infectious species, this rather than any innate factors probably accounts for all the differences in *Necator americanus* frequencies. The action on eosinophil count is a direct result of infection and not a cause (see Table I-13, and below).

The mean red-cell counts for males and females negative and positive for *Necator americanus* are given in Table I-12. No significant differences within the two groups prevail.

Since females characteristically have lower counts than males, the sex difference here is not related to infestation. With regard to eosinophil counts, the literature states that eosinophil percentage levels increase with *Necator americanus* infestation and rise additionally in relation to the degree of infection. Our study supports the first part of this statement, but, lacking evidence of severity of infection, we cannot comment on quantitative differences. Table I-13 gives the pertinent mean values. In addition, mean nutritional and ethnic data are shown for the groups but these data are not significant.

Blood-pressure Values Related to Infestation. — A test was run on the possible relationship of infestation to blood pressure, but no significant differences in diastolic or systolic pressures between persons positive and negative for helminths and for protozoa were found. At least in our sample, blood pressure is unaffected by intestinal infestation.

Schistosomiasis mansoni. — Infestation by this organism was rare and, according to our study, chiefly confined to males. Because of its clinical importance, however, a short account of the findings is pertinent. The distribution by census region of male cases is tabulated below.

Census Region	Number	Percent Positive	Males Examined
1	0	0.00	33
2	3	2.4	124
3	8	10.25	78
4	4	4.08	98
5	4	5.04	74
6	0	0.00	52
7	6	5.66	106
Total	25	4.42	565

One female (Region 14) was found positive, or a rate of 0.25% in a sample of 396 (2.04% of the 49 examined in Region 14). The sex difference is highly significant ($p = .0001$). It is unknown whether innate factors or ecological conditions cause this difference.

CONCLUSIONS

In Puerto Rico the rates of intestinal infestation are high and represent a major public health problem. All classes and subgroups suffer to some extent, but the rural population is probably the major reservoir of disease. Surprisingly, our findings indicate that individual response to infestation is mild with no discernable effect on hemoglobin or cell count. Only the eosinophil count, of those measures marking health status, revealed any close relationship, and then with only one of the helminths. It would be unwise at this time to conclude that ill effects of parasitic infection are actually lacking in Puerto Rico. It may well be that the over-all slight body build and low weight to height ratio characteristic of this population may in the long run be related to this widespread infestation as well as to undernutrition. Furthermore, it may also be true that parasitic infestation operates at a subclinical level and that its most serious effect is in reducing resistance and imparting a general debility that is contributory to a lowered life expectancy and an increased mortality from other causes.

XI. PHYSIOLOGICAL CHARACTERISTICS

A WORKING KNOWLEDGE of the general health status of a population, is a difficult thing to obtain, since health is only relatively definable. Because of its great practical importance, however, in the initial planning of this study, arrangements were made to record such measures of health and physiological function as were feasible in a field study. In doing this our purpose was not only to assist in establishing medical standards for Puerto Rico, standards based on Puerto Ricans rather than other populations, but to provide a method suitable for studying the adaptive health status in relation to nutrition, race, and general environment elsewhere.

The implementation of this part of our work was made possible chiefly through the kindness of Dr. Juan A. Pons and his staff, of the Puerto Rican Department of Public Health. Whatever success we attained is owing to helpful cooperation and advice, and to material aid given by Señor Victor Diaz, who was assigned as our field technician. And to Sr. Diaz goes our special thanks for his technical skill and for his willingness to adapt himself to the rigors of laboratory work under field conditions.

The data obtained in the field concerned pulse rate, systolic and diastolic blood pressure, hemoglobin level, oral temperature, and white- and red-blood cell counts. Differential cell count was also performed in the Public Health Laboratory, but for only a portion of the total sample. In fact, even in the field, data were not secured for all persons for all of the items desired, because (1) a few persons refused to give us a blood sample, (2) some blood samples spoiled, and (3) occasionally, time did not allow all the blood determinations to be completed. In addition, some persons were excluded in the blood pressure, pulse, and temperature readings. Enough data, however, were gathered and from the vast majority of the subjects to maintain the representativeness of the sample tested.

METHODS

Field situations do not allow the accuracy that is possible under the controlled conditions of the clinic or laboratory. For this reason a description of the methods we deemed practical and a discussion of their reliability is given in order that the reader may evaluate the data obtained.

Pulse. — The pulse was counted for 15 or 30 seconds and the rate per minute calculated. A subject was examined after he had been in the "measuring line," frequently seated, for a considerable time and after he had overcome any initial excitement at being studied. The values probably represent the pulse under conditions of very mild activity and are not basal rates.

Temperature. — Temperatures were recorded in degrees Fahrenheit with a standard oral thermometer left in position for one to two minutes. They were taken on a "run of the mill" sample of a population which included those with colds, infections, and other causes which could affect temperature. But it was so recorded that subjects running abnormal fevers could be sorted out from the sample when the standard for those in "good health" was considered. Although we are confident that temperature was read and recorded accurately, we are not confident of what it may mean biologically.

White- and Red-cell Count and Hemoglobin Level. — All the cell counts and hemoglobin determinations were made by Sr. Diaz, a fully trained and qualified laboratory technician. Established procedures for a blood sample drawn by venipuncture were used. As the same investigator, employing the same instruments, worked throughout the whole study, internal comparability is assured. Data on hemoglobin determination was obtained by the Sahli color comparison method. This, although convenient for field situations, is not especially accurate; but with the advantage of internal consistency all our data are comparable. Independent checks of the Sahli determinations were done by more precise methods (colorimetric) in the Public Health Laboratories and confirm that the field equipment was accurate. Cell counts were recorded in thousands per cubic millimeter of blood, and hemoglobin in grams per 100 cubic centimeters. These data are reasonably accurate, internally comparable, and quite useful for the purposes intended.

Blood Pressure. — Blood pressure was taken after the individual had been questioned, a series of anthropometric measurements made, and (the individual seated) a dental examination and his temperature recorded. He had then been at rest some 5 to 10 minutes after being seated. His arm rested on a table at heart level and one reading was taken with standard technique by the auscultatory method, always on the right arm, using a Tycos aneroid sphygmomanometer with a 12 cm arm band. The systolic reading was taken at the appearance of the first sound and the diastolic at the point at which sound became dull and muffled.

Differential Cell Count. — Slides of each blood sample were made and stained in the field. They were read and reported on by technicians in the Laboratory of the Department of Health. While the findings on differential counts are mentioned here, they were only used in analysis in the section on Intestinal Infestation (Chapter X).

RESULTS

A summary of the mean values for males, females, and prisoners is given in Table P-1. Standard errors, ranges, and the number in each subsample are also shown. An analysis and discussion of each measure follows.

Pulse. — Pulse count for Puerto Ricans is similar to readings recorded for other populations. The higher rates for females is also common. Analysis of pulse count for each sex by nutritional and ethnic background is illustrated on Graph 68. As seen from this graph, persons of Ethnic Group 3 (Sample C) exhibit no significant variation with varying nutrition; persons of Nutritional Class 2 analyzed according to their ethnic background (Sample B) show that no significant difference exists between ethnic groups. The difference between males and females is also clearly indicated on Graph 68. Pulse readings for males and females of Nutritional Class 2 and Ethnic Group 3 (Sample A) by various regions on the island are given in Graph 67. Considerable variability is evident here, but no clear pattern that can be related to known regional geographic characteristics is apparent.

Temperature. — No significant difference in temperature between males and females nor between prisoners and civilian males, was observed. All the differences are slight and within the limit of one degree. The means of Samples B and C by sex were also compared, but no significant difference or pattern was revealed.

TABLE P-1

MEAN VALUES FOR VARIOUS PHYSIOLOGICAL CHARACTERISTICS OF THE PUERTO RICAN POPULATION

Measurement	Subsample*	No.	Mean	S.D.	S.E.	Mean ± 2 S.D.	Range
Pulse (count/min.)	P	395	72.74	11.23	.565	50.3-95.20	48-120
	F	1647	82.32	12.82	.316	56.68-107.96	51-141
	M	1361	75.64	13.08	.354	49.48-101.80	44-140
Temperature (Fahrenheit)†	F	1640	98.75	.458	.004	97.83-99.66	96.4-102.1
	M	1358	98.51	.868	.007	96.78-100.25	95.0-102.5
White Count (per mm^3)†	F	1215	8044.6	1521.0	42.9	5002.-11,086.	3100.-13,800.
	M	1094	7974.3	1511.0	45.6	4952.-10,996.	3100.-14,100.
Red Count (thousands/mm^3)†	F	1279	3697.15	525.0	46.4	2647.-4747.	2390.-6800.
	M	1114	4056.03	572.0	54.2	2912.-5200.	2080.-5820.
Hemoglobin (gr./100 cc)	P	341	12.44	1.22	.06	10.00-14.88	6.5-15.0
	F	1619	11.22	1.29	.03	8.65-13.79	3.5-15.2
	M	1473	12.55	1.38	.04	9.79-15.32	2.5-15.0
Systolic Blood Pressure‡	P	394	117.04	14.68	.74	87.68-146.40	78.-182
	F	1646	112.31	17.05	.42	78.21-146.41	74.-278
	M	1509	116.03	15.15	.39	85.73-146.33	68.-200
Diastolic Blood Pressure	P	394	70.01	10.12	.51	49.77-90.25	44.-100
	F	1646	67.82	11.78	.29	44.26-91.38	40.-128
	M	1509	71.19	11.26	.29	48.67-93.71	38.-136

*M = males excluding prisoners; F, females; P, prisoners

†Owing to errors in the coding of field records for prisoners, this data is omitted

‡See Murrill (1955, pp. 277-324) for a complete analysis of blood-pressure findings and causes and patterns of variability. The No. for this table is not the same as Murrill's as some not included in his sample are included here.

White-cell Count. — White-cell counts were determined for 1257 females and 1094 males. (Not enough prisoner counts were done to make analysis of that group meaningful.) There was no significant difference (compare Graphs 71 and 72) between the sexes. Graph 71 illustrates the various effects of nutrition or ethnic background on white count for males; and the same for females is shown in Graph 72. Of not a little interest is the similarity, for both sexes, in low white count for persons of marked Negroid ancestry. Effect of nutritional differences was insignificant.

Red Cell Count. — Sex difference ($t = 5$) in red-cell count for the total sample was highly significant. In Graphs 71 and 72, the effects of nutrition and ethnic background for each sex is indicated. In view of the scale used on these graphs, neither the difference between the sexes nor any differences between either nutritional or ethnic groups are clean. However, there appears to be no self-evident pattern of variation due to either nutritional or ethnic status. There is a suggestion that for females the red-cell count is lower than average for those of more Negroid background; the reverse seems to be true for males. Nutritional background apparently does not affect red-cell characteristics, nor do regional geographic differences. Although there were some significant differences between regions, no broad pattern prevails; for instance, no uniform differences are apparent between coastal and mountain regions. In Chapter X, the relationship between the red-cell count and intestinal infestation is discussed.

Hemoglobin. — Hemoglobin level is always a sensitive barometer of general health status. Any reduction is amount below normal values indicates poor health and extremely low levels indicate a general decline in important physiological processes. In her nutrition studies, Blanco (1946) reviewed the epidemiology of anemia and deficiency diseases in Puerto Rico. She reported on the results of hemoglobin determinations on sections of the population up to that time. Unfortunately, the values are reported in percentage and it is not known on what level the 100% value is set. Yet, whichever the base used, Puerto Ricans have low hemoglobin values. Whether this is a consequence of low caloric intake, infestation with parasites, or a nutritional deficiency in particular vitamins or elements is not clear. Because of this uncertainty, a relatively complete analysis of hemoglobin results is reported here. Since our sample is believed to be representative of the entire island, the data may furnish answers to questions Blanco raised but which, because of restrictions in her data, she could not answer.

In our study hemoglobin determinations were performed on 1473 males, 1619 females, and 341 prisoners. Table P-1 gives the mean, errors, and ranges of hemoglobin values for the male, female, and prison samples. There is a statistically significant sex difference at the 95% confidence level. The mean for the females is 1.33 grams per 100cc. below that for the males. The prisoner's mean is slightly below that of the "free" males, but the difference is not significant. The range and distribution of these values within the population is of some interest. For the males, 8.7% have values of less than 11 grams and only 1% have values of 15 grams or above (14.7 is frequently taken as a "normal" value for healthy persons). Of the 1619 total females, 573 (35.4%) tested for values under 11 grams and only 3 had 15 grams or above. One male individual had a determination of 2.5, another 3.5, and one 4.1 grams. For the females one individual at 3.5, and nine between 5 and 6 grams gave the lowest values. For the prisoners, the lowest recorded value was 6.5, with 10 individuals having less than 10 grams. These are clearly pathologically low levels, yet they were found (and rechecked for accuracy) in persons who had in some cases walked long distances to seek health certificates attesting to their employability.

Table P-2 gives the mean hemoglobin values by various nutritional groups for the three samples. An overlap at the 95% confidence level limit and standard error of difference test indicates that there is: (1) for the males, a significant difference between the mean hemoglobin levels of the high nutritional group (Class 1) and each of the other three groups (Classes 2, 3, and 4); (2) for the females, a statistically significant difference between the mean hemoglobin values of the high (Class 1) and high-middle nutritional group (Class 2) only; (3) for the prisoners, no statistically significant difference between the means of the two nutritional groups included.

For the males (referred to above), the t value is 8.033 between the high and high-middle, and 6.87 between the high and low. The difference is not significant between either the high-middle and low-middle or between the low-middle and low. In the females the only significant difference is between the high and high-middle with $t = 2.75$.

In Chapter X, hemoglobin levels for various groups of individuals according to infestation status are given. There is no statistically significant difference between groups negative for any intestinal parasites and those positive for helminths. Because of this surprising absence of effect from helminth

TABLE P-2

MEAN HEMOGLOBIN MEASUREMENTS IN GRAMS PER 100 cc BY NUTRITIONAL CLASSES

Nutritional Class	Sub-Sample*	Sample Size	Mean	Standard Error	95% Confidence Level
1	M	99	13.27	0.086	13.10-13.44
	F	103	11.63	0.104	11.43-11.84
	P	...	.....	.....	....
2	M	1083	12.50	0.042	12.42-12.59
	F	1171	11.20	0.117	11.09-11.44
	P	283	12.43	0.075	12.28-12.58
3	M	258	12.47	0.084	12.31-12.64
	F	304	11.15	0.084	10.99-11.32
	P	57	12.52	0.144	12.23-12.81
4	M	33	12.39	0.110	12.09-12.53
	F	41	11.27	0.167	10.94-11.69
	P	..	.....	.....	....

*M, males excluding prisoners; F, females; P, prisoners

infection on variation in hemoglobin levels, other explanations were sought. A test for differences between urban and rural residence groups, therefore, was performed. To facilitate setting up the data for the Chi-square test, the hemoglobin measures were arbitrarily divided into high, medium, and low classes. The three groups were adjusted so that the proportion of high to medium to low was approximately 25:50:25, and the resulting distribution is as follows:

RANGE AND NUMBER IN HEMOGLOBIN VALUE GROUPINGS

Sample		Low	Middle	High	Total Number
Male	Range	2.5-11.8	11.9-13.4	13.5-15.8	
	Number	360	748	365	1473
Female	Range	3.5-10.2	10.3-12.0	12.1-15.2	
	Number	335	933	351	1619
Prisoner	Range	6.5-11.8	11.9-13.1	13.2-15.8	
	Number	90	162	89	341

The results of these urban-rural group comparisons are given in Table P-3. In the "high" hemoglobin group the percentage of urban is greater than in the "low" hemoglobin group. A Chi-square test showed that there is a statistically significant difference (except for prisoners) in the proportion of rural to urban people among the high, middle, and low hemoglobin groups (see tabulation below).

	Males	Females	Prisoners
Chi-square	29.32	8.67	3.78
Degrees of Freedom	2	2	2
Probability	.01	.013	.054

Table P-4 gives the mean hemoglobin measures and mean ethnic factor for the same high, medium and low groups as previously used (Table P-3). In all three of these samples the mean ethnic factor consistently increases as the hemoglobin value decreases, that is, the more Negroid the background the lower the values. In order to give sufficient numbers in each cell, ethnic group pairs were combined to make five classes (0 + 1, 2 + 3, 4 + 5, 6 + 7, 8 + 9). The distribution of the numbers of individuals in these classes were arrayed according to their appropriate hemoglobin category (either high, middle, or low) and a Chi-square analysis done. The results are:

	Males	Females	Prisoners
Chi-square	25.05	22.19	12.61
Degrees of Freedom	8	8	6
Probability	.01	.01	.05

The above comparison reveals a highly significant difference between the ethnic groups in terms of hemoglobin level. The general relationship between ethnic and nutritional background with hemoglobin level is plotted on Graph 70. Again, we see a steady depression in hemoglobin level as the ethnic factor of the individual increases and as the nutritional status declines. Graph 69 shows the hemoglobin levels by sex for the 15 geographic regions in Puerto Rico. For this individuals of the same ethnic and nutritional background (Ethnic Group 3 and Nutritional Class 2) were used, thus controlling these two factors. This regional

TABLE P-3

MEAN HEMOGLOBIN VALUES OF HIGH, MEDIUM, AND LOW GROUPS*
WITH THE NUMBER OF RURAL AND URBAN RESIDENTS IN EACH

Category	Males (1473)			Females (1619)			Prisoners (341)		
	H	M	L	H	M	L	H	M	L
Mean Hemoglobin (gr./100 cc)	14.2	12.60	10.75	12.84	11.20	9.46	13.90	12.42	10.93
Total Number	365	748	360	351	933	335	89	162	90
Percent	24.8	50.8	24.4	21.8	57.6	20.7	26.1	47.5	26.4
URBAN Number	142	281	81	158	395	121	27	33	18
Percent	38.9	37.6	22.5	45.0	42.3	36.1	30.3	20.4	20.0
RURAL Number	223	467	279	193	538	214	62	129	72
Percent	61.1	62.4	77.5	55.0	57.7	63.9	69.7	79.6	80.0

* H = Highest 25% of hemoglobin values; M = Middle 59% of hemoglobin values; and
L = Lowest 25% of hemoglobin values.

TABLE P-4

MEAN HEMOGLOBIN MEASUREMENTS FOR HIGH, MEDIUM, AND LOW GROUPS* COMPARED WITH MEAN ETHNIC GROUPS

Group	Hemoglobin Group	Mean Hemoglobin (gr./100 cc)	Mean Ethnic Group (0 - 9)
Males (1473)	High (365)	14.109	3.10
	Middle (748)	12.597	3.31
	Low (360)	10.747	3.65
Females (1619)	High (351)	12.841	2.97
	Middle (933)	11.200	3.14
	Low (335)	9.463	3.16
Prisoners (341)	High (89)	13.903	3.67
	Middle (162)	12.423	4.02
	Low (90)	10.934	4.66

*See Table P-3, note.

comparison reveals a pattern of considerable variation between regions. Apparently, regional factors, as well as ethnic and nutritional, cause variation in hemoglobin level.

To test the relative roles of race and nutrition, an analysis (Graph 70) was made. Shown in the graph are the mean hemoglobin values for all persons of Ethnic Group 3 (Sample B) in each of the four nutritional groups, are presented and also similar values for all persons of Nutritional Class 2 (Sample C) for each of eight ethnic groups. The analysis revealed that, while both factors are of some importance, nutrition appeared to play the major role. While it would not be easy to decide in a particular instance, which was the more important, it is evident that the better nutrition, enjoyed by subjects of Nutritional Class 1, places the mean hemoglobin level of that class clearly above that for any ethnic group or any other nutritional group.

In summary, we found repeated nonhomogeneous distributions of hemoglobin values when various groups were compared. For these no single cause of group differences exists; rather one must assume that multiple causes are acting to determine the individual's status. The low average values for Puerto Rico suggest that whatever the causes they are, in general, acting to depress the island health. What, above all else, stands out from this analysis is, that improvement in nutritional levels would certainly raise hemoglobin values and, in turn, the general health of the population.

Blood Pressure — A full and complete analysis of blood pressure in Puerto Rico is given by Murrill (1955), and anyone particularly interested in this aspect should consult his report. Our presentation here is designed merely to supplement his and to give the broad patterns of variability and group averages. The average blood pressure values for Puerto Ricans are given in Table P-5. We found no correlation between blood pressure and ethnic background, nutritional status, or infestation by parasites. But this was not true for age. A steady increase in mean age parallels mean blood pressure increases. The age-blood pressure values by sex can be seen in Table P-6. Lest the impression that age alone is at work in this increase, however, as clearly pointed out by Murrill, body weight and possibly other factors as well should be considered. When the height weight ratio is held constant, the effect of age increase is largely lost. For the males and females no consistent pattern of change in mean ethnic factor for the various systolic groups is displayed, and the same holds true for the mean nutritional values.

TABLE P-5

MEAN BLOOD PRESSURE VALUES FOR PUERTO RICANS

Category	Diastolic		Systolic	
	Number	Mean	Mean	Standard Error
Males	1518	71.22	116.17	.498
Females	1646	67.82	112.31	.532
Prisoners	395	70.27	117.01	.931

TABLE P-6

CHARACTERISTICS OF INDIVIDUALS ASSORTED ACCORDING TO SYSTOLIC BLOOD PRESSURE

Systolic Blood Pressure Group	Males			
	No. of Individuals	Percentage of Total Sample	Mean Age	Mean Diastolic
60-79	4	.26	27.50	45.00
80-99	168	11.06	33.94	57.54
100-119	734	48.35	29.60	68.35
120-139	503	33.13	29.58	76.45
140-159	91	5.99	34.13	86.49
160-179	12	.79	40.08	96.33
180-199	5	.32	42.20	99.20
200 and over	1	.06	45.00	114.00
Total	1518			
	Females			
79 or less	2	.12	23.5	52.00
80-99	309	18.77	27.64	56.80
100-119	863	52.43	28.03	66.03
120-139	376	22.84	31.16	74.89
140-159	57	3.46	36.67	87.37
160-179	24	1.45	40.33	91.00
180-199	9	.54	35.88	105.67
200-278	6	.36	41.00	127.10
Total	1646			

The distribution of these mean values arrayed by increasing blood pressure does not suggest a correlation.

For a more systematic approach to the relationship of blood pressure to nutrition and ethnic background, see Graphs 74 (males) and 75 (females). The mean blood pressure of grouped individuals of the same nutritional background (Sample B) or the same ethnic (Sample C) are compared for the other variable. For males and females (Sample C) of the same ethnic background (Group 3) a steady decline in systolic pressure and for males diastolic pressure only, a steady decline is shown in blood pressure as nutritional status decreases. A decline in diastolic pressure likewise occurs in the females and in general follows the pattern for the males but is not as dramatic.

In their case possibly the lower blood pressure is a physiologic adaptation to the lower caloric intakes. In Nutritional Class 2 (Sample B) individuals of each sex are compared by varying ethnic origins. There is a strikingly high point in the curves for females of Ethnic Group 7, for both systolic and diastolic pressures, but other than this, no relationship between ethnic background and blood pressure is apparent (as only seven are in this aberrant sample, this deviation probably should be ignored). The mean diastolic and systolic blood pressures by geographic region for samples of males and females who are from Nutritional Class 2 and Ethnic Group 3 only (Sample A) are given in Graph 73. Here again, as in many other characteristics, individuals from Region 10 are unusual in that they exhibit the highest mean pressure for both systolic and diastolic in males and for systolic in females.

One can summarize the blood pressure findings as follows: Variability seems mostly a function of age and body weight differences, with various other causes playing only minor roles. Race, nutrition residence and regional differences, and intestinal infestation rates, are apparently effective at some levels but do not seem to be major factors. Whatever the inherent nature of the individual is, seems to override to a great extent any effects that might be due to differences in the physical environment.

Differential Cell Count. — Data on differential cell counts were only used in connection with intestinal infestation. Several factors modified our confidence in their accuracy, and a preliminary analysis did not reveal any meaningful results. They are, therefore, while recorded and coded, not reported.

XII. RACIAL AND GEOGRAPHIC DISTRIBUTION OF BLOOD TYPES AND TASTERS

THE PURPOSE of obtaining blood-type and taster frequencies in Puerto Rico was threefold: (1) for statistical use by clinicians and medical blood banks; (2) for service as a genetic "marker" in the analysis of our own data; and (3) for addition to the corpus of data of value in studies of human-population genetics and evolution. The representative nature of our sample at the regional and total island level promised to make our results especially useful for the above listed purposes.

A full report of the blood and taster data has been published elsewhere (Thieme, 1952) and gives: (1) ABO and Rh frequencies (phenotype and gene) for each geographic region and ethnic groups; (2) comparisons of actual with calculated sample frequencies for ABO and Rh; (3) the Rh frequencies for persons born in and with present residence in each region; (4) frequencies of nontasters of PTC by sex for each region and ethnic group; and (5) comparisons of the ABO and Rh data from this study with the frequencies reported by Torregrossa (1945a and b). Therefore, only a summary of results is given here, with some basic tabular data. Anyone interested in gene frequencies, tests for internal consistency as well as gene and frequency breakdowns for ethnic, regional, and regional *sedentes* population may consult the more extensive report.

METHODS AND MATERIALS

In the blood grouping a representative sample was sought, but not all persons in the total sample of 3562 were typed, nor were all those typed for ABO examined for Rh. Various difficulties in maintaining the supply of serum, as well as the problem of transporting the blood drawn in the field to the laboratory in usable condition, reduced the number in the typed sample. The number reported does, however, represent the total number typed and none that were typed have been omitted. Because those not typed were not randomly spread through the sample nor were they random by municipios, the blood-type sample is not as accurately representative of the total population as is the total island sample. But when the municipios are combined into regional districts, as has been done, no one section of the island is insufficiently represented in the final sample. The frequencies in a corrected sample, designed to give the exact proportions of the original calculated sample, are not significantly different from the actual results.

A 10 cc sample of blood was drawn by venipuncture; 5 cc were used in typing and 5 cc for other determinations. The citrated samples were delivered to the blood-bank laboratory of the School of Tropical Medicine in San Juan where they were typed, under the direction of Señor N. Dobal, according to standard procedures. The samples were obtained from 3245 individuals typed for ABO, and 2528 for Rh.

Difficulties were encountered with some of the sera used. Unfortunately, 3079 MN determinations had to be discarded due to gross internal inconsistencies in the frequency distribution of the types. In the data analysis given here an attempt is made to use these findings. Also, the Hr (anti-c) testing sera did not give consistent results, so some 1200 of these were not reported. In spite of this, there is good reason to accept the reliability of the ABO and Rh frequencies here reported. The results have internal consistency as seen in D/sigma values, and gene frequencies are what would be expected for a Negro-White mixed population; that is, the Puerto Rican total frequencies are intermediate to reported Negro and White figures, and the extreme Negro and White match their parental groups.

For the determination of the taster and nontaster reaction, phenylthiocarbamide crystals were placed by a toothpick applicator on the tongue of the 3229 subjects tested. While giving no indication of the taste thresholds to known concentrations, this method does give all concentrations as the crystals dissolve, and should discover all tasters. The infliction of this bitter tasting chemical on the palates of our trusting subjects produced the only threat to the otherwise excellent rapport between the Puerto Ricans and ourselves during the study. Unfortunately, so many were tasters!

RESULTS

Blood-type frequencies for the ABO and Rh factors for the total island for both the actual sample and calculated sample are given in Table B-1. The calculated sample was devised to test whether the failure to get all sample subjects typed had a biasing effect on the results. The proportions of the ABO and Rh number for each region were applied to extrapolate its actual sample

TABLE B-1

COMPARISON OF TOTAL ACTUAL SAMPLE WITH TOTAL
CALCULATED SAMPLE FOR PERCENTAGE
FREQUENCIES OF ABO AND Rh TYPES

Sample	ABO					
	O	A_1	A_2	B	$A_1 B$	$A_2 B$
Calculated	53.88	24.88	9.70	9.49	1.01	1.04
Actual	53.99	24.84	9.61	9.52	.99	1.05
Difference	+.11	-.04	-.09	+.03	-.02	+.01

Sample	Rh							
	rh	rh'	rh''	rh'rh''	Rh_0	Rh_1	Rh_2	$Rh_1 Rh_2$
Calculated	8.53	1.16	0.46	0.11	12.82	48.75	15.46	12.71
Actual	8.78	1.23	0.47	0.12	13.21	48.89	14.79	12.50
Difference	+.25	+.07	+.01	+.01	+.39	+.14	-.67	-.21

number up or down to fit the calculated sample. While the proportion of regional types remains unchanged, its share in contributing to the total sample was adjusted to meet the number calculated to fit a representative subsample (N = 3333) of the total population. Only in one case were the differences as high as .67%; in all others they are under .39% and not significant. For this reason our actual sample may be confidently taken to be representative of Puerto Rican island frequencies.

The taster test (PTC) resulted in showing 13.29% of the males and 10.29% of the females to be nontasters. An analysis by region and ethnic group (reported elsewhere, Thieme, 1952) gave the percentage range between regions to be 5.71 - 19.73 for males and 3.70 - 18.26 for females. The sex ratio of frequencies varied appreciably between regions and appeared to be a dependence on race as well. Yet there is no regional or total ethnic heterogeneity: X^2 = 9.63, P = .20 for ethnic, and X^2 = 19.71, P = .10 for regional breakdowns. Negro males seem much more likely to be nontasters than Negro females, and this sex difference is greater than in the Whites. As the taster reaction is presumed to be controlled by a single nonsex-linked gene, these results showing different sex ratios by race seem to call for a slight modification in the theory of inheritance for this trait, a theory that takes into consideration other influences as well as sex.

Of special interest were the several tests carried out which relate to the adequacy of our ethnic classification system and the factors used in its calculation. But first it is necessary to understand that blood-group frequencies vary by ethnic class and geographic region in Puerto Rico. For ABO, the regional distribution tested by Chi-square gives $\chi^2 = 69.99$ with $d.f. = 42$, so $p = .01$ and the distribution is nonhomogeneous. For Rh, $\chi^2 = 135.32$, $d.f. = 70$ and $t = 4.66$; thus, again, a highly significant value is obtained (in this test Rh', Rh'' and Rh'Rh'' were combined to eliminate zero cell values; when this was not done, $t = 5.05$). This variability for ethnic factor is greater than for region, as is apparent by inspection (see Tables 3, 5, 7, and 9 in Thieme, 1952). For instance, Rh⁰ varies from 4% to 25% and A_1 from 26% to 9%, and with expected gradients as ethnic factor change from 1 to 9.

To test the sorting value of our ethnic classification, realizing that regional and racial variation occurs, we first need to ask whether one ethnic class can sort out of the total array of blood groups in each region a combined sample with type frequencies which are homogeneous by regional composition. Using Ethnic Groups 2 and 3 and both ABO and Rh, the results are as follows:

ABO	χ^2	$d.f.$	t	p
Ethnic 2	55.00	42	1.38	.10
Ethnic 2	47.84	42	0.67	.50
Rh				
Ethnic 2	81.03	70	0.97	.10
Ethnic 3	103.16	70	2.57	.01

This is a rigorous test, but the sorting capacity of our ethnic assignment proves to be quite satisfactory: For the different regions the blood-group frequencies for one ethnic group are not significantly different from each other except in the one case.

As a further test designed to find the relative value of each trait used in calculating the ethnic factor, the Chi-square test was applied to samples grouped by region for similar, recorded categories of skin color, hair form, lip thickness and nose shape. The Rh distribution was used because it gives a more strict test for homogeneity. The results are:

	χ^2	$d.f.$	t	p
Skin Color	88.77	70	1.53	1.26
Hair Form	105.33	70	2.72	.007
Nose Shape	109.44	70	3.01	.003
Lip Thickness	116.81	70	3.49	.0005

This analysis indicates that skin-color classes (using 5 groups of equal range) can be used to select homogeneous Rh frequency groups from each region, whereas other trait classes cannot.

As a matter of record, the values of MN frequencies obtained are given below. The typing process for this group was such that our data for N are probably accurate, inasmuch as differences most common in sera titer dictate that error is toward an overenumeration of M at the expense of the MN category but never of N. The fact that anti-M sera is stronger than anti-N accounts for this. Our frequency of type N is 630, out of 3079 individuals tested, or 20.46%. Assuming that the typing error was actually consistent and caused an underenumeration of MN (we got only 343), then the values of M would be 29.99% and of MN 49.54%, giving gene frequencies for M of 54.77 and N of 45.23%. It is admittedly a set of frequencies based on one antisera and an assumption which may not be entirely warranted. However, the results are not aberrant and agree quite closely with what would be expected in a Negro-Southern European mixed population. To justify the above calculation random mating in Puerto Rico is assumed, which we know is not the case, but as Negro and White MN frequencies are not very different, this can be neglected.

It is a pleasure to acknowledge the generous help of Señor Morales Otero, Director of the School of Tropical Medicine, as well as that of Señor Dobal who directed the typing operations. Although cost of typing sera was supplied from our project budget, the considerable material expense involved in typing and recording results were generously borne by the School of Tropical Medicine. The analysis of the data, however, was our sole responsibility.

XIII. CHARACTER OF SUBSAMPLES SELECTED TO REPRESENT GOOD HEALTH IN PUERTO RICO

AN IMPORTANT OBJECTIVE was to establish normative values for good health in Puerto Rico, values which would serve the public authorities and medical practitioners in evaluating the health status of groups or individuals. While "good health" is a relative term and it can only ultimately be measured by longevity and individual life history, the level attained by certain groups, either because of their social status or because selected for certain physical characteristics, furnishes a standard that other members of a population might hope to achieve under suitable conditions. Our data were gathered, then, to give (1) an estimate of what is relatively optimum health in Puerto Rico and (2) represent the goals to be strived for. Ideally, these goals are not high enough, but their achievement by all Puerto Ricans would represent a tremendous step forward and result in vast improvement in all spheres of life, social as well as biological.

Two groups were used in this survey: One included students, who were measured and examined while attending the University of Puerto Rico, and World War II Veterans. The students are individuals not only of superior educational background but high economic and nutritional status as compared to island averages. Since the students, better than any other socially definable subsample of our study, showed the best health status, they were preferred for assessing present as compared to possible island status.

The other subsample was composed of individuals arbitrarily selected from the parent sample on the basis of *a priori* criteria that were thought to be consistent with general standards of good health. They were males and females who were: (1) Nutritional Class 1 or 2 and had (2) a red-cell count over 3×10^6; (3) a white-cell count over 104; (4) a hemoglobin level over 13.0 gr. per 100 cc.; and (5) a blood pressure under 150 systolic and over 50 diastolic.

These are rather mild criteria, to be sure, but were met by only 326 males (17%) and 299 (18%) females. While it would have been desirable to include freedom from intestinal infestation as one criterion, only 48 of the 326 males were known to be negative (of the 210 tested, 162 were positive). Thus, the sample would have been too restricted and the number ineffectively small. The same applies to the females. If lack of infestation is added to these sorting procedures, the utility of this approach is lost as very few in our sample could meet the alleged "normal" level for six "standards" of health. Either such standards should not be applied to this island scene or one quickly, and inevitably, concludes that when only about 75[1] males out of 1916 meet the mild levels set, no subsample of our total can be taken to represent "good health." For reasons such as these only the means of stature and body weight of this arbitrary subsample are given (Table GH-3). The presentation of mean values for many other body dimensions or other characteristics would be meaningless.

ATTRIBUTES OF STUDENT-VETERAN SUBSAMPLE

The descriptive characteristics of the University of Puerto Rico students are given in Table GH-1. Added are the values for veterans of World War II. As can be seen all but 17 of the male students were veterans and of the total male veteran group only 32 were not attending the University. The veterans were included in the subsample designed to exemplify the healthy, because like the students they were a selected group. The students and veterans represent younger, whiter, and better nourished persons than the average for the total sample. The most striking difference between them and the rest is in nutritional status; they are about one level in mean nutritional background above that of the general population.

TABLE GH-1

CHARACTERISTICS OF STUDENTS AND VETERANS

Subsample	Number	Mean Ethnic Factor	Mean Nutritional Class	Mean Age	Mean Skin Color
U. of P. R. Females	108	2.82	1.59	25.30	.....
U. of P. R. Males (including Veterans)	133	2.68	1.51	26.02	13.11
W. W. II Veterans	165	2.95	1.64	26.61	13.84
U. of P. R. Males (non-Veterans)	17	2.47	1.53	23.71	12.41

---

[1] If 162 of the 210 tested for parasites were positive, then about 75 of the sample of 326 males were uninfected, that is, if the proportion holds.

TABLE GH-2

MEAN VALUES FOR CHARACTERS OF UNIVERSITY OF PUERTO RICO STUDENTS AND VETERANS OF WORLD WAR II

The physiological characteristics of the veteran-student subsample are shown in Table GH-2; the anthropometric characteristics are given in Tables 18-21.

Category	U. of P. R. Females	U. of P. R. Males	U. of P. R. Males Non-Vet.	U. of P. R. Males Vet.
Number	108	133	17	165
Pulse	86.31	74.06	76.94	74.91
Systolic Pressure	108.62	114.70	115.88	115.61
Diastolic Pressure	66.77	71.49	71.05	71.62
Hemoglobin (grams per 100 cc)	11.49	13.23	12.69	13.26
Temperature	99.22	98.63	98.86	98.54
White Cell Count (100's per mm^3)	80.43	78.90	79.12	78.52
Red Cell Count (1000's per mm^3)	3593.0	4173.6	4068.8	4156.0

Standards for evaluating part of these blood findings can be secured from the pooled data on man given by Albritton (1951). He gives a mean combined male-female, red-blood count (in millions per cubic millimeter) as 5.1 (males, 5.4 and females, 4.8). By the same approach, the blood-hemoglobin concentration in grams per 100 cc, is 15.8 for the male, and 13.9 for the female (the male-female pooled value is 14.9). By these standards Puerto Rico is low enough, but not at the level one might expect if one relies on some previously published data. For example, Pons (1931) in quoting Suarez, gives 3.3×10^6 for red-cell count and 75% (or, if 100% = 15.0 gr/100 cc, about 11 grams) as normal for Puerto Rico. Suarez' standards of the early 1930's, no longer should apply. In fact, there seems to be no reason why the predicated values for any human population cannot also be expected in Puerto Rico under improved conditions. The rise noted between 1930 and 1948 in hemoglobin and red-cell counts indicates a response to environmental improvement and are obviously not due to changes in the innate nature of the population.

CHARACTERISTICS OF SELECTED SAMPLE

Individuals of this subgroup were selected on the basis of five "health" criteria. For reasons explained above, only the data on mean height and weight for this group are presented. The mean values, compared to total island means, are given in Table GH-3. Although the comparison shows this to be a better average in these two respects, this group still ranks below the height and weight for Nutritional Class 1 (see Tables 62 and 63). No matter what standards or criteria are picked, it seems that a life history of good nutrition remains the best predictor of superiority in both stature and weight and the best determinant of "good health."

TABLE GH-3

"GOOD HEALTH" SAMPLE COMPARED TO TOAL SAMPLE MEANS FOR STATURE AND WEIGHT

Category	Mean Stature (cm)		Mean Weight (lbs)	
	Good Health	Total Sample*	Good Health	Total Sample*
Males	165.29	164.49	134.25	128.59
Females	153.27	152.67	115.22	110.85

*Excluding Prisoners.

CONCLUSIONS

The bodily characteristics of the students, veterans, or members of the selected sample give normative values which can suffice as standards of the Puerto Rican individual at his best. They also serve as public health potentials. Even though this is true, it may well be that the characters of the group defined as Nutritional Class 1 will give as good values for this purpose. These data do support a contention that Puerto Ricans in the long run should be judged by the same medical and biological standards which apply to man in general. Special or more lenient criteria need not be devised for Puerto Ricans. This is mentioned because Puerto Rican medical practitioners in the past have generally gone along with existing conditions and have not expected their patients to meet outside standards— a rationalization, no doubt, of the belief that Puerto Ricans were different and need not be judged except on their own levels.

It was convenient to accept the status quo. Our data, to the contrary, indicate that, when given a healthy environment and a good diet, the Puerto Ricans are like any racially comparable people in responding to such a background. The great forward strides that Puerto Rico is now making, both socially and economically, will undoubtedly eventually substantiate this and result in a biologically changed population.

XIV. THE PUERTO RICAN MIGRANT

POPULATION DENSITY is higher in Puerto Rico than in any other country in the Western Hemisphere, and only a few countries in the world exceed it. High fertility coupled with a rapidly declining death rate promises to make the population pressure even more critical in future years than at present. Two measures have been suggested as humane solutions for this situation: emigration and reduction in fertility. In our study, we attempted to analyze the possible consequence of emigration on the stay-at-home population. More specifically, however, our concern was with the question of whether those who emigrate are a selected sample of the parental population or whether they are merely a random one, and this called for a comparison betwen the migrants and the "sedentes," the persons who remain at home. The results of this comparison have been the subject of a separate paper (Thieme, 1957), and this chapter is a summary of that publication.

THE MIGRANT COMPARED TO THE SEDENTES

Two groups were available for a comparison of migrant and sedentes. One of them was comprised of people who had migrated and returned and the other of subjects from our sample who were same-sex siblings of unmeasured migrants. This latter included brothers of men or sisters of women who had migrated. Both groups can be compared with the general Puerto Rican population. Obviously, it was impossible to measure individuals who had left Puerto Rico and not returned. A qualified estimate of their general characteristics can be obtained, however, from the two groups mentioned. This estimate has to be based on two assumptions. First, one assumes the returned migrant is representative of those who do not return and, second, that members of the same family, not only share similar socioeconomic and nutritional backgrounds, but exhibit considerable genetic similarity. In other words, if the sibling who remains in Puerto Rico is significantly different from the general population, then in all probability, the migrant who is not measured, is significantly different as well. That related persons resemble each other and that the degree of resemblance increases as the genetic relatedness increases is well-known. The order of similarity or concordance between related persons of the same sex is highest for identical twins and decreases through siblings to cousins and so on to unrelated persons. It is with the demonstrable portion of this concordance relationship that we worked in analyzing the migrant problem. The pattern of concordance differs for different characters and is at a moderate correlation level for the sibling comparisons which we used.

In the case of the "returned migrant" one must realize that his experience while out of Puerto Rico may significantly affect his phenotype. One may find in body weight, for example, change owing to differences in diet. Yet such effects can be minimized if characters are chosen that are only slightly responsive to environmental change. This experimental condition is especially feasible for certain measures in adult samples. Howells, (1953) found that male siblings were most alike in longitudinal measures and next in head measures, but in body breadths, as shoulder and hip widths, they were least concordant.

The numbers in the returned-migrant and migrant-sibling samples measured are small, primarily due to the fact that no attempt was made to obtain migration data in our interviews, until examination of the sample was partly completed. As a result, the rate of migration cannot be calculated by comparing these sample numbers. In Tables 22-24 the statistical values for the five sample subgroups of males, females and prisoners used in the migrations code are given, and are for six measures (weight, head length, head width, waist circumference, trunk height, and total stature). In the headings of these tables the description of the five sample subgroups are given. In the previous publication, (Thieme, 1957) the mean values and relevant statistics for each subsample are given for seven body measures and also for ethnic factor, nutritional class, age, and skin color.

When an interview was conducted, the individual was classified as (1) from a family of no migrants; (2) from one in which an unlike-sex sibling had migrated; (3) from one in which a like-sex sibling had migrated; (4) from one in which some other member of family migrated (for instance father or mother); and (5) as a subject who himself had migrated. In the analysis of the data, only those in 3 and 5 (above) were used for comparisons with the total population which was taken as representing the sedentes. In Tables 22-24 the values for the groups 3 and 5 are the ones selected for comparison with the total-population values (see Table 1). All these data are accumulated in a single table in the 1957 publication.

A comparison of the measurements of same-sex siblings of migrants and of returned migrants to the general population (males, females, and prisoners) does not reveal many significant differences. However, it should be mentioned that the parental population includes the group being compared with it in our statistics, so the test used here is a minimum estimate of the significance of the differences. In view of the fact that N in the parental groups is large (1649, 1518, and 395) but small in the subsamples, this is not a large error.

RESULTS

A comparison of those represetive of the migrants with the sedentes shows the migrant to be "Whiter" and less Negroid, and to be better nourished, but of comparable age. In the anthropometric findings, comparisons between sibling and returned migrant subsamples with the total population (for males, females, and prisoners) shows that for the seven measurements (see Thieme, 1957) 32 out of 40 record the migrant as larger. Of these differences only 8 are significant, however, at over the 95% level. Siblings of migrants, when compared to total population, are significantly smaller in the one instance of female waist circumference.

Although the comparisons strongly suggest that the migrants are not a randomly selected sample of the parental population, our data do not show that hereditary features influence migration. Migrants are lighter colored, better nourished, and probably better educated, on the average, than the sedentes. These features are related to economic class in Puerto Rico, and the improved body dimensions of migrants are to be seen, then, as the reflection of a better "biological environment." Although it is certainly suggested it would be unwarranted to conclude that there is clear evidence that a superior segment of the parental population choses to migrate. "Superior" is used here only in the sense that migrants have enjoyed a better socio-economic background which is expressed, through more adequate diet and better health in larger body dimensions. Since this pattern of difference favors the migrant, it is doubtful whether a public policy that urges migration as a solution for over-population in Puerto Rico is wise. The question of the role played by migration in the dispersal of desirable population talents should be carefully examined, before encouragment of it is made an active part of administrative policy.

LITERATURE CITED

Albritton, E. C., ed.
    1951   Standard Values in Blood. Air Force Tech. Rept. No. 6039. The Committee on the Handbook of Biological Data; American Institute of Biological Sciences, National Research Council.

Blanco, Ana T.
    1946   Nutrition Studies in Puerto Rico. Univ. Puerto Rico, Rio Piedras.

Chandler, A. C.
    1944   Introduction to Parasitology. New York.

Gordon, Maxine
    1949   Race Patterns and Prejudice in Puerto Rico. Amer. Soc. Rev., 14: 291-301.
    1950   Cultural Aspects of the Puerto Rican's Race Problem. Amer. Soc. Rev., 15: 382-92.

Howells, W. W.
    1953   Correlations of Brothers in Factor Scores. Amer. J. Phys. Anthropol., 11: 121-40.

Hrdlicka, Ales
    1921   Further Studies of Tooth Morphology. Amer. J. Phys. Anthropol., 4: 141-76.

Martin, R.
    1928   Lehrbuch der Anthropologie in Systematischer Darstellung. Jena, Vol. 1.

Mourant, G. M.
    1949   Some Recent Anthropometric Surveys and Their Value for Practical Purposes. Archiv der Julius Klaus-Stiftung für Vererbungsforschung, Sozialanthropologie und Rassenhygiene, 24: 315-20.

Murrill, Rupert
    1955   Racial Blood Pressure Studies: A Critique of Methodology. Proc. Amer. Phil. Soc., 99: 277-324.

Pederson, P. O.
    1949   The East Greenland Eskimo Dentition. Meddelelser om Gronland, 142: 1-256.

Pons, J. A.
    1931   The Red Cell Count and Hemoglobin in Puerto Rico. Puerto Rican J. Pub. Health and Tropical Med., 7: 203-8.

Puerto Rico Handbook
    1947   Government of Puerto Rico, San Juan.

Roberts, Lydia
    1949   Patterns of Living in Puerto Rican Families. Univ. Puerto Rico, Rio Piedras.

Shourie, K. L.
    1949   A Dental Survey of Puerto Rican Children. Univ. of Rochester School of Medicine and Dentistry, Division of Dental Research. (Draft Report.)

Simpson, G. G.
    1941   Large Pleistocene Felines of North America. Amer. Mus. Novitates, No. 1136.

Stafne, E. C.
    1932   Supernumerary Teeth. Dental Cosmos, 74: 653-59.

Steward, J. H., E. Manners, E. Wolf, E. Padilla, S. Mintz, and R. Scheele
    1956   The People of Puerto Rico. Urbana. Ill.: Univ. Illinois Press.

Thieme, F. P.
    1950   Problems and Methods of Population Surveys. In Origin and Evolution of Man. Cold Spring Harbor Symposia on Quantitative Biology, Vol. 15.
    1952   The Geographical and Racial Distribution of ABO and Rh Blood Types and Tasters of PTC in Puerto Rico. Amer. J. Human Genetics, 4: 94-112.
    1957   A Comparison of Puerto Rico Migrants and Sedentes. Papers Mich. Acad. of Sci., Arts and Letters, 42: 249-56.

Torregrossa, M. V.
    1945a Incidence of the Rh Agglutinogen Among Puerto Ricans. Puerto Rico J. Pub. Health, 21: 166-68.
    1945b Incidence of the Eight Rh Types Among 179 Puerto Ricans. Proc. Soc. Exper. Biol., 60: 215-18.

2

Summary Tables and Graphs

A STUDY IN HUMAN BIOLOGY 153

INDEX TO TABLES

(See page 155 for code explanation)

TABLE NUMBER	MEASURE NUMBER	MEASUREMENT AND SORTING USED	SAMPLE USED						SEX		
			T	A	B	C	D	E	X	M	F	P
		GENERAL ANTHROPOMETRIC TABLES										
1	1-25	Statistical values for all measurements	X	.	.	.	.	.	.	X	X	X
2-4	1	Weight by Age	X	.	.	.	.	.	.	X	X	X
5	1	Weight by Age (3-year grouping)	X	.	.	.	.	.	.	X	X	X
6-8	5	Stature by Age	X	.	.	.	.	.	.	X	X	X
9	5	Stature by Age (3-year grouping)	X	.	.	.	.	.	.	X	X	X
10	1	Weight by Residence (Urban-Rural)	X	.	.	.	.	.	.	X	X	X
11	5	Stature by Residence (Urban-Rural)	X	.	.	.	.	.	.	X	X	X
12	1	Weight by Season of Year	X	.	.	.	.	.	.	X	X	X
13	10	Abdominal Fold by Season of Year	X	.	.	.	.	.	.	X	X	.
14	1	Weight by Number of Living Children	X	.	.	.	.	.	.	.	X	.
15	5	Stature by Number of Living Children	X	.	.	.	.	.	.	.	X	.
16	..	No. of Deceased Children by Nutritional Class	X	.	.	.	.	X	.	.	X	.
17	..	No. of Deceased Children by Ethnic Group	X	.	.	.	.	.	.	.	X	.
		SELECTED SUBSAMPLES										
18-21	1-26	Measurements on 3 subsamples (University of Puerto Rico Students; World War II Veterans)	.	.	.	.	.	.	X	X	X	.
22-24	1, 5, 7, 12 13, 21	Measurements on Migrants and Sedentes	.	.	.	.	.	.	X	X	X	X
		TABLES SHOWING GEOGRAPHICAL, NUTRITIONAL, AND ETHNIC VARIATION *										
25-48	1-25	Each measurement‡ By Geographic Regions	X†	.	.	.	.	.	X†	X	X	X
49-61	1-25	Each measurement‡ by 15 Geographic Regions	X†	.	.	.	.	.	X†	X	X	X
62-70	1-25	Each measurement‡ by 4 Nutritional Classes	X	.	.	.	.	X	.	X	X	X
71-95	1-25	Each measurement‡ by 8 Ethnic Groups	X	.	.	.	.	.	.	X	X	X
96-111	**	Ethnic 3 and Nutritional 2 sample by 15 Geographic Regions	.	X	.	.	.	.	.	X§	X§	.
112-119	**	Nutritional Class 2 sample by 8 Ethnic Groups	.	.	X	.	.	.	.	X§	X§	.
120-125	**	Ethnic Group 3 sample by 4 Nutritional Classes	.	.	.	X	.	.	.	X§	X§	.
126-127	Indices	Various Indices for Total Sample and Nutritional Class	X	.	.	.	.	.	.	X	X	.
		DENTAL TABLES										
128-133	...	Frequency of Carious, Noncarious and Missing Teeth by 15 Regions	X	.	.	.	.	.	.	X	X	X
134-137	...	Frequency of Carious, Noncarious and Missing Teeth by Ethnic Group	X	.	.	.	X	.	.	X	X	X
138-139	...	Frequency of Carious, Noncarious and Missing Teeth by Nutritional Class	X	.	.	.	.	X	.	X	X	X

*Tables of measurements arranged in numerical order of measurement number (except Tables 49-61 and 112-).
†Selected is "permanent" residents of each region.
‡Abdominal Fold not included for Males and Females.
§Prisoners combined with other males in these A, B, and C samples.
**16 selected measurements.

INDEX TO GRAPHS

(See p 155 for code explanation)

GRAPH NUMBER	MEASURE NUMBER	MEASUREMENTS AND SORTING USED*	GRAPH NUMBER	MEASUREMENTS AND SORTING USED	SAMPLE			
					T	A	B	C
		SAMPLE A* by 15 Regions (Ethnic group 3 and Nutritional Class 2 only)		DENTAL CONDITIONS				
1	1	Weight	46	Noncarious teeth by Age		X		
2	4	Total Arm Length	47	Noncarious teeth by Region		X		
3	5	Stature	48	Noncarious teeth by Ethnic and Nutritional			X	X
4	6	Leg Length	49	Noncarious teeth by Site–Upper, Lower Left	X			
5	7	Trunk Height	50	Noncarious teeth-Upper Left by Ethnic group	X			
6	8	Biacromial Diameter	51	Noncarious-Lower Left by Ethnic group	X			
7–8	12–13	Head Width and Length	52	Noncarious–Upper Left by Nutritional Class	X			
9	14	Bizygomatic Diameter	53	Noncarious–Lower Left by Nutritional Class	X			
10	15	Bigonial Diameter		INDICES	T	D	E	
11	16	Total Face Height	54–55	Cephalic and Nasal	X	X	X	X
12–13	18–19	Nose Width and Length	56–57	Bigonial/Bizygomatic	X	X	X	X
14–15	23	Leg Circumference	58	Waist Circumference/Stature	X	X	X	X
			59–60	Leg Length/Stature	X	X	X	X
		SAMPLE B† by Ethnic Group (Nutritional Class 2 only)	61–62	Trunk Height/Stature	X	X	X	X
			63	Bigonial/Head Width	X	X	X	X
		SAMPLE C† by Nutritional Class (Ethnic Group 3 only)	64	Bizygomatic/Head Width	X	X	X	X
			65	Total Arm Length/Stature	X	X	X	X
			66	Arm Circumference/Leg Circumference	X	X	X	X
16–17	1	Weight		PHYSIOLOGICAL MEASURES	A	B	C	
18–19	4	Total Arm Length	67	Pulse	X		X	
20–21	5	Stature	68	Pulse		X		X
22–23	6	Leg Length	69	Hemoglobin	X		X	X
24–25	7	Trunk Height	70	Hemoglobin			X	X
26–27	8	Biacromial Diameter	71–72	Blood Count, Red and White		X	X	X
28–29	12–13	Head Length, Width and C.I.	73–75	Blood Pressure, Diastolic and Systolic		X	X	X
30–31	14	Bizygomatic Diameter	76	Mean Values for 6 measures for Males Grouped by Occupation				
32–33	15	Bigonial Diameter						
34–35	16	Total Face Height						
36–37	18	Nose Height						
38–39	19	Nose Width						
40–41	22	Arm Circumference						
42–43	23	Leg Circumference						
44–45	25	Age (at last birthday)						

*All Graphs, except 50–53, give mean values for males including prisoners, and for females.
†All mean values shown with a vertical bar indicating the 2 S.E. distance above and below the mean.

CODE TO TABLES AND GRAPHS

SAMPLE CODE

T = Total Sample.
A = Persons of Ethnic Group 3 and Nutritional Class 2 only.
B = Persons of Nutritional Class 2 only.
C = Persons of Ethnic Group 3 only.
D = Total Sample Arrayed by Ethnic Groups.
E = Total Sample arrayed by Nutritional Class.
X = Special selected Subsample.*

SEX CODE

M = Males, excluding Prisoners
F = Females
P = Prisoners

*For the subsample in each of 15 geographic regions (Tables 23-58) only those resident all their life, from birth to 20 years, or over 20 years are included.

MEASURE NUMBER (See pp. 13-14 for descriptions):

1. Weight
2. Upper Arm Length
3. Lower Arm Length
4. Total Arm Length
5. Stature
6. Leg Length
7. Trunk Height
8. Biacromial Diameter
9. Bicristal Diameter
10. Abdominal Fold
11. Knee Width
12. Head Width
13. Head Length
14. Bizygomatic Diameter
15. Bigonial Diameter
16. Total Face Height
17. Upper Face Height
18. Nose Height
19. Nose Width
20. Chest Circumference
21. Waist Circumference
22. Arm Circumference
23. Leg Circumference
24. Skin Color
25. Age
26. Ethnic Group
27. Nutritional Class

REFERENCE TABLE FOR IDENTIFICATION OF DATA IN GRAPHS 1-76

Graph No.	Table No.	Graph No.	Table No.
1	96	24	118, 123
2	97	25	118, 123
3	98	26	118, 123
4	99	27	118, 123
5	100	28	116, 117, 123, 124, 126
6	101	29	116, 117, 123, 124, 126
7	102, 103	30	116, 125
8	102, 103	31	116, 125
9	104	32	117, 122
10	105	33	117, 122
11	106	34	115, 121
12	107, 108	35	115, 121
13	107, 108	36	114, 121
14	110	37	114, 121
15	110	38	112, 120
16	112, 120	39	112, 120
17	112, 120	40	119, 125
18	113, 124	41	119, 125
19	113, 124	42	115, 122
20	114, 121	43	115, 122
21	114, 121	44	119, 125
22	113, 124	45	119, 125
23	113, 124	46-76	No table references

TABLE 1

MEANS, STANDARD DEVIATION (S.D.), AND RANGE FOR EACH MEASUREMENT ON THE TOTAL SAMPLE

MEASUREMENT	MALES**			FEMALES			PRISONERS		
	Mean	S.D.	Range	Mean	S.D.	Range	Mean	S.D.	Range
1. Weight (lbs)	128.59	19.38	86-227	110.85	21.52	67-245	133.91	17.80	90-227
2. Upper Arm Length	31.24	2.09	20-38	28.32	1.92	20-35	31.52	2.02	27-35
3. Lower Arm Length	23.16	1.88	17-31	20.86	1.62	15-28	23.45	1.76	20-30
4. Total Arm Length	73.10	3.91	59-89	66.41	3.69	55-81	73.49	3.74	63-84
5. Stature	164.49	6.43	145-191	152.67	5.73	134-173	163.95	6.39	146-184
6. Leg Length	79.47	4.58	67-97	72.77	4.58	62-88	79.23	4.42	69-95
7. Trunk Height	53.58	3.03	44-63	50.46	2.80	41-65	53.02	3.02	45-61
8. Biacromial Diameter	37.39	1.99	25-45	33.28	1.71	23-42	37.56	1.81	20-43
9. Bicristal Diameter	25.70	2.45	19-38	24.85	2.48	19-40	24.21	2.27	20-32
10. Abdominal Fold*	4.68	3.64	1-30	9.54	6.64	1-48	4.35	2.30	1-28
11. Knee Width*	89.35	11.59	72-107	81.21	4.84	65-108	89.42	9.68	79-104
12. Head Width*	150.29	5.75	133-170	144.03	5.37	126-162	149.87	5.46	135-167
13. Head Length*	184.89	7.53	158-210	175.96	6.86	145-201	185.12	7.27	165-205
14. Bizygomatic Diameter*	135.87	5.58	107-157	128.18	5.01	112-144	136.90	5.22	115-151
15. Bigonial Diameter*	98.52	5.97	81-125	91.57	5.23	75-111	98.69	6.46	83-123
16. Total Face Height*	121.27	6.85	100-143	113.51	6.45	87-132	123.35	6.94	101-142
17. Upper Face Height*	71.50	5.11	55-96	68.20	5.01	47-85	72.19	5.40	53-88
18. Nose Height*	54.28	4.27	36-72	51.63	4.26	38-67	54.01	5.40	43-69
19. Nose Width*	36.05	3.46	26-50	32.59	3.13	21-47	36.62	3.61	26-51
20. Chest Circumference	85.04	5.01	69-114	----	----	----	86.46	5.04	75-109
21. Waist Circumference	72.92	7.78	58-114	65.63	8.17	50-119	75.82	7.11	60-108
22. Arm Circumference	24.33	2.48	17-38	22.35	2.84	15-40	24.70	1.97	20-35
23. Leg Circumference	32.38	2.64	22-44	31.21	2.96	21-49	33.51	2.57	22-42
24. Skin Color***	15.67	----	7-28	14.79	----	7-32	16.19	----	10-27
25. Age (last birthday)	29.82	----	17-60	29.25	----	17-58	28.25	----	17-49
26. Ethnic Factor****	3.45	----	0-8	3.57	----	0-9	4.05	----	1-8

Number in Samples: M = 1518, F = 1649, P = 395; Total = 3562. Except for females, N = 1517 for measure 10 and 1520 for 21.

* Measured in millimeters, all others in centimeters.
** Excluding Prisoners.
***Von Luschan Color Scale.
**** See page 11 for explanation.

TABLE 2
WEIGHT BY AGE - MALES

Table Group Numbers Age	(lbs) Mean M	Standard Deviation σ	Standard Error S.E.M	Number N
17	139.00	4.00	2.82	2
18	120.82	10.76	2.24	23
19	120.65	13.76	2.31	35
20	124.69	17.49	1.77	97
21	123.05	14.64	1.54	90
22	123.90	16.95	1.56	118
23	125.22	16.20	1.66	95
24	128.68	19.44	2.24	75
25	129.54	19.62	2.16	82
26	131.02	16.49	1.88	77
27	129.25	20.42	2.85	51
28	130.75	19.18	2.51	58
29	129.12	14.99	2.00	56
30	129.65	17.03	2.18	61
31	131.22	22.38	3.78	35
32	132.35	20.82	3.21	42
33	132.63	22.47	3.51	41
34	130.79	20.17	2.91	48
35	129.62	16.51	2.46	45
36	137.30	19.96	3.32	36
37	135.18	22.17	4.26	27
38	124.13	17.99	2.95	37
39	131.82	18.55	3.18	34
40	132.09	24.54	3.11	62
42	132.98	19.96	2.57	60
45	129.53	22.98	2.72	71
48	130.57	26.16	4.94	28
51	126.44	16.99	4.00	18
56	135.21	31.74	8.48	14

TABLE 3
WEIGHT BY AGE - FEMALES

Table Group Numbers Age	(lbs) Mean M	Standard Deviation σ	Standard Error S.E.M	Number N
17	97.33	7.42	3.03	6
18	111.48	16.32	2.93	31
19	107.20	13.68	2.06	44
20	105.69	14.56	1.31	123
21	104.56	14.39	1.56	85
22	104.76	15.12	1.64	85
23	106.76	18.81	1.71	120
24	107.00	20.72	2.18	90
25	107.52	18.02	1.87	92
26	112.61	21.26	3.03	49
27	113.36	18.98	2.39	63
28	109.43	19.55	2.08	88
29	108.55	17.52	2.24	61
30	110.45	20.96	2.19	91
31	117.04	19.16	4.08	22
32	111.77	22.19	2.93	57
33	123.25	28.40	4.14	47
34	114.27	23.36	3.52	44
35	112.10	23.22	2.64	77
36	114.13	24.69	3.64	46
37	121.93	29.00	4.37	44
38	112.25	22.30	2.78	64
39	118.14	19.85	6.40	34
40	111.16	20.98	2.85	54
42	117.12	26.45	4.18	40
45	122.05	26.00	3.53	54
48	119.88	23.59	5.72	17
54	114.95	23.51	5.13	21

TABLE 4
WEIGHT BY AGE - MALE PRISONERS

Table Group Numbers Age	(lbs) Mean M	Standard Deviation σ	Standard Error S.E.M	Number N
17	129.00			1
18	131.38	18.99	5.26	13
19	124.22	13.39	3.15	18
20	129.18	13.88	3.47	16
21	130.40	12.66	2.70	22
22	133.78	18.77	3.04	38
23	131.29	12.65	3.06	17
24	135.14	15.74	3.43	21
25	132.57	11.67	2.28	26
26	131.90	18.16	4.06	20
27	134.50	13.00	3.75	12
28	136.43	19.52	4.07	23
29	132.61	13.09	3.63	13
30	128.30	17.68	3.95	20
31	130.50	10.53	3.04	12
32	131.88	13.65	3.31	17
33	140.06	22.61	5.84	15
34	139.00	13.94	4.64	9
35	136.92	17.82	4.76	14
36	122.50	4.38	2.19	4
37	129.28	19.18	7.25	7
38	145.94	18.56	4.25	19
39	142.25	7.08	3.54	4
40	134.00	21.45	7.15	9
42	150.85	27.38	7.31	14
45	129.00	10.04	3.34	9
49	155.50	28.39	1.76	2

TABLE 5
WEIGHT BY AGE (3 year age groups)

Table Group Numbers Age*	(lbs) Mean M	Standard Deviation σ	Standard Error S.E.M	Number N
	Males			
18	121.33	12.81	1.65	60
21	123.90	16.50	94	305
24	127.65	18.49	1.16	252
27	130.45	18.50	1.35	186
30	129.82	17.72	1.43	152
33	131.87	21.11	1.84	131
36	133.57	19.52	1.87	108
39	129.81	21.69	1.88	133
42	132.98	19.96	2.57	60
45	129.53	22.98	2.72	71
48	130.57	26.16	4.94	28
55	130.28	24.93	4.40	32
	Prisoners			
18	127.28	16.10	2.84	32
21	131.84	16.28	1.86	76
24	133.07	13.50	1.68	64
27	134.36	17.91	2.41	55
30	130.13	14.89	2.22	45
33	136.43	17.98	2.80	41
36	132.48	17.67	3.53	25
39	142.12	19.17	3.38	32
42	150.85	27.38	7.31	14
45	129.00	10.04	3.34	9
48	155.50	28.39	1.76	2
	Females			
18	108.11	14.84	1.64	81
21	105.09	14.70	85	293
24	107.06	19.19	1.10	302
27	111.45	19.87	1.40	200
30	110.62	19.74	1.49	174
33	116.16	25.14	2.06	148
36	115.25	25.58	1.98	167
39	113.18	26.17	2.12	152
42	117.12	26.45	4.18	40
45	122.05	26.00	3.53	54
48	119.88	23.59	5.72	17
55	114.95	23.51	5.13	21

*Average age of the group.

TABLE 6
TOTAL STATURE BY AGE - MALES

Table Group Numbers	(lbs) Mean M	Standard Deviation σ	Standard Error S.E.M	Number N
Age				
17	163.50	4.50	3.18	2
18	163.69	7.05	1.47	23
19	163.65	7.09	1.19	35
20	163.62	6.50	66	97
21	164.14	6.46	68	90
22	163.75	6.05	55	118
23	164.12	6.32	64	95
24	164.14	5.90	68	75
25	165.06	6.25	69	82
26	165.07	6.21	70	77
27	162.72	6.09	85	51
28	165.27	6.14	80	58
29	165.42	6.49	86	56
30	165.86	6.10	78	61
31	166.11	7.29	1.23	35
32	164.78	6.49	1.00	42
33	164.51	6.73	1.05	41
34	165.27	6.19	89	48
35	164.77	6.13	91	45
36	166.02	6.37	1.06	36
37	165.66	6.94	1.33	27
38	163.45	6.53	1.07	37
39	164.50	5.57	95	34
40	164.45	6.57	83	62
42	164.95	7.25	93	60
45	164.36	6.30	74	71
48	162.57	4.75	89	28
51	164.22	5.88	1.38	18
56	164.92	9.11	2.43	14

TABLE 7
TOTAL STATURE BY AGE - FEMALE

Table Group Numbers	(cm) Mean M	Standard Deviation σ	Standard Error S.E.M	Number N
Age				
17	152.33	5.05	2.06	6
18	152.32	4.56	82	31
19	152.25	4.80	72	44
20	152.78	5.66	50	123
21	151.89	5.05	54	85
22	152.09	5.86	63	85
23	152.22	5.92	54	120
24	151.44	6.32	66	90
25	151.98	6.31	65	92
26	154.65	5.19	74	49
27	154.34	6.41	80	63
28	152.92	6.16	65	88
29	152.60	6.76	86	61
30	152.15	5.90	61	91
31	155.50	6.05	1.28	22
32	152.29	6.41	84	57
33	153.14	6.14	89	47
34	153.63	6.31	95	44
35	152.93	5.50	62	77
36	153.89	4.87	71	46
37	151.59	5.05	76	44
38	152.81	5.60	70	64
39	154.38	5.65	96	34
40	151.40	5.85	79	54
42	153.50	5.49	86	40
45	152.90	5.07	68	54
48	154.52	5.22	1.26	17
54	151.28	5.71	1.24	21

TABLE 8
TOTAL STATURE BY AGE - PRISONERS

Table Group Numbers	(cm) Mean M	Standard Deviation σ	Standard Error S.E.M	Number N
Age				
17	165.00			1
18	163.61	7.33	2.03	13
19	162.33	5.72	1.34	18
20	162.93	6.11	1.52	16
21	163.90	6.56	1.39	22
22	163.39	7.02	1.14	38
23	164.00	5.92	1.43	17
24	164.19	5.50	1.20	21
25	164.46	5.80	1.13	26
26	163.50	5.68	1.27	20
27	165.08	6.36	1.83	12
28	166.43	6.17	1.28	23
29	164.46	6.11	1.69	13
30	159.95	5.34	1.19	20
31	162.58	4.91	1.41	12
32	163.05	6.69	1.62	17
33	166.46	8.42	2.17	15
34	163.88	5.97	1.99	9
35	164.00	6.51	1.74	14
36	161.50	4.03	2.01	4
37	164.28	5.88	2.22	7
38	164.94	4.24	97	19
39	171.25	2.48	1.24	4
40	161.66	6.93	2.31	9
42	167.07	7.55	2.01	14
45	162.44	4.33	1.44	9
49	167.50	9.50	6.71	2

TABLE 9
TOTAL STATURE BY AGE (3 year groups)

Table Group Numbers	(yrs) Mean M	Standard Deviation σ	Standard Error S.E.M	Number N
Age*		Males		
18	163.66	7.01	.90	60
21	163.80	6.22	.35	305
24	164.43	6.24	.39	252
27	164.49	6.20	.45	186
30	165.76	6.42	.52	152
33	164.87	6.60	.57	131
36	165.41	6.42	.61	108
39	164.18	6.45	.55	133
42	164.95	7.25	.93	60
45	164.36	6.30	.74	71
48	162.57	4.75	.89	28
55	164.53	7.40	1.30	32
		Prisoners		
18	162.93	6.47	1.14	32
21	163.44	6.73	.77	76
24	164.25	5.72	.71	64
27	165.07	6.18	.83	55
30	161.95	5.91	.88	45
33	164.48	7.39	1.15	41
36	163.68	6.03	1.20	25
39	164.81	5.63	.99	32
42	167.07	7.55	2.01	14
45	162.44	4.33	1.44	9
48	167.50	9.50	6.71	2
		Females		
18	152.28	4.82	.53	81
21	152.32	5.61	.32	293
24	151.92	6.03	.34	302
27	153.79	6.10	.43	200
30	152.73	6.36	.48	174
33	152.96	6.28	.51	148
36	152.84	5.32	.41	167
39	152.66	5.82	.47	152
42	153.50	5.49	.86	40
45	152.90	5.07	.68	54
48	154.52	5.22	1.26	17
55	151.28	5.71	1.24	21

*Average age of the group.

TABLE 10
WEIGHT BY RESIDENCE CATEGORY

Table Group Numbers	(lbs) Mean M	Standard Deviation σ	Standard Error S.E.M	Number N
Residence*		Males		
1	130.54	21.30	.94	511
2	130.32	18.67	1.80	107
3	127.27	18.20	.60	900
		Prisoners		
1	132.59	20.44	2.01	103
2	134.00	31.00	8.97	2
3	134.37	16.66	.97	290
		Females		
1	112.87	23.43	.89	681
2	109.74	18.50	1.89	95
3	109.39	20.13	.68	873

*Code 1 = Urban
2 = Rural with Neighbors
3 = Rural Alone

TABLE 11
STATURE BY RESIDENCE CATEGORY

Table Group Numbers	(cm) Mean M	Standard Deviation σ	Standard Error S.E.M	Number N
Residence*		Males		
1	164.15	6.46	.28	511
2	165.93	6.47	.62	107
3	164.50	6.43	.21	900
		Prisoners		
1	163.17	6.61	.65	103
2	160.50	6.50	4.59	2
3	164.25	6.29	.36	290
		Females		
1	153.06	5.90	.22	681
2	153.23	6.07	.62	95
3	152.29	5.91	.20	873

*Code 1 = Urban
2 = Rural with neighbors
3 = Rural alone

TABLE 12
WEIGHT BY SEASON OF THE YEAR

Table Group Numbers	(lbs) Mean M	Standard Deviation σ	Standard Error S.E.M	Number N
Season*		Males		
4	130.66	18.27	.91	402
5	130.27	19.46	.95	413
6	126.84	21.49	1.59	182
7	128.03	18.09	1.45	154
8	125.01	19.05	1.18	259
9	126.80	19.98	1.92	108

*Code 4 = June, July
5 = August, September
6 = October
7 = November
8 = December
9 = January

TABLE 13
ABDOMINAL FOLD THICKNESS BY SEASON OF THE YEAR

Table Group Numbers	(mm) Mean M	Standard Deviation σ	Standard Error S.E.M	Number N
Season*		Males		
4	5.78	4.57	.22	401
5	3.70	3.58	.17	413
6	3.87	3.58	.26	182
7	3.33	2.10	.16	154
8	2.93	2.14	.13	259
9	3.28	2.28	.21	108

*Code 4 = June, July
5 = August, September
6 = October
7 = November
8 = December
9 = January

TABLE 14
WEIGHT BY NUMBER OF LIVING CHILDREN

Table Group Numbers	(lbs) Mean M	Standard Deviation σ	Standard Error S.E.M	Number N
Living Children		Females		
0	110.73	20.42	.89	517
1	111.12	19.99	1.34	220
2	109.31	21.36	1.44	219
3	107.10	20.15	1.48	185
4	111.89	22.50	1.78	159
5	112.73	23.20	2.23	108
6	107.43	19.73	2.09	89
7	114.16	26.20	3.41	59
8	118.09	20.40	3.60	32
9	116.80	26.16	5.13	26
10	122.70	16.71	8.67	17
11	103.85	16.84	6.36	7
12	135.85	17.28	6.53	7
13	122.00	5.00	3.53	2
14	126.00	14.00	9.89	2

TABLE 15
TOTAL STATURE BY NUMBER OF LIVING CHILDREN

Table Group Numbers	(cm) Mean M	Standard Deviation σ	Standard Error S.E.M	Number N
Living Children		Females		
0	153.38	5.76	.25	517
1	152.69	5.91	.39	220
2	152.08	5.71	.38	219
3	151.92	5.95	.43	185
4	152.20	6.14	.48	159
5	152.85	6.12	.58	108
6	151.62	5.54	.58	89
7	151.77	5.47	.71	59
8	153.06	5.12	.90	32
9	153.26	5.96	1.16	26
10	154.41	5.56	1.35	17
11	151.00	6.34	2.39	7
12	156.57	3.56	3.56	7
13	156.50	8.50	6.01	2
14	157.00	2.00	1.41	2

TABLE 16
NUMBER OF DECEASED CHILDREN PER WOMAN BY NUTRITIONAL CLASS

Table Group Numbers	Mean M	Standard Deviation σ	Standard Error S.E.M	Number N
NC				
1	.36	.82	.08	103
2	.73	1.32	.03	400
3	.97	1.50	.08	302
4	1.10	1.71	.26	42

TABLE 17
NUMBER OF DECEASED CHILDREN PER WOMAN BY ETHNIC GROUP

Table Group Numbers	Mean M	Standard Deviation σ	Standard Error S.E.M	Number N
EG				
1	1.12	1.75	.23	56
2	.76	1.28	.05	426
3	.69	1.28	.04	705
4	.81	1.53	.10	230
5	.68	1.04	.11	76
6	.94	1.55	.18	72
7	.66	1.11	.17	39
8	.62	.98	.35	8

TABLE 18
VARIOUS MEASUREMENTS FOR THREE SUB-SAMPLES

Table Group Numbers*	Mean M	Standard Deviation σ	Standard Error S.E.M	Number N
	WEIGHT (lbs)			
4	138.55	17.86	1.39	165
5	137.13	19.32	1.67	133
6	113.83	21.80	2.07	108
	UPPER ARM LENGTH (cm)			
4	31.53	1.62	.12	165
5	31.61	1.78	.15	133
6	28.32	1.70	.16	108
	LOWER ARM LENGTH (cm)			
4	22.96	1.77	.13	165
5	22.72	1.45	.12	133
6	20.60	1.37	.13	108
	TOTAL LEG LENGTH (cm)			
4	80.12	3.87	.30	165
5	79.85	3.99	.34	133
6	73.99	3.45	.33	108
	BICRISTAL DIAMETER (cm)			
4	26.21	1.94	.15	165
5	26.42	1.95	.16	133
6	25.93	2.72	.26	109
	ABDOMINAL FOLD THICKNESS (mm)			
4	4.59	3.15	.24	165
5	4.38	3.47	.30	133
6	12.75	7.87	.75	108

*Code: 4 = Male Veterans of World War II.
5 = University of Puerto Rico Males
6 = University of Puerto Rico Females

TABLE 19
VARIOUS MEASUREMENTS FOR THREE SUB-SAMPLES

Table Group Numbers*	Mean M	Standard Deviation σ	Standard Error S.E.M	Number N
	HEIGHT (cm)			
4	166.72	5.46	.42	165
5	166.66	5.49	.47	133
6	154.39	4.98	.47	108
	BIACROMIAL DIAMETER (cm)			
4	37.81	1.78	.13	165
5	37.60	1.75	.15	133
6	33.29	1.87	.17	108
	TOTAL ARM LENGTH (cm)			
4	73.17	3.22	.25	165
5	72.92	3.11	.27	133
6	65.95	3.22	.30	108
	TRUNK HEIGHT (cm)			
4	55.18	2.63	.20	165
5	55.54	2.58	.22	133
6	51.85	2.09	.20	108
	BIZYGOMATIC DIAMETER (mm)			
4	137.75	4.98	.38	165
5	137.80	5.22	.45	133
6	127.65	4.55	.43	108
	WAIST CIRCUMFERENCE (cm)			
4	71.81	7.32	.57	165
5	70.32	7.22	.62	133
6	61.54	7.15	.68	108

*Code: 4 = Male Veterans of World War II.
5 = University of Puerto Rico Males
6 = University of Puerto Rico Females

TABLE 20
VARIOUS MEASUREMENTS FOR THREE SUB-SAMPLES

Table Group Numbers*	Mean M	Standard Deviation σ	Standard Error S.E.M	Number N
	BIGONIAL DIAMETER (mm)			
4	99.09	58.56	.454	165
5	99.20	56.32	.487	133
6	92.57	47.61	.457	108
	HEAD WIDTH (mm)			
4	152.56	56.23	.438	165
5	153.36	55.17	.477	133
6	144.29	49.26	.473	108
	TOTAL FACE HEIGHT (mm)			
4	122.61	59.51	.462	165
5	122.87	59.23	.512	133
6	113.14	51.53	.498	108
	NOSE WIDTH (mm)			
4	36.18	30.60	.238	165
5	35.94	29.83	.259	133
6	32.78	32.18	.308	108
	AGE (yrs)			
4	26.61	38.21	.297	165
5	26.02	40.76	.353	133
6	25.29	58.01	.557	108
	SKIN COLOR (von Luschan)			
6	13.86	32.30	.310	108
4	13.83	35.29	.273	165
5	13.11	26.96	.233	133
	CHEST CIRCUMFERENCE (cm)			
4	86.64	56.40	.439	165
5	85.14	57.00	.494	133

*Code: 4 = Male Veterans of World War II.
5 = University of Puerto Rico Males
6 = University of Puerto Rico Females

TABLE 21
VARIOUS MEASUREMENTS FOR THREE SUB-SAMPLES

Table Group Numbers*	(yrs) Mean M	Standard Deviation σ	Standard Error S.E.M	Number N
	KNEE WIDTH (mm)			
4	90.37	3.95	.30	165
5	89.86	3.83	.33	133
6	81.57	4.68	.45	108
	HEAD LENGTH (mm)			
4	187.95	6.92	.53	165
5	188.70	6.83	.59	133
6	178.39	6.50	.62	108
	UPPER FACE HEIGHT (mm)			
4	73.23	4.55	.35	165
5	74.02	4.25	.36	133
6	70.50	4.31	.41	108
	NOSE HEIGHT (mm)			
4	56.31	3.63	.28	165
5	56.99	3.71	.32	133
6	53.87	4.08	.39	108
	ARM CIRCUMFERENCE (cm)			
4	25.01	2.24	.17	165
5	24.79	2.51	.21	133
6	22.45	2.87	.27	108
	LEG CIRCUMFERENCE (cm)			
4	33.18	2.45	.19	165
5	32.76	2.52	.21	133
6	30.67	2.49	.23	108
	ETHNIC GROUP			
4	2.94	1.19	.08	165
5	2.67	.87	.07	133
6	2.82	1.10	.10	108

*Code: 4 = Male Veterans of World War II.
5 = University of Puerto Rico Males
6 = University of Puerto Rico Females

TABLE 22
VARIOUS MEASUREMENTS OF MIGRANTS AND SEDENTES

Table Group Numbers*	Mean M	Standard Deviation σ	Standard Error S.E.M	Number N
	WEIGHT (lbs)	Males		
2	126.85	16.93	2.18	60
3	131.21	20.71	2.22	87
4	127.54	19.87	2.67	55
5	136.40	25.36	5.67	20
		Females		
2	109.27	19.41	2.15	81
3	112.61	20.97	2.12	97
4	111.28	22.93	3.27	49
5	118.11	21.78	5.28	17
		Prisoners		
1	133.37	16.63	.98	286
2	132.11	18.40	2.84	42
3	136.20	17.87	2.32	59
4	107.00			1
5	151.14	20.38	1.49	7
	HEAD LENGTH (cm)	Males		
2	185.16	6.59	.85	60
3	185.08	6.84	.73	87
4	184.74	6.36	.85	55
5	184.35	6.27	1.40	20
		Females		
2	176.60	6.28	.69	81
3	176.19	6.78	.68	97
4	176.95	8.24	1.17	49
5	175.41	7.28	1.76	17
		Prisoners		
1	184.87	7.25	.42	286
2	185.52	7.02	1.08	42
3	186.20	7.22	.94	59
4	176.00			1
5	185.28	4.00	1.51	7

*Code: 1 = No Migrants in Family
2 = Unlike Sex Sibling Migrant
3 = Like Sex Sibling Migrant
4 = Other Member of Family Migrant
5 = Migrant Who Has Returned

TABLE 23
VARIOUS MEASUREMENTS OF MIGRANTS AND SEDENTES

Table Group Numbers*	Mean M	Standard Deviation σ	Standard Error S.E.M	Number N
	TRUNK HEIGHT	Males		
2	54.35	2.61	.33	60
3	54.64	2.72	.29	87
4	53.50	2.76	.37	55
5	55.30	3.01	.67	20
		Females		
2	51.00	2.46	.27	81
3	51.13	2.77	.28	97
4	51.48	3.05	.43	49
5	52.23	2.27	.55	17
		Prisoners		
1	53.54	3.06	.17	286
2	53.83	3.11	.47	42
3	54.42	2.91	.37	59
4	49.00			1
5	55.57	2.89	1.09	7
	TOTAL STATURE	Males		
2	164.61	60.98	7.86	60
3	165.65	56.44	6.04	87
4	162.10	70.00	9.43	55
5	164.25	64.24	14.36	20
		Females		
2	152.13	55.44	6.15	81
3	152.95	56.73	5.75	97
4	153.67	55.96	7.99	49
5	154.41	53.31	12.93	17
		Prisoners		
1	163.84	65.18	3.84	286
2	163.78	56.80	8.76	42
3	164.27	64.54	8.40	59
4	159.00			1
5	167.28	82.87	31.32	7

*Code: 1 = No Migrants in Family
2 = Unlike Sex Sibling Migrant
3 = Like Sex Sibling Migrant
4 = Other Member of Family Migrant
5 = Migrant Who Has Returned

TABLE 24
VARIOUS MEASUREMENTS OF MIGRANTS AND SEDENTES

Table Group Numbers*	Mean M	Standard Deviation σ	Standard Error S.E.M	Number N
NC	HEAD WITH (mm)			
2	149.85	5.35	.69	60
3	150.87	5.76	.61	87
4	149.61	5.84	.78	55
5	152.00	7.36	1.64	20
2	143.56	5.14	.57	81
3	143.77	5.87	.59	97
4	144.36	5.10	.72	49
5	145.11	4.02	.97	17
1	149.86	5.55	.32	286
2	150.95	4.69	.72	42
3	148.96	5.57	.72	59
4	151.00			1
5	151.28	4.09	1.54	7
	WAIST CIRCUMFERENCE (cm)			
2	72.41	6.39	.82	60
3	71.95	13.02	1.39	87
4	73.74	7.15	.96	55
5	75.40	9.59	2.14	20
2	60.97	20.48	2.27	81
3	60.98	19.89	2.01	97
4	65.79	7.42	1.06	49
5	63.47	17.77	4.31	17
1	76.52	6.45	.38	286
2	76.73	7.82	1.20	42
3	77.35	8.16	1.06	59
4	68.00			1
5	81.28	13.70	5.17	7

*Code: 1 = No Migrants in Family
2 = Unlike Sex Sibling Migrant
3 = Like Sex Sibling Migrant
4 = Other Member of Family Migrant
5 = Migrant Who Has Returned

TABLE 25
WEIGHT BY GEOGRAPHIC REGION

Table Group Numbers	(lbs) Mean M	Standard Deviation σ	Standard Error S.E.M	Number N
Region		Males		
1	128.78	16.24	1.99	66
2	128.69	21.25	1.82	136
3	127.88	15.68	1.61	94
4	133.92	12.59	1.71	54
5	131.46	18.35	1.41	169
6	132.55	15.89	2.51	40
7	125.96	20.79	2.55	66
8	132.16	19.30	2.94	43
9	130.40	20.60	3.96	27
10	131.00	20.55	4.28	23
11	128.46	23.14	2.82	67
12	131.84	22.99	3.25	50
13	125.17	17.55	1.73	102
14	127.75	17.48	1.73	102
15	131.48	21.29	2.36	81
		Females		
1	109.37	22.04	2.44	81
2	110.97	18.26	1.55	138
3	113.45	21.91	2.42	82
4	114.00	20.84	4.44	22
5	114.77	20.77	1.98	109
6	109.76	17.95	2.16	69
7	116.79	26.11	2.31	127
8	102.95	15.26	1.83	69
9	112.85	17.19	4.59	14
10	113.70	16.85	3.07	30
11	109.18	19.99	2.74	53
12	109.78	23.01	2.97	60
13	104.13	17.37	1.45	143
14	108.10	21.94	2.16	103
15	113.70	23.12	2.31	100

TABLE 26
UPPER ARM LENGTH BY GEOGRAPHIC REGION

Table Group Numbers	(cm) Mean M	Standard Deviation σ	Standard Error S.E.M	Number N
Region		Males		
1	31.32	1.87	.23	66
2	31.22	2.14	.18	136
3	31.38	2.14	.21	94
4	30.90	2.26	.30	54
5	31.64	2.36	.18	169
6	31.62	1.86	.29	40
7	31.12	2.17	.26	66
8	31.44	1.76	.26	43
9	31.26	1.59	.30	27
10	31.60	1.96	.40	23
11	31.00	1.89	.23	67
12	30.65	1.77	.24	50
13	30.98	2.00	.19	102
14	31.56	1.94	.19	102
15	31.25	2.14	.23	81
		Females		
1	27.93	1.80	.20	81
2	28.74	2.14	.18	138
3	28.47	1.86	.20	82
4	28.62	2.07	.44	22
5	29.23	1.94	.18	109
6	28.45	1.88	.22	69
7	28.43	2.05	.18	127
8	27.97	1.48	.17	69
9	28.55	1.62	.43	14
10	28.46	1.43	.26	30
11	27.83	1.86	.25	53
12	28.03	1.88	.24	60
13	27.73	1.86	.15	143
14	27.91	1.86	.18	103
15	28.51	1.99	.19	100

TABLE 27
LOWER ARM LENGTH BY GEOGRAPHICAL REGION

Table Group Numbers	(cm) Mean M	Standard Deviation σ	Standard Error S.E.M	Number N
Region		Males		
1	22.78	1.63	.20	66
2	23.17	2.10	.17	136
3	23.42	1.91	.19	94
4	25.23	2.69	.36	54
5	24.47	2.08	.15	169
6	23.42	1.40	.22	40
7	23.32	1.88	.23	66
8	23.39	1.85	.28	43
9	22.44	1.78	.34	27
10	23.26	2.20	.46	23
11	22.90	1.80	.21	67
12	22.48	1.89	.26	50
13	22.61	1.60	.15	102
14	22.78	1.56	.15	102
15	22.96	1.90	.20	81
		Females		
1	20.57	1.64	.18	81
2	21.22	1.76	.14	138
3	21.17	1.73	.18	82
4	21.21	1.45	.30	22
5	21.36	1.67	.15	109
6	21.02	1.40	.16	69
7	21.03	1.76	.15	127
8	20.80	1.26	.15	69
9	21.04	1.36	.36	14
10	20.99	1.60	.29	30
11	20.68	1.52	.20	53
12	20.60	1.72	.22	60
13	20.30	1.52	.12	143
14	20.55	1.61	.15	103
15	20.93	1.55	.15	100

TABLE 28
TOTAL ARM LENGTH BY GEOGRAPHIC REGION

Table Group Numbers	(cm) Mean M	Standard Deviation σ	Standard Error S.E.M	Number N
Region		Males		
1	73.10	3.28	.40	66
2	73.10	4.59	.39	136
3	73.76	4.24	.43	94
4	74.89	4.29	.58	54
5	75.34	4.27	.32	169
6	73.98	3.11	.49	40
7	72.95	4.05	.49	66
8	73.51	3.39	.51	43
9	72.45	3.53	.67	27
10	73.32	3.74	.77	23
11	72.38	3.86	.47	67
12	71.56	3.82	.54	50
13	72.09	3.87	.38	102
14	72.92	3.82	.37	102
15	72.62	3.98	.44	81
		Females		
1	65.81	3.24	.36	81
2	67.29	3.83	.32	138
3	67.17	3.60	.39	82
4	67.55	3.21	.68	22
5	68.36	3.99	.38	109
6	66.55	3.56	.42	69
7	66.54	4.14	.36	127
8	65.65	3.34	.40	69
9	66.43	2.81	.75	14
10	66.64	3.05	.55	30
11	65.39	3.50	.48	53
12	65.71	3.78	.48	60
13	65.03	3.49	.29	143
14	65.44	3.52	.34	103
15	66.93	3.55	.35	100

TABLE 29
TOTAL STATURE BY GEOGRAPHIC REGION

Table Group Numbers	(cm) Mean M	Standard Deviation σ	Standard Error S.E.M	Number N
Region		Males		
1	165.06	6.08	.74	66
2	164.20	7.18	.61	136
3	165.31	6.39	.65	94
4	166.24	6.12	.83	54
5	166.77	6.54	.50	169
6	163.95	5.17	.81	40
7	164.57	6.33	.77	66
8	165.48	6.19	.94	43
9	164.18	6.84	1.31	27
10	165.91	5.60	1.16	23
11	164.43	5.96	.72	67
12	162.64	6.39	.90	50
13	163.11	6.25	.61	102
14	164.25	5.49	.54	102
15	164.75	6.49	.72	81
		Females		
1	152.19	5.98	.66	81
2	153.68	5.77	.49	138
3	152.98	6.13	.67	82
4	153.40	5.37	1.14	22
5	155.16	6.27	.60	109
6	153.10	5.30	.63	69
7	152.83	6.31	.55	127
8	151.02	5.19	.62	69
9	154.64	4.28	1.14	14
10	154.50	4.28	.89	30
11	152.33	5.77	.79	53
12	152.30	5.85	.75	60
13	150.91	5.54	.46	143
14	151.46	5.72	.56	103
15	153.35	5.48	.54	100

TABLE 30
TOTAL LEG LENGTH BY GEOGRAPHICAL REGION

Table Group Numbers	(cm) Mean M	Standard Deviation σ	Standard Error S.E.M	Number N
Region		Males		
1	79.87	4.39	.54	66
2	79.51	5.15	.44	136
3	80.58	4.58	.47	94
4	81.88	4.84	.65	54
5	82.36	5.14	.39	169
6	79.17	3.71	.58	40
7	79.03	4.48	.55	66
8	78.93	4.57	.69	43
9	78.70	4.35	.83	27
10	78.69	4.33	.90	23
11	78.88	4.06	.49	67
12	78.06	4.41	.62	50
13	78.19	4.67	.46	102
14	78.15	4.15	.41	102
15	79.38	4.37	.48	81
		Females		
1	72.51	4.00	.44	81
2	73.85	4.27	.36	130
3	73.62	4.47	.49	82
4	73.59	4.61	.98	22
5	75.00	4.58	.43	109
6	73.97	3.54	.42	69
7	72.55	4.38	.38	127
8	71.30	3.19	.38	69
9	72.50	3.84	1.02	14
10	73.23	2.97	.54	30
11	72.60	4.10	.56	53
12	72.23	4.12	.53	60
13	71.62	4.03	.33	143
14	71.66	3.95	.38	103
15	72.64	3.77	.37	100

TABLE 31
TRUNK HEIGHT BY GEOGRAPHIC REGION

Table Group Numbers	(cm) Mean M	Standard Deviation σ	Standard Error S.E.M	Number N
Region		Males		
1	53.06	3.21	.42	66
2	52.84	3.38	.28	136
3	53.29	2.83	.43	94
4	54.19	3.09	.42	54
5	53.32	2.92	.22	169
6	53.06	2.40	.38	40
7	53.73	2.87	.35	66
8	54.34	2.22	.33	43
9	53.87	3.40	.65	27
10	55.23	2.60	.54	23
11	54.05	2.88	.35	67
12	53.52	3.04	.43	50
13	53.82	2.62	.25	102
14	54.43	2.66	.26	102
15	53.93	3.33	.37	81
		Females		
1	49.94	2.84	.31	81
2	50.42	2.70	.23	138
3	49.85	2.93	.32	82
4	51.30	2.96	.63	22
5	49.95	3.06	.29	109
6	50.06	2.97	.35	69
7	50.52	2.91	.25	127
8	50.37	2.81	.33	69
9	51.97	1.72	.46	14
10	51.12	2.41	.43	30
11	50.24	2.71	.37	53
12	50.40	2.62	.33	60
13	50.19	2.58	.21	143
14	50.63	2.63	.25	103
15	51.33	2.29	.22	100

TABLE 32
BIACROMIAL DIAMETER BY GEOGRAPHIC REGION

Table Group Numbers	Mean M	Standard Deviation σ	Standard Error S.E.M	Number N
Region		Males		
1	37.21	1.62	.20	66
2	37.23	2.11	.18	136
3	37.78	1.95	.20	94
4	39.11	1.68	.23	54
5	38.25	2.11	.16	169
6	38.05	1.67	.26	40
7	37.30	1.78	.21	66
8	37.67	1.88	.28	43
9	37.48	1.50	.28	27
10	37.26	1.79	.37	23
11	37.18	1.79	.21	67
12	37.66	2.20	.31	50
13	36.81	1.78	.17	102
14	37.36	1.66	.16	102
15	37.59	2.31	.25	81
		Females		
1	32.67	2.04	.22	81
2	33.61	1.69	.14	138
3	34.20	1.59	.17	82
4	33.95	1.63	.34	22
5	33.75	1.82	.17	109
6	33.29	1.57	.19	69
7	33.77	1.88	.16	127
8	33.25	1.59	.19	69
9	34.00	1.13	.30	14
10	34.30	1.44	.26	30
11	33.34	1.38	.19	53
12	33.37	1.80	.23	60
13	32.86	1.71	.14	143
14	33.34	2.11	.27	103
15	33.63	1.56	.15	100

TABLE 33
BICRISTAL DIAMETER BY GEOGRAPHIC REGION

Table Group Numbers	(cm) Mean M	Standard Deviation σ	Standard Error S.E.M	Number N
Region		Males		
1	25.47	2.24	.27	66
2	25.39	2.18	.18	136
3	26.13	2.53	.26	94
4	27.85	1.88	.25	54
5	26.70	2.07	.15	169
6	25.10	2.48	.39	40
7	24.81	2.79	.34	66
8	24.72	2.69	.41	43
9	25.95	1.94	.37	27
10	25.40	2.41	.50	23
11	26.23	2.22	.27	67
12	25.05	2.09	.29	50
13	25.24	2.23	.22	102
14	25.55	2.66	.26	102
15	25.58	2.96	.32	81
		Females		
1	24.76	1.95	.21	80
2	25.18	2.44	.20	138
3	24.83	2.29	.25	82
4	25.33	2.02	.43	22
5	25.11	2.52	.24	109
6	24.69	2.44	.29	69
7	24.53	3.12	.27	127
8	23.83	2.36	.28	69
9	24.96	2.80	.74	14
10	25.05	2.06	.37	30
11	25.23	2.43	.33	53
12	24.72	2.50	.32	60
13	24.44	2.30	.19	143
14	24.28	2.08	.20	103
15	24.77	2.47	.24	100

TABLE 34
KNEE WIDTH BY GEOGRAPHICAL REGION

Table Group Numbers	(mm) Mean M	Standard Deviation σ	Standard Error S.E.M	Number N
Region		Males		
1	89.03	4.19	.51	66
2	88.86	4.93	.42	136
3	89.47	5.12	.52	94
4	90.51	5.85	.79	54
5	90.00	5.32	.40	168
6	89.15	3.36	.53	40
7	90.25	4.72	.58	66
8	89.69	4.36	.66	43
9	89.70	3.82	.73	27
10	90.39	4.42	.92	23
11	89.01	4.46	.54	67
12	90.10	4.21	.59	50
13	89.18	4.22	.41	102
14	89.36	4.17	.41	102
15	89.49	4.56	.50	81
		Females		
1	81.19	5.21	.57	81
2	80.87	4.91	.41	138
3	81.59	4.25	.46	82
4	81.78	3.81	.81	22
5	82.82	5.23	.50	109
6	81.59	4.35	.52	69
7	81.80	5.55	.49	127
8	79.90	4.37	.52	69
9	82.16	3.04	.81	14
10	81.29	2.85	.52	30
11	81.08	4.33	.59	53
12	81.80	5.34	.68	60
13	80.20	4.33	.36	143
14	80.65	4.79	.47	103
15	81.56	4.96	.49	100

TABLE 35
HEAD WIDTH BY GEOGRAPHIC GROUP

Table Group Numbers	(mm) Mean M	Standard Deviation σ	Standard Error S.E.M	Number N
Region		Males		
1	151.60	6.28	.77	66
2	149.98	5.86	.50	136
3	149.04	5.67	.58	94
4	148.12	5.31	.72	54
5	148.13	6.19	.47	169
6	148.82	6.44	1.01	40
7	148.75	4.89	.60	66
8	150.62	6.99	1.06	43
9	151.44	6.44	1.23	27
10	149.17	5.59	1.16	23
11	151.71	5.94	.72	67
12	149.38	4.60	.65	50
13	151.34	5.49	.54	102
14	151.58	5.56	.55	102
15	151.50	5.53	.61	81
		Females		
1	145.02	5.20	.57	81
2	143.95	4.96	.42	138
3	143.95	5.43	.59	82
4	145.40	3.28	.70	22
5	142.14	5.65	.54	109
6	144.02	4.43	.53	69
7	142.88	5.46	.48	127
8	142.97	4.67	.56	69
9	146.71	4.26	1.13	14
10	143.26	5.19	.94	30
11	145.58	5.28	.72	53
12	144.20	5.06	.65	60
13	144.79	5.33	.44	143
14	144.41	4.92	.48	103
15	144.09	5.80	.58	100

TABLE 36
HEAD LENGTH BY GEOGRAPHIC REGION

Table Group Numbers	(cm) Mean M	Standard Deviation σ	Standard Error S.E.M	Number N
Region		Males		
1	183.00	6.60	.81	66
2	185.17	7.74	.66	136
3	185.24	7.48	.77	94
4	186.75	6.85	.93	54
5	188.77	7.07	.54	169
6	187.17	6.93	1.09	40
7	187.12	7.02	.86	66
8	185.23	7.07	1.07	43
9	184.55	7.50	1.44	27
10	185.47	6.68	1.39	23
11	182.85	7.04	.86	67
12	186.80	7.63	1.07	50
13	182.36	7.88	.77	102
14	182.91	6.28	.62	102
15	184.66	6.53	.72	81
		Females		
1	173.45	6.45	.71	81
2	176.89	6.85	.58	138
3	175.03	7.25	.80	82
4	174.45	5.28	1.12	22
5	181.60	6.48	.62	109
6	177.68	6.89	.82	69
7	177.33	6.64	.58	127
8	175.49	6.27	.75	69
9	176.92	5.51	1.47	14
10	177.10	7.20	1.31	30
11	174.43	5.79	.79	53
12	175.96	7.28	.94	60
13	172.84	5.83	.48	143
14	174.87	6.51	.64	103
15	175.48	6.43	.64	100

TABLE 37
BIZYGOMATIC DIAMETER BY GEOGRAPHIC REGION

Table Group Numbers	(mm) Mean M	Standard Deviation σ	Standard Error S.E.M	Number N
Region		Males		
1	136.83	4.50	.55	66
2	135.41	5.88	.50	136
3	134.62	5.45	.56	94
4	135.53	5.28	.71	54
5	135.29	5.76	.44	169
6	136.42	5.24	.82	40
7	136.04	4.94	.60	66
8	136.00	5.30	.80	43
9	137.44	5.87	1.13	27
10	136.21	6.04	1.26	23
11	136.74	5.34	.65	67
12	135.90	5.10	.72	50
13	135.36	6.05	.59	102
14	136.00	5.94	.58	102
15	137.16	5.72	.63	81
		Females		
1	128.39	4.99	.55	81
2	127.85	5.06	.43	138
3	127.36	4.26	.47	82
4	130.40	4.80	1.02	22
5	127.77	5.78	.55	109
6	128.79	4.88	.58	69
7	128.27	5.19	.46	127
8	127.18	4.66	.56	69
9	130.21	3.31	.88	14
10	128.40	4.99	.89	30
11	128.60	4.99	.68	53
12	128.23	4.96	.64	60
13	128.16	5.17	.43	143
14	127.80	5.19	.51	103
15	128.54	5.06	.50	100

TABLE 38
BIGONIAL DIAMETER BY GEOGRAPHIC REGION

Table Group Numbers	(mm) Mean M	Standard Deviation σ	Standard Error S.E.M	Numbers N
Region		Males		
1	98.58	5.08	.62	66
2	98.30	5.24	.44	136
3	98.08	6.63	.68	93
4	98.85	5.39	.73	54
5	98.90	6.08	.46	169
6	99.55	5.77	.91	40
7	98.37	5.85	.72	66
8	99.01	5.35	.81	43
9	101.48	6.32	1.21	27
10	95.79	5.96	1.24	23
11	100.16	6.37	.77	67
12	96.53	5.04	.71	50
13	98.57	5.71	.56	102
14	98.53	6.37	.63	102
15	98.84	7.02	.78	81
		Females		
1	91.32	4.58	.50	81
2	91.77	5.05	.43	138
3	90.74	4.36	.48	82
4	89.97	5.07	1.08	22
5	90.66	4.92	.47	109
6	91.08	5.40	.65	69
7	92.08	6.04	.53	127
8	91.60	4.88	.58	69
9	93.25	3.74	1.00	14
10	92.45	5.10	.93	30
11	91.70	5.68	.78	53
12	92.53	5.54	.71	60
13	91.47	5.33	.44	143
14	91.96	5.72	.56	103
15	90.80	5.42	.54	100

TABLE 39
TOTAL FACE HEIGHT BY GEOGRAPHIC REGION

Table Group Numbers	(mm) Mean M	Standard Deviation σ	Standard Error S.E.M	Number N
Region		Males		
1	122.39	7.66	.94	66
2	121.03	6.87	.58	136
3	120.27	6.95	.71	94
4	120.53	6.67	.90	54
5	120.83	6.91	.53	169
6	121.84	5.61	.88	40
7	122.03	6.46	.79	66
8	122.61	6.89	1.05	43
9	123.60	7.13	1.37	27
10	120.44	5.93	1.23	23
11	122.01	6.56	.80	67
12	121.73	8.45	1.19	50
13	122.49	7.21	.71	102
14	122.13	6.92	.68	102
15	123.00	6.55	.72	81
		Females		
1	112.97	5.84	.64	81
2	112.09	6.19	.52	138
3	113.10	5.34	.58	82
4	113.58	5.60	1.19	22
5	115.03	6.23	.59	109
6	113.55	5.70	.68	69
7	114.36	6.86	.60	127
8	112.86	6.01	.72	69
9	117.77	6.78	1.81	14
10	113.60	6.17	1.12	30
11	113.01	6.73	.92	53
12	113.71	6.83	.88	60
13	114.08	6.83	.57	143
14	114.32	5.89	.58	103
15	113.96	6.60	.66	100

TABLE 40
UPPER FACE HEIGHT BY GEOGRAPHICAL REGION

Table Group Numbers	(mm) Mean M	Standard Deviation σ	Standard Error S.E.M	Number N
Region		Males		
1	71.74	5.53	.68	66
2	70.52	5.20	.44	136
3	70.57	4.98	.51	94
4	69.73	5.34	.72	54
5	70.68	5.61	.43	169
6	72.64	4.31	.68	40
7	71.35	5.52	.67	66
8	71.36	5.19	.79	43
9	72.81	5.23	1.00	27
10	69.30	5.01	1.04	23
11	71.28	4.88	.59	67
12	70.87	6.37	.90	50
13	72.51	4.93	.48	102
14	73.51	4.84	.47	102
15	73.91	5.25	.58	81
		Females		
1	67.63	4.69	.52	81
2	67.62	5.08	.43	138
3	67.82	4.08	.45	82
4	68.62	4.24	.90	22
5	70.17	5.19	.49	109
6	69.66	4.24	.51	69
7	68.08	5.20	.46	127
8	66.15	4.64	.55	69
9	69.05	6.36	1.70	14
10	67.41	5.30	.96	30
11	67.22	4.77	.65	53
12	67.85	4.58	.59	60
13	68.06	5.09	.42	143
14	69.38	4.63	.45	103
15	68.73	4.79	.47	100

TABLE 41
NOSE HEIGHT BY GEOGRAPHIC REGION

Table Group Numbers	(mm) Mean M	Standard Deviation σ	Standard Error S.E.M	Number N
Region		Males		
1	54.91	5.00	.61	66
2	53.79	4.42	.37	136
3	53.49	5.04	.52	94
4	53.63	4.46	.60	54
5	52.76	4.52	.34	169
6	53.44	3.02	.47	40
7	54.04	4.08	.50	66
8	54.04	4.03	.61	43
9	55.62	3.44	.66	27
10	53.82	4.59	.95	23
11	55.35	4.19	.51	67
12	54.17	4.65	.65	50
13	54.92	3.89	.38	102
14	55.30	4.54	.44	102
15	55.47	4.84	.53	81
		Females		
1	51.10	4.14	.46	81
2	51.43	4.27	.36	138
3	51.25	3.97	.43	82
4	51.79	4.45	.95	22
5	52.89	4.13	.39	109
6	52.27	4.28	.51	69
7	51.24	4.18	.37	127
8	50.50	4.34	.52	69
9	53.25	6.68	1.78	14
10	51.27	4.31	.78	30
11	51.80	3.70	.50	53
12	51.84	4.22	.54	60
13	51.55	4.22	.35	143
14	52.35	4.38	.43	103
15	51.47	4.25	.42	100

TABLE 42
NOSE WIDTH BY GEOGRAPHIC REGION

Table Group Numbers	(mm) Mean M	Standard Deviation σ	Standard Error S.E.M	Number N
Region		Males		
1	35.43	3.90	.48	66
2	36.09	3.05	.26	136
3	36.48	3.83	.39	94
4	38.22	3.61	.49	54
5	38.11	4.08	.31	169
6	35.77	4.11	.65	40
7	35.83	3.06	.37	66
8	35.58	3.02	.46	43
9	36.37	2.86	.55	27
10	35.36	3.37	.70	23
11	36.25	3.29	.40	67
12	36.72	3.92	.55	50
13	35.06	2.99	.29	102
14	34.87	3.29	.32	102
15	36.00	2.63	.29	81
		Females		
1	32.03	3.65	.40	81
2	33.03	3.14	.26	138
3	32.06	2.99	.33	82
4	32.50	2.50	.53	22
5	34.29	3.08	.29	109
6	32.72	3.27	.39	69
7	33.56	3.44	.30	127
8	31.79	2.73	.32	69
9	32.78	2.22	.59	14
10	32.20	3.23	.59	30
11	33.33	3.12	.42	53
12	32.41	3.42	.44	60
13	31.57	2.78	.23	143
14	31.22	2.72	.26	103
15	32.69	2.67	.26	100

TABLE 43
CHEST CIRCUMFERENCE BY GEOGRAPHIC REGION

Table Group Numbers	(cm) Mean M	Standard Deviation σ	Standard Error S.E.M	Number N
Region		Males		
1	84.65	5.01	.61	66
2	84.51	6.02	.51	136
3	84.99	5.26	.54	94
4	87.07	4.82	.65	54
5	84.12	6.06	.46	169
6	86.10	5.45	.86	40
7	84.95	6.37	.78	66
8	85.67	5.27	.80	43
9	84.33	4.94	.95	27
10	85.34	5.70	1.19	23
11	84.53	6.78	.82	67
12	85.74	6.67	.94	50
13	85.30	6.12	.60	102
14	85.30	5.53	.58	102
15	86.64	6.29	.69	81

TABLE 44
WAIST CIRCUMFERENCE BY GEOGRAPHIC REGION

Table Group Numbers	(cm) Mean M	Standard Deviation σ	Standard Error S.E.M	Number N
Region		Males		
1	72.76	82.26	1.012	66
2	72.28	79.74	.683	136
3	72.80	62.84	.648	94
4	76.43	62.22	.846	54
5	75.29	54.73	.420	169
6	75.81	68.46	1.082	40
7	72.83	80.98	.996	66
8	73.43	75.55	1.151	43
9	71.31	74.49	1.433	27
10	71.87	68.79	1.434	23
11	72.97	96.66	1.180	67
12	73.32	75.71	1.070	50
13	72.26	78.14	.773	102
14	72.24	69.69	.689	102
15	75.68	56.28	.625	81
		Females		
1	65.48	56.20	.646	76
2	65.02	75.30	.650	134
3	66.98	50.57	.596	70
4	67.90	77.61	1.829	18
5	66.39	77.23	.758	104
6	65.94	94.32	.883	62
7	67.86	58.15	.738	114
8	63.39	59.33	.742	64
9	65.52	57.90	1.547	14
10	64.93	60.72	1.147	28
11	69.60	26.17	.378	48
12	65.01	88.27	1.139	60
13	64.56	68.01	.510	140
14	64.48	77.55	.800	94
15	65.59	86.49	.944	84

TABLE 45
ARM CIRCUMFERENCE BY GEOGRAPHIC REGION

Table Group Numbers	(cm) Mean M	Standard Deviation σ	Standard Error S.E.M	Number N
Region		Males		
1	24.14	2.31	.28	66
2	24.57	2.53	.21	136
3	24.60	2.37	.24	94
4	26.24	2.00	.27	54
5	25.02	2.55	.19	169
6	24.81	2.02	.31	40
7	23.26	2.21	.27	66
8	24.31	1.92	.29	43
9	23.88	1.95	.38	27
10	24.00	2.61	.54	23
11	23.81	2.74	.33	67
12	25.12	2.60	.36	50
13	23.51	2.07	.20	102
14	24.08	2.52	.24	102
15	24.50	2.55	.28	81
		Females		
1	21.94	1.63	.18	80
2	22.70	2.88	.24	138
3	22.25	2.61	.28	82
4	22.90	2.54	.54	22
5	22.59	2.87	.27	109
6	21.87	2.37	.28	69
7	23.10	3.25	.28	127
8	21.65	2.26	.27	69
9	22.55	2.61	.69	14
10	22.47	2.13	.38	30
11	22.33	2.73	.37	53
12	22.02	3.14	.40	60
13	21.69	2.49	.20	143
14	21.95	2.66	.26	103
15	22.50	2.87	.28	100

TABLE 46
LEG CIRCUMFERENCE BY GEOGRAPHICAL REGIONS

Table Group Numbers	(cm) Mean M	Standard Deviation σ	Standard Error S.E.M	Number N
Region		Males		
1	32.56	2.16	.26	66
2	32.41	2.68	.23	136
3	32.46	2.37	.24	94
4	33.25	1.62	.21	54
5	32.50	2.49	.19	168
6	32.62	2.23	.35	40
7	32.25	2.85	.35	66
8	33.13	2.81	.42	43
9	32.44	2.08	.40	27
10	32.82	2.20	.45	23
11	32.26	2.94	.35	67
12	32.96	2.58	.36	50
13	32.07	2.50	.24	102
14	32.08	2.56	.25	102
15	32.55	2.59	.28	81
		Females		
1	30.90	2.99	.33	81
2	31.39	3.04	.25	138
3	31.48	2.37	.26	82
4	30.68	1.06	.22	22
5	30.99	2.39	.22	109
6	30.98	2.38	.28	69
7	32.14	3.05	.27	127
8	30.65	2.16	.26	69
9	30.86	2.66	.71	14
10	31.86	1.54	.28	30
11	31.33	2.45	.33	53
12	31.60	2.93	.37	60
13	30.43	2.50	.20	143
14	30.88	3.02	.29	103
15	31.37	2.81	.28	100

TABLE 47
SKIN COLOR BY GEOGRAPHIC REGION

Table Group Numbers	* Mean M	Standard Deviation σ	Standard Error S.E.M	Number N
Region		Males		
1	14.66	3.08	.37	66
2	15.58	4.25	.36	136
3	17.48	4.76	.49	94
4	20.29	5.45	.74	54
5	20.24	5.08	.39	169
6	16.17	4.18	.66	40
7	16.06	3.49	.42	66
8	14.62	3.07	.46	43
9	14.25	2.82	.54	27
10	14.00	2.08	.43	23
11	14.23	2.90	.35	67
12	16.36	4.09	.57	50
13	13.72	2.22	.21	102
14	13.13	2.48	.24	102
15	14.96	2.62	.29	81
		Females		
1	14.49	2.95	.32	81
2	15.15	4.00	.34	138
3	14.27	3.18	.35	82
4	17.95	4.63	.69	22
5	15.49	3.58	.44	109
6	16.33	3.90	.43	69
7	14.69	3.37	.34	127
8	13.28	1.62	.40	69
9	13.66	3.33	.43	14
10	14.15	2.36	.60	30
11	14.43	3.01	.32	53
12	13.67	2.20	.38	60
13	13.17	2.37	.18	143
14	14.43	3.06	.23	103
15			.30	100

*Von Luschan Scale

TABLE 48
AGE BY GEOGRAPHIC REGIONS

Table Group Numbers	(yrs) Mean M	Standard Deviation σ	Standard Error S.E.M	Number N
Region		Males		
1	29.04	7.96	.97	66
2	29.13	7.63	.65	136
3	28.04	7.27	.75	94
4	28.59	6.90	.93	54
5	29.32	8.23	.63	169
6	34.55	9.89	1.56	40
7	33.10	9.69	1.19	66
8	27.60	8.64	1.31	43
9	29.40	7.21	1.38	27
10	27.91	7.51	1.56	23
11	34.19	11.12	1.35	67
12	30.00	10.20	1.44	50
13	32.31	9.43	.93	102
14	31.48	8.79	.87	102
15	31.45	8.27	.91	81

TABLE 49
WEIGHT BY GEOGRAPHIC REGION

Table Group Numbers	(lbs) Mean M	Standard Deviation σ	Standard Error S.E.M	Number N
Region		Prisoners		
1	129.16	4.14	1.69	6
2	137.88	17.58	3.38	27
3	132.98	16.60	1.89	77
4	137.61	18.31	3.28	31
5	142.27	19.20	4.52	18
6	134.47	20.03	2.52	63
7	135.31	10.52	2.41	19
8	145.00	5.00	3.53	2
9	131.50	22.50	3.55	40
10	122.71	7.88	2.97	7
11	130.61	14.22	2.78	26
12	131.76	19.67	3.93	25
13	130.54	17.36	5.23	11
14	135.00	11.02	2.84	15
15	133.07	15.24	2.88	28

TABLE 50
UPPER ARM LENGTH BY GEOGRAPHIC REGION

Table Group Numbers	(cm) Mean M	Standard Deviation σ	Standard Error S.E.M	Number N
Region		Prisoners		
1	29.80	1.23	.50	6
2	32.25	1.91	.36	27
3	31.91	1.82	.20	77
4	31.91	2.03	.36	31
5	32.91	1.92	.45	18
6	32.02	2.06	.25	63
7	31.64	1.80	.41	19
8	33.96	.50	.35	2
9	30.90	1.93	.30	40
10	31.63	1.57	.59	7
11	30.86	1.55	.30	26
12	30.24	1.72	.34	25
13	30.47	1.31	.39	11
14	31.35	1.68	.43	15
15	30.24	2.74	.51	28

TABLE 51
PRISONERS BY GEOGRAPHIC REGION

Table Group Numbers	(cm) Mean M	Standard Deviation σ	Standard Error S.E.M	Number N
Region	TOTAL STATURE			
1	159.50	6.21	2.53	6
2	166.51	6.86	1.32	27
3	164.83	6.35	.72	77
4	165.61	5.33	.95	31
5	168.11	6.63	1.56	18
6	163.30	6.24	.78	63
7	164.31	5.28	1.21	19
8	167.50	1.50	1.06	2
9	163.75	6.80	1.07	40
10	165.57	2.64	.99	7
11	162.07	6.41	1.25	26
12	161.76	5.47	1.09	25
13	162.36	5.70	1.71	11
14	162.66	4.74	1.22	15
15	161.35	6.75	1.27	28
	LOWER ARM LENGTH			
1	23.00	1.36	.55	6
2	23.63	1.65	.31	27
3	23.42	1.59	.17	77
4	23.87	1.48	.26	31
5	24.50	1.80	.42	18
6	23.67	1.68	.21	63
7	23.42	1.55	.35	19
8	24.01			2
9	23.52	1.66	.26	40
10	24.14	1.57	.59	7
11	22.65	1.54	.30	26
12	22.44	1.49	.29	25
13	22.55	1.75	.52	11
14	23.47	1.97	.50	15
15	23.46	1.91	.36	28

TABLE 52
PRISONERS BY GEOGRAPHIC REGION

Table Group Numbers	Mean M	Standard Deviation σ	Standard Error S.E.M	Number N
Region	TOTAL LEG LENGTH (cm)			
1	75.33	5.42	2.21	6
2	80.55	3.57	.68	27
3	79.67	4.25	.48	77
4	80.87	4.15	.74	31
5	82.66	4.60	1.08	18
6	79.30	4.17	.52	63
7	79.10	4.06	.93	19
8	79.50	.50	.35	2
9	78.45	4.35	.68	40
10	79.57	2.11	.79	7
11	78.50	4.62	.90	26
12	77.92	4.55	.91	25
13	77.81	4.91	1.48	11
14	77.33	3.54	.91	15
15	77.60	4.45	.84	28
	HEAD LENGTH (cm)			
1	186.16	8.22	3.35	6
2	183.62	8.03	1.54	27
3	184.36	7.47	.85	77
4	186.25	6.65	1.19	31
5	189.66	8.70	2.05	18
6	186.52	7.58	.95	63
7	186.57	6.63	1.52	19
8	184.50	6.50	4.59	2
9	185.02	7.51	1.18	40
10	180.57	5.62	2.12	7
11	183.50	6.71	1.31	26
12	184.16	5.87	1.17	25
13	184.00	4.08	1.23	11
14	186.33	5.17	1.33	15
15	183.61	6.03	1.13	28

TABLE 53
PRISONERS BY GEOGRAPHIC REGION

Table Group Numbers	Mean M	Standard Deviation σ	Standard Error S.E.M	Number N
Region	TRUNK HEIGHT (cm)			
1	52.93	1.52	.62	6
2	54.18	3.58	.68	27
3	53.18	2.90	.33	77
4	53.38	3.15	.56	31
5	53.37	2.41	.56	18
6	52.63	2.77	.34	63
7	52.78	2.33	.53	19
8	55.39	2.00	1.41	2
9	53.16	3.62	.57	40
10	54.05	2.50	.94	7
11	51.84	3.38	.66	26
12	53.12	2.71	.54	25
13	52.63	2.34	.70	11
14	52.66	2.45	.63	15
15	52.66	3.14	.59	28
	HEAD WIDTH (mm)			
1	149.00	5.13	2.09	6
2	149.81	5.93	1.14	27
3	149.59	7.77	.88	77
4	150.29	4.58	.82	31
5	148.05	4.85	1.14	18
6	149.39	5.74	.72	63
7	148.10	5.19	1.19	19
8	150.00	3.00	2.12	2
9	151.45	5.85	.92	40
10	148.85	4.95	1.87	7
11	150.26	6.58	1.29	26
12	148.32	6.20	1.24	25
13	150.18	4.96	1.49	11
14	151.86	4.78	1.23	15
15	151.32	5.21	.98	28

TABLE 54
PRISONERS BY GEOGRAPHIC REGION

Table Group Numbers	Mean M	Standard Deviation σ	Standard Error S.E.M	Number N
Region	\multicolumn{4}{c|}{BIZYGOMATIC DIAMETER (mm)}			
1	135.83	4.00	1.63	6
2	137.48	5.06	.97	27
3	137.05	4.82	.54	77
4	137.67	4.77	.85	31
5	137.55	5.21	1.22	18
6	137.14	5.09	.64	63
7	137.78	5.00	1.14	19
8	137.00	2.00	1.41	2
9	136.97	6.19	.97	40
10	137.85	4.78	1.81	7
11	135.69	5.05	.99	26
12	134.72	4.44	.88	25
13	133.63	4.77	1.44	11
14	137.60	6.48	1.67	15
15	137.39	5.09	.96	28
	\multicolumn{4}{c|}{BIACROMIAL DIAMETER (cm)}			
1	36.75	2.00	.81	6
2	37.74	2.14	.41	27
3	37.89	1.91	.21	77
4	37.85	1.85	.33	31
5	38.41	2.09	.49	18
6	37.42	2.05	.25	63
7	37.65	1.58	.36	19
8	40.13	2.50	1.76	2
9	37.56	1.90	.30	40
10	37.95	1.77	.66	7
11	36.62	1.75	.34	26
12	37.36	1.80	.36	25
13	36.28	1.28	.38	11
14	37.41	1.39	.36	15
15	37.25	1.74	.32	28

TABLE 55
PRISONERS BY GEOGRAPHIC REGION

Table Group Numbers	Mean M	Standard Deviation σ	Standard Error S.E.M	Number N
Region	\multicolumn{4}{c|}{BICRISTAL DIAMETER (cm)}			
1	25.02	1.74	.71	6
2	24.23	1.89	.36	27
3	23.92	2.12	.24	77
4	24.52	2.42	.43	31
5	23.52	1.84	.43	18
6	24.21	2.31	.29	63
7	25.39	1.53	.35	19
8	26.03	1.00	.70	2
9	23.87	2.62	.41	40
10	23.14	1.33	.50	7
11	24.62	2.14	.42	26
12	24.32	1.64	.32	25
13	24.82	2.00	.60	11
14	24.14	2.10	.54	15
15	24.00	2.06	.38	28
	\multicolumn{4}{c|}{TOTAL FACE HEIGHT (mm)}			
1	121.14	3.95	1.61	6
2	125.28	7.25	1.39	27
3	124.74	6.77	.77	77
4	124.82	6.95	1.24	31
5	128.19	7.88	1.85	18
6	122.96	7.20	.90	63
7	119.88	6.38	1.46	19
8	120.21	3.00	2.12	2
9	122.04	5.40	.85	40
10	122.43	5.16	1.95	7
11	123.11	6.41	1.25	26
12	122.04	5.24	1.04	25
13	124.18	5.81	1.75	11
14	120.80	7.85	2.02	15
15	121.40	7.58	1.43	28

TABLE 56
PRISONERS BY GEOGRAPHIC REGION

Table Group Numbers	Mean M	Standard Deviation σ	Standard Error S.E.M	Number N
Region	\multicolumn{4}{c|}{BIGONIAL DIAMETER (mm)}			
1	100.88	5.14	2.10	6
2	97.97	6.85	1.31	27
3	97.99	6.81	.77	77
4	99.45	6.37	1.14	31
5	100.05	7.15	1.68	18
6	98.73	6.20	.78	63
7	99.81	5.26	1.20	19
8	101.08	3.50	2.47	2
9	98.73	7.10	1.12	40
10	100.08	3.45	1.30	7
11	97.34	6.56	1.28	26
12	98.52	4.84	.96	25
13	97.08	5.24	1.58	11
14	101.26	7.14	1.84	15
15	98.40	4.73	.89	28
	\multicolumn{4}{c|}{ABDOMINAL FOLD THICKNESS (mm)}			
1	4.53	.70	.28	6
2	4.00	1.26	.24	27
3	4.50	1.65	.18	77
4	4.41	4.57	.82	31
5	4.03	.75	.17	18
6	5.18	2.66	.33	63
7	5.84	1.98	.45	19
8	9.05	4.50	3.18	2
9	3.51	2.10	.33	40
10	3.21	.66	.25	7
11	4.52	1.90	.37	26
12	3.16	2.27	.45	25
13	4.34	1.80	.54	11
14	4.11	1.08	.27	15
15	3.60	1.62	.30	28

TABLE 57
PRISONERS BY GEOGRAPHIC REGION

Table Group Numbers	Mean M	Standard Deviation σ	Standard Error S.E.M	Number N
Region	\multicolumn{4}{c|}{KNEE WIDTH (mm)}			
1	92.00	3.60	1.47	6
2	90.37	4.69	.90	27
3	89.92	4.42	.50	77
4	91.74	4.01	.72	31
5	91.77	4.38	1.03	18
6	90.92	4.34	.54	63
7	91.52	4.08	.93	19
8	91.50	.50	.35	2
9	89.80	4.70	.74	40
10	89.42	4.63	1.75	7
11	89.92	3.35	.65	26
12	88.64	3.46	.69	25
13	87.81	4.94	1.49	11
14	90.60	3.51	.90	15
15	91.46	4.52	.85	28
	\multicolumn{4}{c|}{UPPER FACE HEIGHT (mm)}			
1	71.52	2.00	.81	6
2	73.39	5.60	1.07	27
3	73.52	4.81	.54	77
4	73.06	5.30	.95	31
5	74.02	6.47	1.52	18
6	71.46	5.05	.63	63
7	68.01	4.73	1.08	19
8	68.29			2
9	71.00	5.06	.80	40
10	72.32	4.03	1.52	7
11	71.89	5.84	1.14	26
12	71.72	4.54	.90	25
13	71.77	4.13	1.24	11
14	71.16	7.25	1.87	15
15	70.95	5.55	1.04	28

TABLE 58
PRISONERS BY GEOGRAPHIC REGION

Table Group Numbers	Mean M	Standard Deviation σ	Standard Error S.E.M	Number N
Region	NOSE HEIGHT (mm)			
1	55.02	2.81	1.14	6
2	54.92	4.27	.82	27
3	55.16	4.06	.46	77
4	55.28	4.28	.77	31
5	54.36	4.78	1.12	18
6	53.00	3.81	.47	63
7	52.40	3.63	.83	19
8	54.04	1.50	1.06	2
9	53.02	3.95	.62	40
10	52.63	2.72	1.03	7
11	54.64	3.85	.75	26
12	53.36	3.80	.76	25
13	54.70	3.83	1.15	11
14	53.44	4.72	1.22	15
15	53.32	3.96	.74	28
	CHEST CIRCUMFERENCE (cm)			
1	85.16	1.50	.61	6
2	87.33	4.88	.94	27
3	86.20	4.43	.50	77
4	87.26	5.91	1.06	31
5	86.22	5.94	1.40	18
6	86.61	5.67	.71	63
7	87.00	4.19	.96	19
8	91.00	3.00	2.12	2
9	85.97	5.81	.91	40
10	83.57	3.44	1.30	7
11	85.23	4.07	.79	26
12	85.56	5.89	1.17	25
13	86.63	5.56	1.67	11
14	87.46	5.11	1.32	15
15	87.50	4.67	.88	28

TABLE 59
PRISONERS BY GEOGRAPHIC REGION

Table Group Numbers	Mean M	Standard Deviation σ	Standard Error S.E.M	Number N
Region	NOSE WIDTH (mm)			
1	35.16	3.40	1.39	6
2	37.00	4.23	.81	27
3	37.14	3.70	.42	77
4	36.06	2.86	.51	31
5	42.05	2.95	.93	18
6	36.52	3.34	.42	63
7	37.94	3.22	.73	19
8	37.50	1.50	1.06	2
9	35.90	3.13	.49	40
10	35.42	2.92	1.10	7
11	35.69	3.69	.72	26
12	35.92	2.96	.59	25
13	34.63	1.63	.49	11
14	35.40	3.34	.86	15
15	35.67	3.39	.64	28
	WAIST CIRCUMFERENCE (cm)			
1	74.12	2.87	1.17	6
2	76.81	5.74	1.10	27
3	74.12	6.27	.71	77
4	77.35	8.05	1.44	31
5	75.56	6.49	1.53	18
6	76.83	7.97	1.00	63
7	76.46	4.97	1.14	19
8	74.43	.50	.35	2
9	75.99	8.57	1.35	40
10	69.98	4.58	1.73	7
11	76.75	4.92	.96	26
12	75.64	8.94	1.78	25
13	75.24	7.54	2.27	11
14	76.44	5.72	1.47	15
15	76.70	6.54	1.23	28

TABLE 60
PRISONERS BY GEOGRAPHIC REGION

Table Group Numbers	Mean M	Standard Deviation σ	Standard Error S.E.M	Number N
Region	ARM CIRCUMFERENCE (cm)			
1	23.91	.95	.38	6
2	24.90	2.24	.43	27
3	24.75	2.40	.27	77
4	24.57	1.64	.29	31
5	26.02	1.74	.41	18
6	24.32	1.92	.24	63
7	24.73	1.54	.35	19
8	25.61	1.50	1.06	2
9	24.43	2.04	.32	40
10	23.72	1.14	.43	7
11	24.40	1.76	.34	26
12	25.12	1.77	.35	25
13	24.23	2.04	.61	11
14	24.96	1.54	.39	15
15	25.15	1.71	.32	28
	SKIN COLOR*			
1	16.66	3.52	1.44	6
2	17.81	5.19	.99	27
3	18.62	4.96	.56	77
4	16.80	4.55	.81	31
5	25.22	1.39	.32	18
6	17.38	4.20	.53	63
7	17.05	4.50	1.03	19
8	13.50	.50	.35	2
9	14.87	2.26	.35	40
10	17.14	4.20	1.58	7
11	14.73	3.37	.66	26
12	13.84	2.83	.56	25
13	13.00	1.34	.40	11
14	14.73	2.96	.76	15
15	15.60	3.46	.65	28

*von Luschan Scale

TABLE 61
PRISONERS BY GEOGRAPHIC REGION

Table Group Numbers	Mean M	Standard Deviation σ	Standard Error S.E.M	Number N
Region	LEG CIRCUMFERENCE (cm)			
1	33.83	1.34	.54	6
2	34.25	2.04	.39	27
3	33.62	2.59	.29	77
4	33.80	2.75	.49	31
5	35.11	.46	.10	18
6	33.14	2.50	.31	63
7	33.68	1.62	.37	19
8	36.50	1.50	1.06	2
9	33.02	2.41	.38	40
10	31.71	1.67	.63	7
11	33.30	1.53	.30	26
12	32.72	2.33	.46	25
13	33.63	1.13	.34	11
14	34.13	1.09	.28	15
15	33.53	2.00	.37	28
	AGE (years)			
1	26.33	6.45	2.63	6
2	29.18	6.22	1.19	27
3	29.36	6.68	.76	77
4	28.09	7.62	1.37	31
5	27.33	6.24	1.47	18
6	27.77	7.24	.91	63
7	31.73	6.20	1.42	19
8	20.50	1.50	1.06	2
9	29.47	7.62	1.20	40
10	26.71	5.56	2.10	7
11	26.19	6.87	1.34	26
12	25.64	5.58	1.11	25
13	26.81	8.05	2.42	11
14	30.53	7.87	2.03	15
15	26.85	7.28	1.37	28

TABLE 62
VARIOUS MEASUREMENTS BY NUTRITIONAL CLASS

Table Group Numbers	Mean M	Standard Deviation σ	Standard Error S.E.M	Number N
NC	WEIGHT (lbs)	Male		
1	145.26	21.83	2.18	100
2	127.10	17.64	.88	400
3	125.80	20.98	1.26	274
4	121.20	17.59	2.97	35
		Female		
1	124.26	25.10	2.47	103
2	110.12	22.61	1.13	400
3	107.83	19.70	1.13	302
4	103.78	18.33	2.82	42
	UPPER ARM LENGTH (cm)	Male		
1	31.65	1.80	.17	100
2	31.27	2.14	.10	400
3	31.07	2.06	.12	274
4	31.06	2.17	.36	35
		Female		
1	28.38	1.92	.18	103
2	28.39	1.92	.09	400
3	28.22	1.90	.10	302
4	28.43	1.85	.28	42
	TOTAL ARM LENGTH (cm)	Male		
1	73.43	2.84	.28	100
2	73.47	4.28	.21	400
3	72.78	4.18	.25	274
4	72.42	3.76	.63	35
		Female		
1	66.24	3.69	.36	103
2	66.26	3.57	.17	400
3	66.07	3.72	.21	302
4	66.50	3.92	.60	42

TABLE 63
VARIOUS MEASUREMENTS BY NUTRITIONAL CLASS

Table Group Numbers	Mean M	Standard Deviation σ	Standard Error S.E.M	Number N
NC	STATURE (cm)	Male		
1	167.86	5.75	.57	100
2	164.77	6.76	.33	400
3	163.34	6.38	.38	274
4	163.11	5.98	1.01	35
		Female		
1	155.05	5.84	.57	103
2	152.91	6.07	.30	400
3	151.96	5.82	.33	302
4	151.07	5.28	.81	42
	LOWER ARM LENGTH (cm)	Male		
1	22.92	1.42	.14	100
2	23.40	2.03	.10	400
3	23.05	2.00	.11	274
4	22.91	1.98	.33	35
		Female		
1	20.74	1.57	.15	103
2	20.95	1.59	.07	400
3	20.72	1.74	.10	302
4	20.95	1.57	.24	42
	TOTAL LEG LENGTH (cm)	Male		
1	80.56	3.85	.38	100
2	80.00	5.17	.25	400
3	79.00	4.90	.29	274
4	78.20	4.40	.74	35
		Female		
1	73.95	3.91	.38	103
2	73.08	4.24	.20	400
3	72.66	4.38	.25	302
4	71.76	3.81	.58	42

TABLE 64
VARIOUS MEASUREMENTS BY NUTRITIONAL CALSS

Table Group Numbers	Mean M	Standard Deviation σ	Standard Error S.E.M	Number N
NC	TRUNK HEIGHT (cm)	Male		
1	55.87	2.52	.25	100
2	53.57	2.89	.14	400
3	52.82	3.10	.18	274
4	53.39	3.21	.54	35
		Female		
1	51.89	2.96	.29	103
2	50.37	2.86	.14	400
3	49.83	2.57	.14	302
4	49.69	2.70	.41	42
	BIACROMIAL DIAMETER (cm)	Male		
1	38.07	1.83	.18	100
2	37.52	2.04	.10	400
3	37.21	2.32	.13	274
4	36.58	2.12	.35	35
		Female		
1	33.76	2.04	.20	103
2	33.36	1.90	.09	400
3	33.10	1.86	.10	302
4	32.53	1.83	.28	42
	KNEE WIDTH (mm)	Male		
1	91.15	4.29	.42	100
2	89.14	5.95	.17	400
3	88.67	6.70	.40	274
4	88.29	4.79	.81	35
		Female		
1	83.31	6.15	.60	103
2	81.11	5.04	.25	400
3	80.55	4.68	.26	322
4	79.66	4.37	.67	42

TABLE 65
VARIOUS MEASUREMENTS BY NUTRITIONAL CLASS

Table Group Numbers	Mean M	Standard Deviation σ	Standard Error S.E.M	Number N
NC	HEAD LENGTH (mm)	Male		
1	189.67	6.33	.63	100
2	184.87	7.70	.38	400
3	184.55	7.03	.42	274
4	183.57	6.66	1.12	35
		Female		
1	177.69	7.56	.74	103
2	175.79	6.54	.32	400
3	175.80	7.01	.40	302
4	174.57	6.62	1.02	42
	BIACROMIAL DIAMETER (cm)	Male		
1	138.33	4.95	.49	100
2	135.59	5.67	.28	400
3	136.01	5.38	.32	274
4	135.80	4.80	.81	35
		Female		
1	129.02	5.35	.52	103
2	128.35	4.93	.24	400
3	128.05	5.16	.29	302
4	126.64	5.42	.83	42
	KNEE WIDTH (mm)	Male		
1	123.33	5.59	.55	100
2	121.35	6.21	.30	400
3	120.58	7.70	.46	274
4	121.38	5.54	.93	35
		Female		
1	113.51	6.59	.64	103
2	113.40	6.27	.31	400
3	113.20	6.79	.38	322
4	115.24	7.78	1.20	42

TABLE 66
VARIOUS MEASUREMENTS BY NUTRITIONAL CLASS

Table Group Numbers NC	Mean M	Standard Deviation σ	Standard Error S.E.M	Number N
	NOSE HEIGHT (mm) Male			
1	56.68	4.02	.40	100
2	53.99	4.21	.20	400
3	53.87	4.57	.27	274
4	53.66	3.28	.55	35
	Female			
1	53.21	4.26	.41	103
2	51.82	3.94	.19	400
3	51.48	4.46	.25	302
4	51.49	4.40	.67	42
	SKIN COLOR (von Luschan) Male			
1	12.83	2.54	.25	100
2	16.83	4.70	.23	400
3	16.24	4.33	.26	274
4	15.14	2.58	.43	35
	Female			
1	12.50	2.08	.20	103
2	14.72	3.40	.10	1202
3	15.61	3.90	.22	302
4	16.60	3.86	.59	42
	ARM CIRCUMFERENCE (cm) Male			
1	25.90	2.72	.27	100
2	24.21	2.24	.10	400
3	24.14	2.67	.16	274
4	23.23	2.22	.37	35
	Female			
1	23.90	3.03	.29	103
2	22.23	2.79	.13	400
3	22.09	2.93	.16	302
4	21.70	2.26	.34	42

TABLE 67
VARIOUS MEASUREMENTS BY NUTRITIONAL CLASS

Table Group Numbers NC	Mean M	Standard Deviation σ	Standard Error S.E.M	Number N
	BICRISTAL DIAMETER (cm) Male			
1	26.63	24.12	2.40	100
2	25.59	25.09	1.22	400
3	26.10	24.16	1.44	274
4	24.92	18.05	3.04	35
	Female			
1	26.15	26.41	2.58	103
2	24.85	24.65	1.22	400
3	25.21	22.89	1.30	302
4	24.72	24.41	3.76	42
	ABDOMINAL FOLD THICKNESS (mm) Male			
1	6.22	50.70	5.06	100
2	4.33	40.45	2.00	400
3	4.11	31.74	1.89	274
4	3.64	15.29	2.58	35
	Female			
1	15.72	88.64	8.82	101
2	9.25	65.72	3.28	400
3	8.42	56.48	3.36	282
4	7.41	40.98	6.73	37
	LEG CIRCUMFERENCE (cm) Male			
1	33.80	24.02	2.38	100
2	32.11	24.67	1.22	400
3	32.18	28.08	1.67	274
4	31.34	19.02	3.20	35
	Female			
1	32.43	33.30	3.27	103
2	30.98	29.71	1.48	400
3	30.86	28.30	1.61	302
4	30.04	20.39	3.14	42

TABLE 68
VARIOUS MEASUREMENTS BY NUTRITIONAL CLASS

Table Group Numbers NC	Mean M	Standard Deviation σ	Standard Error S.E.M	Number N
	HEAD WIDTH (mm) Male			
1	153.07	5.58	.55	100
2	149.52	6.12	.30	400
3	149.61	5.86	.35	274
4	150.82	5.59	.94	35
	Female			
1	144.65	5.07	.50	103
2	144.04	5.22	.26	400
3	143.80	5.63	.32	302
4	142.57	4.80	.74	42
	BIGONIAL DIAMETER (mm) Male			
1	100.45	5.50	.54	100
2	98.23	7.06	.35	400
3	98.71	6.33	.38	274
4	96.88	6.03	1.01	35
	Female			
1	93.25	5.62	.55	103
2	91.63	4.78	.23	400
3	90.89	5.09	.29	302
4	91.13	4.66	.71	42
	UPPER FACE HEIGHT (mm) Male			
1	73.76	4.22	.42	100
2	71.33	4.85	.24	400
3	71.16	6.00	.36	274
4	71.60	4.56	.77	35
	Female			
1	69.01	4.96	.48	103
2	68.22	4.68	.23	400
3	68.33	5.59	.32	302
4	68.66	5.19	.80	42

TABLE 69
VARIOUS MEASUREMENTS BY NUTRITIONAL CLASS

Table Group Numbers NC	Mean M	Standard Deviation σ	Standard Error S.E.M	Number N
	NOSE WIDTH (mm) Male			
1	35.55	2.82	.28	100
2	36.28	3.66	.18	400
3	36.38	3.64	.21	274
4	34.97	2.59	.43	35
	Female			
1	32.02	3.06	.30	103
2	32.43	3.06	.15	400
3	32.98	3.46	.19	302
4	33.16	3.75	.57	42
	WAIST CIRCUMFERENCE (cm) Male			
1	74.37	11.42	1.14	100
2	73.35	8.46	.42	400
3	72.75	11.38	.68	274
4	71.80	6.07	1.02	35
	Female			
1	67.48	10.75	1.07	101
2	65.36	8.09	.40	400
3	64.86	8.51	.50	283
4	65.90	10.41	1.71	37
	AGE (years) Male			
1	27.56	6.04	.60	100
2	28.80	7.65	.38	400
3	31.31	9.78	.59	274
4	34.42	9.24	1.56	35
	Female			
1	28.60	7.17	.70	103
2	29.06	7.56	.37	400
3	30.05	8.26	.47	302
4	33.16	9.30	1.43	42

TABLE 70
VARIOUS MEASUREMENTS BY NUTRITIONAL CLASS

Table Group Numbers	Mean M	Standard Deviation σ	Standard Error S.E.M	Number N
NC	CHEST CIRCUMFERENCE (cm)		Males	
1	87.82	6.89	.69	100
2	85.01	5.71	.17	400
3	84.31	6.05	.36	274
4	83.74	6.10	1.03	35
	NUMBER OF LIVING CHILDREN		Females	
1	1.52	2.29	.22	103
2	2.45	2.60	.07	400
3	3.04	2.79	.16	302
4	4.55	2.87	.08	42

TABLE 71
WEIGHT BY ETHNIC GROUP

Table Group Numbers	Mean M	Standard Deviation σ	Standard Error S.E.M	Number N
EG			Males	
1	127.82	21.85	3.09	50
2	127.14	19.95	1.07	343
3	125.37	16.43	.82	400
4	127.96	17.86	1.30	188
5	130.92	18.48	2.51	54
6	136.14	18.00	2.28	62
7	135.75	19.80	2.27	76
8	140.16	20.46	2.48	68
			Prisoners	
1	115.33	11.58	6.69	3
2	137.44	22.12	2.90	58
3	130.73	16.29	1.23	175
4	129.87	16.89	2.63	41
5	131.23	10.64	2.95	13
6	138.84	16.82	2.72	38
7	139.58	17.30	2.77	39
8	140.92	16.09	3.04	28
			Females	
1	106.58	16.66	2.22	56
2	108.13	21.00	1.01	426
3	110.18	20.64	1.03	400
4	113.93	22.20	1.46	230
5	115.25	23.97	2.75	76
6	127.63	21.31	2.51	72
7	120.41	29.80	4.77	39
8	127.50	25.41	8.98	8

TABLE 72
UPPER ARM LENGTH BY ETHNIC GROUP

Table Group Numbers	Mean M	Standard Deviation σ	Standard Error S.E.M	Number N
EG			Males	
1	31.33	2.02	.28	50
2	31.08	2.13	.11	343
3	31.11	1.43	.07	400
4	31.34	2.00	.14	188
5	31.18	1.94	.26	54
6	31.84	2.04	.25	62
7	31.58	2.37	.27	76
8	31.83	2.40	.28	68
			Prisoners	
1	29.00	1.63	.94	3
2	31.63	1.63	.21	58
3	30.99	1.98	.14	175
4	31.30	1.74	.27	41
5	31.44	2.12	.58	13
6	32.61	1.69	.27	38
7	32.38	1.88	.30	39
8	32.59	2.02	.38	28
			Females	
1	28.22	1.74	.23	56
2	28.05	1.87	.08	426
3	28.30	1.94	.09	400
4	28.46	1.77	.11	230
5	28.79	1.99	.22	76
6	29.47	1.80	.21	72
7	29.62	1.63	.26	39
8	29.92	1.91	.67	8

TABLE 73
LOWER ARM LENGTH BY ETHNIC GROUP

Table Group Numbers	Mean M	Standard Deviation σ	Standard Error S.E.M	Number N
EG			Males	
1	22.96	1.89	.26	50
2	22.73	1.73	.08	343
3	22.79	1.33	.06	400
4	23.13	1.74	.12	188
5	23.24	1.53	.20	54
6	24.19	1.97	.24	62
7	25.14	2.02	.23	76
8	25.90	1.83	.22	68
			Prisoners	
1	22.33	1.30	.75	3
2	23.44	1.72	.22	58
3	23.13	1.74	.13	175
4	23.09	1.51	.23	41
5	23.23	1.43	.39	13
6	24.06	1.51	.24	38
7	24.20	1.93	.30	39
8	24.25	1.63	.30	28
			Females	
1	20.83	1.54	.20	56
2	20.55	1.61	.07	426
3	20.84	1.55	.07	400
4	20.89	1.67	.10	230
5	21.65	1.73	.19	76
6	21.83	1.70	.20	72
7	22.49	1.78	.28	39
8	21.42	2.16	.76	8

TABLE 74
TOTAL ARM LENGTH BY ETHNIC GROUP

Table Group Numbers	Mean M	Standard Deviation σ	Standard Error S.E.M	Number N
EG		Males		
1	72.51	3.73	.52	50
2	72.27	4.03	.21	343
3	72.87	3.65	.14	677
4	73.15	3.90	.28	188
5	73.28	3.59	.48	54
6	75.38	3.65	.46	62
7	76.03	4.09	.46	76
8	77.41	3.84	.46	68
		Prisoners		
1	68.00	2.94	1.69	3
2	73.57	3.30	.43	58
3	72.41	3.90	.29	175
4	72.91	2.80	.43	41
5	73.20	3.49	.96	13
6	75.49	3.26	.52	38
7	75.56	3.80	.60	39
8	76.03	3.69	.69	28
		Females		
1	65.96	3.50	.46	56
2	65.55	3.64	.17	426
3	66.35	3.51	.17	400
4	66.82	3.34	.21	230
5	68.26	3.74	.42	76
6	69.32	3.78	.44	72
7	70.16	3.49	.55	39
8	68.63	3.57	1.26	8

TABLE 75
TOTAL STATURE BY ETHNIC GROUP

Table Group Numbers	Mean M	Standard Deviation σ	Standard Error S.E.M	Numbers N
EG		Males		
1	164.76	6.59	.93	50
2	163.44	6.76	.36	343
3	163.84	5.94	.22	677
4	164.22	6.05	.44	188
5	164.20	4.82	.65	54
6	167.14	6.08	.77	62
7	168.43	6.62	.75	76
8	170.11	6.06	.73	68
		Prisoners		
1	156.66	7.09	4.09	3
2	164.63	6.20	.81	58
3	162.62	6.40	.48	175
4	161.48	6.11	.95	41
5	162.69	4.13	1.14	13
6	166.81	5.13	.83	38
7	167.48	5.74	.91	39
8	166.96	7.06	1.33	28
		Females		
1	151.37	6.46	.86	56
2	151.97	5.71	.27	426
3	153.05	6.15	.30	400
4	153.47	5.36	.35	230
5	153.84	5.21	.59	76
6	155.25	5.62	.66	72
7	155.84	5.83	.93	39
8	156.00	5.63	1.99	8

TABLE 76
TOTAL LEG LENGTH BY ETHNIC GROUP

Table Group Numbers	(cm) Mean M	Standard Deviation σ	Standard Error S.E.M	Number N
EG		Males		
1	79.02	4.41	.62	50
2	78.62	4.54	.24	343
3	78.63	4.26	.16	677
4	79.37	4.35	.31	188
5	79.12	3.31	.45	54
6	82.30	4.30	.54	62
7	83.88	4.50	.51	76
8	85.38	4.21	.51	68
		Prisoners		
1	76.33	3.74	2.16	3
2	79.22	4.58	.60	58
3	78.18	4.41	.33	175
4	77.46	3.57	.55	41
5	79.00	3.35	.92	13
6	81.55	3.04	.49	38
7	81.71	3.93	.63	39
8	82.17	4.54	.85	28
		Females		
1	72.28	4.04	.54	56
2	72.07	3.83	.18	426
3	72.98	4.15	.20	400
4	73.40	3.76	.24	230
5	74.30	4.48	.51	76
6	75.36	4.20	.49	72
7	76.25	3.93	.63	39
8	75.87	4.04	1.43	8

TABLE 77
TRUNK HEIGHT BY ETHNIC GROUP

Table Group Numbers	(cm) Mean M	Standard Deviation σ	Standard Error S.E.M	Number N
EG		Males		
1	53.83	3.03	.42	50
2	53.42	3.07	.16	343
3	54.09	2.93	.11	677
4	53.35	2.98	.21	188
5	53.31	2.80	.38	54
6	53.43	2.69	.34	62
7	53.61	3.03	.34	76
8	54.06	3.10	.37	68
		Prisoners		
1	51.00	2.44	1.41	3
2	53.93	2.78	.36	58
3	52.63	2.99	.22	175
4	52.49	3.20	.50	41
5	52.64	2.37	.65	13
6	53.75	3.30	.53	38
7	53.69	2.70	.43	39
8	52.87	2.72	.51	28
		Females		
1	49.85	3.06	.40	56
2	50.51	2.97	.14	426
3	50.58	2.82	.13	400
4	50.66	2.75	.18	230
5	50.19	2.51	.28	76
6	50.26	2.86	.33	72
7	49.91	2.70	.43	39
8	50.24	3.10	1.09	8

TABLE 78
BIACROMIAL DIAMETER BY ETHNIC GROUP

Table Group Numbers	(cm) Mean M	Standard Deviation σ	Standard Error S.E.M	Number N
EG		Males		
1	36.64	1.81	.25	50
2	36.94	2.00	.10	343
3	37.21	1.90	.07	677
4	37.47	2.17	.15	188
5	38.01	1.91	.25	54
6	38.50	1.78	.22	62
7	38.87	1.94	.22	76
8	39.59	2.12	.25	68
		Prisoners		
1	34.33	.67	.38	3
2	37.35	2.08	.27	58
3	37.20	1.90	.14	175
4	37.56	2.36	.36	41
5	37.23	1.67	.46	13
6	37.94	1.61	.26	38
7	38.55	1.64	.26	39
8	38.67	1.81	.34	28
		Females		
1	32.80	2.44	.32	56
2	33.02	1.72	.07	426
3	33.33	1.76	.08	400
4	33.56	1.72	.11	230
5	33.54	1.62	.18	76
6	34.52	1.92	.22	72
7	34.46	2.26	.36	39
8	34.58	1.78	.63	8

TABLE 79
BICRISTAL DIAMETER BY ETHNIC GROUP

Table Group Numbers	(cm) Mean M	Standard Deviation σ	Standard Error S.E.M	Number N
EG		Males		
1	26.15	2.64	.37	50
2	25.51	2.45	.13	343
3	25.45	1.94	.09	400
4	25.35	2.60	.18	188
5	25.47	2.65	.36	54
6	26.22	2.78	.35	62
7	27.01	2.27	.26	76
8	27.46	1.72	.20	68
		Prisoners		
1	23.33	.60	.35	3
2	25.01	2.53	.33	58
3	24.02	2.24	.16	175
4	24.08	2.20	.34	41
5	23.78	2.18	.60	13
6	24.54	1.77	.28	38
7	24.32	2.14	.34	39
8	23.62	2.01	.38	28
		Females		
1	24.95	2.64	.35	56
2	24.88	2.25	.10	426
3	24.82	2.52	.12	400
4	25.12	2.63	.17	230
5	24.89	2.97	.34	76
6	25.66	2.72	.32	72
7	25.07	3.24	.51	39
8	23.70	2.04	.72	8

TABLE 80
ABDOMINAL FOLD THICKNESS BY ETHNIC GROUP

Table Group Numbers	(mm) Mean M	Standard Deviation σ	Standard Error S.E.M	Number N
EG		Males		
1	5.19	3.51	.49	50
2	4.65	3.44	.18	343
3	3.63	3.37	.16	400
4	3.87	2.50	.18	188
5	5.04	4.61	.62	54
6	5.03	4.13	.52	62
7	7.32	6.42	.73	76
8	7.38	4.37	.53	68
		Prisoners		
1	2.33	.47	.27	3
2	4.99	2.39	.31	58
3	4.38	2.55	.19	175
4	4.39	2.78	.43	41
5	3.87	.91	.25	13
6	4.16	1.54	.24	38
7	4.00	1.20	.19	39
8	3.94	1.31	.24	28
		Females		
1	7.93	5.10	.76	45
2	9.87	6.73	.32	426
3	9.78	7.02	.35	400
4	9.33	6.57	.45	207
5	9.30	6.26	.76	68
6	11.61	6.78	.83	66
7	10.23	9.41	1.59	35
8	9.02	5.69	2.32	6

TABLE 81
KNEE WIDTH BY ETHNIC GROUP

Table Group Numbers	(mm) Mean M	Standard Deviation σ	Standard Error S.E.M	Number N
EG		Males		
1	89.36	4.62	.65	50
2	89.07	4.47	.24	343
3	89.00	4.50	.17	677
4	89.54	4.18	.35	188
5	88.72	4.57	.62	54
6	89.62	4.93	.62	62
7	91.01	5.41	.62	76
8	92.09	5.02	.61	68
		Prisoners		
1	85.66	3.56	2.05	3
2	91.13	4.66	.61	58
3	89.86	4.37	.33	175
4	89.41	5.19	.81	41
5	90.69	3.78	1.04	13
6	91.36	4.27	.69	38
7	91.53	3.76	.60	39
8	91.53	4.04	.76	28
		Females		
1	80.20	5.16	.69	56
2	80.84	4.81	.23	426
3	81.23	4.85	.24	400
4	81.55	4.77	.31	230
5	81.74	4.07	.46	76
6	84.49	4.95	.58	72
7	83.29	7.57	1.21	39
8	83.39	5.91	2.08	8

TABLE 82
HEAD WIDTH BY ETHNIC GROUP

Table Group Numbers	(mm) Mean M	Standard Deviation σ	Standard Error S.E.M	Number N
EG		Males		
1	151.74	5.49	.77	50
2	150.67	5.97	.32	343
3	150.80	5.78	.22	677
4	149.85	5.88	.42	188
5	150.61	5.88	.80	54
6	147.95	5.74	.72	62
7	148.40	6.29	.72	76
8	147.30	5.82	.70	68
		Prisoners		
1	150.00	2.44	1.41	3
2	150.25	5.14	.67	58
3	149.98	5.43	.40	175
4	150.21	5.43	.84	41
5	149.92	7.06	1.95	13
6	149.89	6.91	1.12	38
7	149.17	4.98	.79	39
8	148.75	5.41	1.02	28
		Females		
1	144.26	5.35	.71	56
2	144.56	5.22	.25	426
3	144.23	5.38	.26	400
4	143.51	5.43	.35	230
5	142.59	5.55	.63	76
6	144.05	5.55	.65	72
7	141.94	5.50	.88	39
8	141.37	3.02	1.06	8

TABLE 83
HEAD LENGTH BY ETHNIC GROUP

Table Group Numbers	(mm) Mean M	Standard Deviation σ	Standard Error S.E.M	Number N
EG		Males		
1	183.04	6.93	.98	50
2	183.42	7.63	.41	343
3	184.14	6.97	.26	677
4	184.92	7.58	.55	188
5	185.75	7.12	.96	54
6	189.95	6.86	.87	62
7	189.51	6.89	.79	76
8	190.60	6.74	.81	68
		Prisoners		
1	183.66	4.76	2.74	3
2	183.37	6.17	.81	58
3	183.70	6.97	.52	175
4	185.19	7.49	1.17	41
5	188.46	6.81	1.89	13
6	187.28	7.36	1.19	38
7	187.53	6.65	1.06	39
8	189.82	8.11	1.53	28
		Females		
1	174.66	7.57	1.01	56
2	174.22	6.66	.32	426
3	176.00	6.72	.33	400
4	176.97	6.32	.41	230
5	178.60	7.20	.82	76
6	182.48	6.38	.75	72
7	182.58	6.69	1.07	39
8	180.62	3.00	1.06	8

TABLE 84
BIZYGOMATIC DIAMETER BY ETHNIC GROUP

Table Group Numbers	(mm) Mean M	Standard Deviation σ	Standard Error S.E.M	Number N
EG		Males		
1	134.66	4.60	.65	50
2	135.41	5.44	.29	343
3	136.31	5.30	.20	677
4	135.95	6.09	.44	188
5	135.81	6.29	.85	54
6	134.53	6.18	.78	62
7	135.38	5.81	.66	76
8	136.36	5.13	.62	68
		Prisoners		
1	132.33	1.55	.90	3
2	136.84	4.94	.64	58
3	136.41	5.31	.40	175
4	137.63	5.00	.78	41
5	137.07	5.68	1.57	13
6	137.31	6.12	.99	38
7	137.35	5.04	.80	39
8	138.21	4.61	.87	28
		Females		
1	127.75	4.05	.54	56
2	128.39	5.02	.24	426
3	128.22	4.93	.24	400
4	128.42	5.00	.32	230
5	128.19	5.55	.63	76
6	130.02	4.80	.56	72
7	128.61	4.68	.75	39
8	129.50	4.18	1.47	8

TABLE 85
BIGONIAL DIAMETER BY ETHNIC GROUP

Table Group Numbers	(mm) Mean M	Standard Deviation σ	Standard Error S.E.M	Number N
EG		Males		
1	99.10	6.85	.96	50
2	98.21	7.63	.41	343
3	98.86	3.23	.16	400
4	98.19	6.19	.45	188
5	97.94	6.58	.89	54
6	98.21	5.32	.67	62
7	99.48	6.04	.69	76
8	100.10	5.62	.68	68
		Prisoners		
1	97.33	4.98	2.87	3
2	99.39	6.12	.80	58
3	98.62	6.43	.48	175
4	98.84	6.05	.94	41
5	97.11	6.14	1.70	13
6	98.94	6.50	1.05	38
7	98.07	6.25	1.00	39
8	98.92	7.65	1.44	28
		Females		
1	90.87	4.41	.58	56
2	91.71	5.30	.25	426
3	92.12	5.00	.24	400
4	91.54	5.65	.37	230
5	91.88	5.05	.57	76
6	91.13	5.11	.60	72
7	91.18	4.78	.76	39
8	91.55	4.55	1.61	8

TABLE 86
TOTAL FACE HEIGHT BY ETHNIC GROUP

Table Group Numbers	(mm) Mean M	Standard Deviation σ	Standard Error S.E.M	Number N
EG		Males		
1	120.52	6.14	.86	50
2	120.62	7.04	.37	343
3	120.28	6.35	.24	677
4	121.91	7.00	.50	188
5	120.92	7.24	.98	54
6	123.30	7.50	.95	62
7	121.61	7.63	.87	76
8	120.60	8.07	.97	68
		Prisoners		
1	115.33	.99	.57	3
2	122.56	6.00	.78	58
3	122.46	6.66	.50	175
4	121.39	6.88	1.07	41
5	122.01	7.18	1.99	13
6	127.28	6.54	1.06	38
7	124.64	7.94	1.27	39
8	127.77	7.29	1.37	28
		Females		
1	113.61	6.66	.88	56
2	112.81	5.89	.28	426
3	113.23	6.28	.31	400
4	113.78	6.75	.44	230
5	115.21	7.41	.84	76
6	115.94	6.53	.77	72
7	117.56	7.20	1.15	39
8	119.34	3.86	1.36	8

TABLE 87
UPPER FACE HEIGHT BY ETHNIC GROUP

Table Group Numbers	(mm) Mean M	Standard Deviation σ	Standard Error S.E.M	Number N
EG		Males		
1	71.16	4.05	.57	50
2	71.43	4.97	.26	343
3	71.80	2.95	.14	400
4	72.02	5.27	.38	188
5	71.23	5.94	.80	54
6	72.74	6.68	.84	62
7	72.39	5.23	.60	76
8	68.98	6.96	.84	68
		Prisoners		
1	67.00			3
2	71.45	5.03	.66	58
3	72.08	5.00	.37	175
4	70.96	5.62	.87	41
5	70.36	6.42	1.78	13
6	73.84	5.19	.84	38
7	73.15	6.15	.98	39
8	74.03	6.41	1.21	28
		Females		
1	68.48	4.90	.65	56
2	67.95	4.51	.21	426
3	67.93	4.78	.23	400
4	68.82	5.11	.33	230
5	68.54	6.05	.69	76
6	70.24	5.62	.66	72
7	70.91	6.16	.98	39
8	73.28	3.74	1.32	8

TABLE 88
NOSE HEIGHT BY ETHNIC GROUP

Table Group Numbers	(mm) Mean M	Standard Deviation σ	Standard Error S.E.M	Number N
EG		Males		
1	54.71	4.36	.61	50
2	54.78	4.34	.23	343
3	54.61	2.83	.14	400
4	54.50	4.17	.30	188
5	53.95	4.98	.67	54
6	53.99	5.07	.64	62
7	51.83	4.03	.46	76
8	50.68	5.01	.60	68
		Prisoners		
1	50.66	1.48	.86	3
2	52.90	3.57	.46	58
3	54.16	4.23	.31	175
4	53.20	4.14	.64	41
5	52.32	4.38	1.21	13
6	54.41	3.77	.61	38
7	54.28	5.13	.82	38
8	54.75	4.93	.93	28
		Females		
1	51.16	4.40	.58	56
2	50.74	4.16	.20	426
3	51.58	3.90	.19	400
4	51.88	4.57	.30	230
5	51.19	4.84	.55	76
6	52.44	5.07	.59	72
7	52.61	4.31	.69	39
8	53.03	1.53	.54	8

TABLE 89
NOSE WIDTH BY ETHNIC GROUP

Table Group Number	(mm) Mean M	Standard Deviation σ	Standard Error S.E.M	Number N
EG		Males		
1	34.08	3.18	.45	50
2	34.69	2.92	.15	343
3	35.38	2.20	.10	400
4	36.44	2.93	.21	188
5	37.25	2.95	.40	54
6	39.25	3.34	.42	62
7	39.34	3.41	.39	76
8	42.38	3.31	.40	68
		Prisoners		
1	33.66	1.41	.81	3
2	34.77	3.01	.39	58
3	35.24	2.78	.20	175
4	36.07	3.37	.52	41
5	38.07	2.38	.66	13
6	38.23	2.86	.46	38
7	39.94	2.94	.47	39
8	42.57	2.90	.54	28
		Females		
1	30.92	2.64	.35	56
2	31.37	2.57	.12	426
3	32.14	2.76	.13	400
4	33.95	2.59	.17	230
5	34.93	2.72	.31	76
6	36.51	3.46	.40	72
7	37.84	3.40	.54	39
8	35.50	3.42	1.21	8

TABLE 90
CHEST CIRCUMFERENCE BY ETHNIC GROUP

Table Group Numbers	(cm) Mean M	Standard Deviation σ	Standard Error S.E.M	Number N
EG		Males		
1	84.76	7.03	.99	50
2	84.72	6.21	.33	343
3	84.94	5.69	.21	677
4	84.65	5.33	.38	188
5	85.39	6.24	.85	54
6	85.60	5.77	.73	62
7	86.05	6.60	.75	76
8	86.96	6.32	.76	68
		Prisoners		
1	81.33	4.92	2.84	3
2	87.98	5.83	.76	58
3	86.02	5.06	.38	175
4	86.44	4.86	.76	41
5	84.92	4.32	1.19	13
6	87.37	4.40	.71	38
7	85.82	4.37	.70	39
8	86.93	4.86	.91	28

TABLE 91
WAIST CIRCUMFERENCE BY ETHNIC GROUP

Table Group Numbers	(cm) Mean M	Standard Deviation σ	Standard Error S.E.M	Number N
EG		Males		
1	72.66	7.49	1.06	50
2	72.72	8.14	.43	343
3	72.75	7.58	.29	677
4	72.38	6.97	.50	188
5	73.81	8.04	1.09	54
6	74.00	7.98	1.01	62
7	75.82	7.41	.85	76
8	77.56	7.54	.91	68
		Prisoners		
1	69.33	3.36	1.94	3
2	79.24	8.43	1.10	58
3	75.20	7.45	.56	175
4	74.79	7.73	1.20	41
5	74.42	3.61	1.00	13
6	76.06	6.52	1.05	38
7	74.37	5.05	.80	39
8	75.56	5.72	1.08	28
		Females		
1	66.42	9.97	1.50	44
2	65.45	7.96	.38	426
3	64.98	7.78	.38	400
4	66.17	8.91	.62	207
5	65.99	8.29	1.00	68
6	70.41	8.04	.99	66
7	66.76	9.66	1.63	35
8	70.96	6.67	2.72	6

TABLE 92
ARM CIRCUMFERENCE BY ETHNIC GROUP

Table Group Numbers	(cm) Mean M	Standard Deviation σ	Standard Error S.E.M	Number N
EG		Males		
1	24.19	2.60	.36	50
2	24.01	2.49	.13	343
3	23.97	1.82	.08	400
4	24.31	2.36	.17	188
5	24.78	2.15	.29	54
6	25.62	2.60	.33	62
7	25.68	2.47	.28	76
8	26.77	2.77	.33	68
		Prisoners		
1	22.66	.72	.41	3
2	24.58	2.24	.29	58
3	24.41	1.90	.14	175
4	24.50	1.57	.24	41
5	24.97	1.30	.36	13
6	25.05	1.93	.31	38
7	25.28	2.00	.31	39
8	25.81	2.22	.42	28
		Females		
1	22.08	2.40	.32	56
2	22.11	2.90	.13	426
3	22.25	2.65	.13	400
4	22.66	2.83	.18	230
5	22.87	3.35	.38	76
6	24.93	3.42	.40	72
7	23.42	3.80	.60	39
8	23.55	2.75	.97	8

TABLE 93
LEG CIRCUMFERENCE BY ETHNIC GROUP

Table Group Numbers	(cm) Mean M	Standard Deviation σ	Standard Error S.E.M	Number N
EG		Males		
1	32.08	2.75	.38	50
2	32.05	2.70	.14	343
3	31.87	2.46	.12	400
4	32.54	1.08	.07	188
5	32.62	2.18	.29	54
6	33.32	1.92	.24	62
7	33.69	2.74	.31	76
8	33.73	2.26	.27	68
		Prisoners		
1	31.66	2.44	1.41	3
2	33.57	2.79	.36	58
3	33.05	2.45	.18	175
4	33.07	2.27	.35	41
5	33.31	2.30	.63	13
6	33.95	2.77	.45	38
7	34.77	2.31	.37	39
8	34.86	2.45	.46	28
		Females		
1	30.52	2.67	.35	56
2	30.90	3.02	.14	463
3	30.93	2.81	.10	705
4	31.72	2.91	.19	230
5	32.12	3.25	.37	76
6	33.15	2.82	.33	72
7	32.10	3.49	.55	39
8	32.88	3.10	1.09	8

TABLE 94
SKIN COLOR BY ETHNIC GROUP

Table Group Numbers	* Mean M	Standard Deviation σ	Standard Error S.E.M	Number N
EG		Males		
1	10.80	1.74	.24	50
2	12.44	1.80	.09	343
3	14.47	1.78	.08	400
4	17.46	1.85	.13	188
5	20.20	2.70	.36	54
6	22.41	2.64	.33	62
7	23.90	1.62	.18	76
8	25.77	1.31	.15	68
		Prisoners		
1	10.66	.60	.34	3
2	12.77	1.37	.17	58
3	14.09	1.64	.12	175
4	17.21	1.49	.23	41
5	18.76	2.55	.70	13
6	22.15	1.73	.28	38
7	24.10	1.45	.23	39
8	25.32	1.10	.20	28
		Females		
1	10.60	1.69	.21	56
2	12.45	1.69	.07	463
3	14.14	1.86	.07	705
4	16.82	2.14	.14	230
5	19.70	2.46	.28	76
6	22.08	2.80	.33	72
7	24.03	2.28	.36	39
8	20.50	6.14	2.17	8

*von Luschan Scale

TABLE 95
AGE BY ETHNIC GROUP

Table Group Numbers	(yrs) Mean M	Standard Deviation σ	Standard Error S.E.M	Number N
EG		Males		
1	32.18	9.71	1.37	50
2	30.98	8.87	.47	343
3	30.10	8.55	.42	400
4	28.71	7.99	.58	188
5	29.35	8.14	1.10	54
6	28.66	7.44	.94	62
7	27.31	7.90	.90	76
8	29.42	7.80	.94	68
		Prisoners		
1	25.66	10.15	5.86	3
2	30.48	7.48	.98	58
3	28.04	7.33	.55	175
4	27.51	6.35	.99	41
5	22.53	3.50	.97	13
6	27.84	5.99	.97	38
7	28.23	6.76	1.08	39
8	29.42	6.66	1.25	28
		Females		
1	28.80	6.45	.86	56
2	30.56	8.40	.40	426
3	28.46	7.20	.35	400
4	29.29	7.96	.52	230
5	28.68	7.62	.87	76
6	30.20	7.82	.92	72
7	30.43	7.87	1.26	39
8	27.25	4.86	1.72	8

TABLE 96
PERSONS OF ETHNIC GROUP 3 AND NUTRITIONAL CLASS 2 ANALYZED BY DIFFERENT GEOGRAPHIC REGION

Table Group Numbers	Mean M	Standard Deviation σ	Standard Error S.E.M	Number N
	WEIGHT	Sample - A		
Region				
*99	127.77	17.49	.39	636
99	107.98	18.48	.80	534
*99 = Total Sample		Males		
1	126.39	15.28	2.89	28
2	124.09	15.08	1.82	69
3	127.26	14.63	1.81	65
4	132.92	15.78	3.09	26
5	125.81	16.32	2.93	31
6	129.74	18.37	3.15	34
7	137.16	22.35	4.01	31
8	128.90	15.65	2.91	29
9	131.37	19.44	3.55	30
10	125.31	15.14	3.79	16
11	128.06	20.49	3.46	35
12	131.14	19.50	3.69	28
13	125.67	15.57	1.75	79
14	125.65	17.24	1.99	75
15	128.00	18.99	2.45	60
		Females		
1	110.35	15.32	3.43	20
2	108.00	16.64	2.08	64
3	105.86	18.83	2.84	44
4	99.50	20.32	10.21	4
5	108.39	15.63	2.81	31
6	106.90	17.08	3.12	30
7	109.80	17.59	2.46	51
8	103.25	14.17	2.36	36
9	115.50	20.32	7.18	8
10	117.46	13.87	3.85	13
11	106.28	20.25	4.77	18
12	110.72	23.10	4.62	25
13	105.73	17.80	1.98	81
14	108.33	18.01	2.39	57
15	110.25	23.81	3.30	52

TABLE 97
PERSONS OF ETHNIC GROUP 3 AND NUTRITIONAL CLASS 2 ANALYZED BY VARIOUS GEOGRAPHIC REGIONS

Table Group Numbers	(cm) Mean M	Standard Deviation σ	Standard Error S.E.M	Number N
	TOTAL ARM LENGTH	Sample - A		
Region		Males		
1	72.02	2.73	.52	28
2	72.22	4.08	.49	69
3	72.61	3.05	.38	65
4	73.88	3.85	.76	26
5	73.97	3.89	.70	31
6	73.15	3.84	.66	34
7	72.73	4.02	.72	31
8	72.24	3.37	.63	29
9	72.54	3.78	.69	30
10	70.85	4.93	1.23	16
11	71.85	3.79	.64	35
12	72.01	3.34	.63	28
13	72.09	3.84	.43	79
14	72.47	3.24	.37	75
15	72.88	3.52	.45	60
		Females		
1	66.36	3.22	.72	20
2	67.36	3.72	.47	64
3	66.43	3.19	.48	44
4	66.76	3.54	1.77	4
5	66.71	3.29	.59	31
6	65.90	3.26	.60	30
7	65.73	3.64	.51	51
8	65.01	2.38	.40	36
9	67.51	3.13	1.11	8
10	66.71	3.05	.85	13
11	64.23	2.89	.68	18
12	66.21	3.90	.78	25
13	65.37	3.36	.37	81
14	65.95	3.22	.43	57
15	66.84	3.57	.49	52

TABLE 98
PERSONS OF ETHNIC GROUP 3 AND NUTRITIONAL CLASS 2 ANALYZED BY VARIOUS GEOGRAPHIC REGIONS

Table Group Numbers	(cm) Mean M	Standard Deviation σ	Standard Error S.E.M	Number N
Regions	STATURE	Sample - A		
*99	163.64	5.94	.24	636
99	152.40	5.75	.25	534
*99 = Total Sample		Males		
1	163.29	6.04	1.14	28
2	162.81	5.86	.70	69
3	163.72	5.40	.67	65
4	164.23	5.04	.99	26
5	163.48	5.54	1.00	31
6	162.76	5.76	.99	34
7	165.06	6.24	1.12	31
8	165.62	5.70	1.06	29
9	164.27	7.15	1.31	30
10	163.38	5.40	1.35	16
11	162.89	6.24	1.05	35
12	163.39	5.25	.99	28
13	163.04	5.94	.67	79
14	163.97	5.78	.67	75
15	163.95	6.46	.83	60
		Females		
1	153.85	4.73	1.06	20
2	153.58	6.13	.77	64
3	152.00	6.29	.95	44
4	153.50	4.77	2.39	4
5	153.42	6.24	1.12	31
6	152.43	6.45	1.18	30
7	151.86	6.50	.91	51
8	150.58	4.19	.70	36
9	155.13	3.86	1.36	8
10	155.38	4.07	1.13	13
11	150.67	4.69	1.10	18
12	153.52	5.64	1.13	25
13	151.21	5.46	.61	81
14	151.86	5.50	.73	57
15	153.10	5.63	.78	52

TABLE 99
PERSONS OF ETHNIC GROUP 3 AND NUTRITIONAL CLASS 2 ANALYZED BY DIFFERENT GEOGRAPHIC REGIONS

Table Group Numbers	(cm) Mean M	Standard Deviation σ	Standard Error S.E.M	Number N
Region	TOTAL LEG LENGTH	Sample - A Males		
1	78.43	3.95	.75	28
2	78.09	4.36	.52	69
3	79.43	3.52	.44	65
4	79.62	4.71	.92	26
5	79.13	4.66	.84	31
6	78.65	4.19	.72	34
7	78.74	4.53	.81	31
8	78.90	4.44	.82	29
9	78.30	4.07	.74	30
10	77.38	4.35	1.09	16
11	78.60	4.42	.75	35
12	78.71	3.88	.73	28
13	78.05	4.63	.52	79
14	78.24	4.02	.47	75
15	78.85	4.19	.54	60
		Females		
1	73.00	3.67	.82	20
2	73.59	4.09	.51	64
3	72.52	3.82	.58	44
4	74.75	6.42	3.21	4
5	72.81	3.59	.64	31
6	73.67	3.65	.67	30
7	71.45	4.01	.56	51
8	71.03	2.53	.42	36
9	74.00	3.08	1.09	8
10	72.85	2.77	.77	13
11	71.22	3.03	.71	18
12	73.04	3.53	.71	25
13	71.64	4.04	.45	81
14	71.95	4.24	.56	57
15	73.12	4.16	.58	52

TABLE 100
PERSONS OF ETHNIC GROUP 3 AND NUTRITIONAL CLASS 2 ANALYZED BY VARIOUS GEOGRAPHIC REGIONS

Table Group Numbers	(cm) Mean M	Standard Deviation σ	Standard Error S.E.M	Number N
Region	TRUNK HEIGHT	Sample - A Males		
1	53.21	2.98	.56	28
2	52.92	2.64	.32	69
3	52.54	2.93	.36	65
4	54.48	3.17	.62	26
5	52.84	2.16	.39	31
6	52.63	2.84	.49	34
7	54.29	2.71	.49	31
8	54.43	2.13	.40	29
9	53.92	4.17	.76	30
10	54.46	2.75	.69	16
11	52.74	3.21	.54	35
12	53.38	2.23	.42	28
13	53.71	2.25	.25	79
14	53.90	2.37	.27	75
15	53.77	3.03	.39	60
		Females		
1	50.93	2.36	.53	20
2	50.55	2.64	.33	64
3	49.96	3.23	.49	44
4	50.44	1.30	.65	4
5	50.31	3.50	.63	31
6	49.50	2.81	.51	30
7	50.48	2.86	.40	51
8	50.25	2.51	.42	36
9	51.37	1.94	.69	8
10	51.76	2.41	.67	13
11	50.44	2.56	.60	18
12	50.60	2.80	.56	25
13	50.31	2.30	.26	81
14	50.95	2.13	.28	57
15	50.82	2.41	.33	52

TABLE 101
PERSONS OF ETHNIC GROUP 3 AND NUTRITIONAL CLASS 2 ANALYZED BY VARIOUS GEOGRAPHIC REGIONS

Table Group Numbers	(cm) Mean M	Standard Deviation σ	Standard Error S.E.M	Number N
Region	BIACROMIAL DIAMETER	Sample - A Male		
1	36.65	1.70	.32	28
2	36.84	1.82	.22	69
3	37.13	1.64	.20	65
4	38.56	1.55	.30	26
5	37.55	1.39	.25	31
6	36.98	2.03	.35	34
7	37.69	1.80	.32	31
8	37.75	1.61	.30	29
9	36.95	1.82	.33	30
10	36.98	1.73	.43	16
11	36.98	1.90	.32	35
12	37.51	1.76	.33	28
13	36.94	1.70	.19	79
14	37.09	1.76	.20	75
15	37.17	2.25	.29	60
		Females		
1	32.59	2.73	.61	20
2	33.56	1.61	.20	64
3	33.19	1.75	.26	44
4	34.11	1.09	.55	4
5	33.06	1.91	.34	31
6	33.16	1.20	.22	30
7	33.23	1.59	.22	51
8	32.92	1.35	.23	36
9	33.96	.97	.34	8
10	33.41	1.42	.40	13
11	32.48	1.16	.27	18
12	33.37	1.68	.34	25
13	32.90	1.63	.18	81
14	33.36	1.78	.24	57
15	33.24	1.55	.22	52

TABLE 102

PERSONS OF ETHNIC GROUP 3 AND NUTRITIONAL CLASS 2 ANALYZED BY VARIOUS GEOGRAPHIC REGIONS

Table Group Numbers	(mm) Mean M	Standard Deviation σ	Standard Error S.E.M	Number N
Region	HEAD WIDTH	Sample - A Males		
1	150.18	6.30	1.19	28
2	150.78	5.25	.63	69
3	150.42	5.32	.66	65
4	148.58	4.73	.93	26
5	149.97	6.61	1.19	31
6	149.44	5.47	.94	34
7	149.84	5.12	.92	31
8	150.62	7.44	1.38	29
9	152.27	5.62	1.03	30
10	148.81	4.17	1.04	16
11	150.60	6.11	1.03	35
12	149.14	6.09	1.15	28
13	152.54	5.13	.58	79
14	150.39	5.44	.63	75
15	151.48	5.04	.65	60
		Females		
1	146.85	4.68	1.05	20
2	144.88	4.89	.61	64
3	143.86	4.58	.69	44
4	141.25	4.49	2.25	4
5	142.39	5.55	1.00	31
6	142.17	4.55	.83	30
7	142.49	5.21	.73	51
8	143.58	4.06	.68	36
9	145.88	1.76	.62	8
10	145.23	4.84	1.34	13
11	144.67	5.08	1.20	18
12	146.04	5.23	1.05	25
13	145.47	5.16	.57	81
14	144.42	4.54	.60	57
15	143.42	6.40	.89	52

TABLE 103

PERSONS OF ETHNIC GROUP 3 AND NUTRITIONAL CLASS 2 ANALYZED BY VARIOUS GEOGRAPHIC REGIONS

Table Group Numbers	(mm) Mean M	Standard Deviation σ	Standard Error S.E.M	Number N
Region	HEAD LENGTH	Sample - A Males		
1	181.57	7.79	1.47	28
2	183.19	6.48	.78	69
3	183.54	8.00	.99	65
4	184.50	6.05	1.19	26
5	185.58	5.86	1.05	31
6	185.18	7.06	1.21	34
7	187.03	6.35	1.14	31
8	184.59	6.37	1.18	29
9	184.23	7.63	1.39	30
10	182.19	9.45	2.36	16
11	181.77	6.39	1.08	35
12	184.71	6.50	1.23	28
13	183.25	6.74	.76	79
14	182.97	6.98	.81	75
15	184.70	5.52	.71	60
		Females		
1	175.15	5.04	1.13	20
2	175.75	7.14	.89	64
3	174.93	6.89	1.04	44
4	171.75	4.66	2.33	4
5	180.71	6.32	1.14	31
6	176.50	6.52	1.19	30
7	175.27	4.53	.63	51
8	176.11	6.48	1.08	36
9	178.13	4.37	1.55	8
10	178.23	8.29	2.30	13
11	174.94	6.03	1.42	18
12	175.20	5.63	1.13	25
13	173.26	5.09	.57	81
14	175.04	6.07	.80	57
15	174.96	6.68	.93	52

TABLE 104

PERSONS OF ETHNIC GROUP 3 AND NUTRITIONAL CLASS 2 ANALYZED BY VARIOUS GEOGRAPHIC REGIONS

Table Group Numbers	(mm) Mean M	Standard Deviation σ	Standard Error S.E.M	Number N
Region	BIZYGOMATIC DIAMETER	Sample - A Male		
1	135.86	5.70	1.08	28
2	135.50	5.35	.64	69
3	135.92	4.90	.61	65
4	137.65	5.20	1.02	26
5	136.65	5.60	1.01	31
6	137.06	4.27	.73	34
7	137.65	4.93	.89	31
8	136.17	4.70	.87	29
9	138.20	5.24	.96	30
10	135.25	5.94	1.49	16
11	136.11	4.43	.75	35
12	134.79	4.84	.92	28
13	136.54	5.10	.57	79
14	135.65	5.73	.66	75
15	137.22	5.45	.70	60
		Females		
1	129.05	5.02	1.12	20
2	128.34	4.85	.61	64
3	126.55	4.99	.75	44
4	128.75	1.48	.74	4
5	126.45	6.00	1.08	31
6	127.47	4.80	.88	30
7	127.78	4.43	.62	51
8	127.83	4.14	.69	36
9	130.13	3.10	1.10	8
10	128.54	5.44	1.51	13
11	128.00	4.43	1.05	18
12	128.60	4.92	.99	25
13	128.12	5.20	.58	81
14	127.75	4.57	.61	57
15	127.85	5.10	.71	52

TABLE 105

PERSONS OF ETHNIC GROUP 3 AND NUTRITIONAL CLASS 2 ANALYZED BY VARIOUS GEOGRAPHIC REGIONS

Table Group Numbers	(mm) Mean M	Standard Deviation σ	Standard Error S.E.M	Number N
Region	BIGONIAL DIAMETER	Sample - A Males		
1	98.10	4.01	.76	28
2	97.16	5.59	.67	69
3	98.56	6.21	.77	65
4	99.18	5.11	1.00	26
5	97.32	5.54	1.00	31
6	99.12	6.29	1.08	34
7				
8	100.50	4.89	.88	31
8	99.70	6.11	1.13	29
9	101.73	5.27	.96	30
10	95.84	6.38	.51	16
11	97.79	5.24	.89	35
12	96.89	5.42	1.03	28
13	99.01	5.72	.64	79
14	97.71	6.15	.71	75
15	98.97	6.54	.84	60
		Females		
1	91.09	3.92	.88	20
2	91.92	4.66	.58	64
3	90.65	4.89	.74	44
4	89.77	2.59	1.29	4
5	91.39	5.58	1.00	31
6	89.31	5.17	.94	30
7	91.21	5.73	.80	51
8	91.87	4.30	.72	36
9	94.18	3.66	1.29	8
10	91.91	5.64	1.56	13
11	90.47	6.50	1.53	18
12	93.39	6.18	1.24	25
13	91.79	5.07	.56	81
14	92.27	5.42	.72	57
15	90.14	5.72	.79	52

TABLE 106
PERSONS OF ETHNIC GROUP 3 AND NUTRITIONAL CLASS 2 ANALYZED BY VARIOUS GEOGRAPHIC REGIONS

Table Group Numbers	(mm) Mean M	Standard Deviation σ	Standard Error S.E.M	Number N
Region	TOTAL FACE HEIGHT	Sample - A Males		
1	117.71	8.42	1.59	28
2	121.02	5.88	.71	69
3	119.91	5.62	.70	65
4	124.01	6.32	1.24	26
5	120.45	4.81	.86	31
6	123.36	6.91	1.19	34
7	121.64	5.92	1.06	31
8	121.65	7.21	1.34	29
9	123.45	6.30	1.15	30
10	121.70	6.01	1.50	16
11	121.22	6.18	1.05	35
12	121.98	5.98	1.13	28
13	123.04	6.55	.74	79
14	121.27	5.71	.66	75
15	121.81	6.38	.82	60
		Females		
1	113.58	6.57	1.47	20
2	111.97	5.64	.71	64
3	113.23	5.61	.85	44
4	111.80	3.04	1.52	4
5	113.56	6.47	1.16	31
6	112.86	6.54	1.20	30
7	113.48	6.32	.88	51
8	113.39	5.88	.98	36
9	116.34	8.07	2.85	8
10	113.27	6.17	1.71	13
11	112.26	7.01	1.65	18
12	114.22	6.49	1.30	25
13	114.27	6.44	.72	81
14	114.21	5.98	.79	57
15	113.16	5.89	.82	52

TABLE 107
PERSONS OF ETHNIC GROUP 3 AND NUTRITIONAL CLASS 2 ANALYZED BY VARIOUS GEOGRAPHIC REGIONS

Table Group Numbers	(mm) Mean M	Standard Deviation σ	Standard Error S.E.M	Number N
Region	NOSE HEIGHT	Sample - A Males		
1	54.34	5.08	.96	28
2	54.10	3.69	.45	69
3	54.41	4.13	.51	65
4	57.25	3.89	.76	26
5	54.58	3.44	.62	31
6	53.30	4.11	.70	34
7	53.86	3.52	.63	31
8	53.86	3.21	.60	29
9	54.23	4.17	.76	30
10	52.83	3.87	.97	16
11	55.17	4.07	.69	35
12	53.85	3.46	.65	28
13	55.13	3.79	.43	79
14	54.75	4.22	.49	75
15	54.58	3.36	.43	60
		Females		
1	51.49	3.88	.87	20
2	51.56	3.69	.46	64
3	51.34	3.90	.59	44
4	50.58	1.66	.83	4
5	52.67	3.38	.60	31
6	51.94	4.36	.80	30
7	51.11	4.06	.57	51
8	50.10	4.78	.80	36
9	49.78	3.35	1.19	8
10	51.96	3.41	.95	13
11	50.51	3.50	.83	18
12	52.30	3.20	.64	25
13	51.50	4.31	.48	81
14	51.82	3.97	.53	57
15	50.82	4.12	.57	52

TABLE 108
PERSONS OF ETHNIC GROUP 3 AND NUTRITIONAL CLASS 2 ANALYZED BY VARIOUS GEOGRAPHIC REGIONS

Table Group Numbers	(mm) Mean M	Standard Deviation σ	Standard Error S.E.M	Number N
Region	NOSE WIDTH	Sample - A Males		
1	35.25	2.71	.51	28
2	35.14	2.37	.90	69
3	35.66	3.08	.38	65
4	36.04	2.70	.53	26
5	36.06	2.78	.50	31
6	35.56	3.05	.52	34
7	35.32	2.67	.48	31
8	35.41	2.63	.49	29
9	35.10	3.20	.58	30
10	34.25	2.61	.65	16
11	36.23	2.64	.45	35
12	35.61	3.31	.63	28
13	35.22	2.58	.29	79
14	34.71	3.05	.35	75
15	35.33	2.63	.34	60
		Females		
1	32.35	3.77	.84	20
2	32.53	2.89	.36	64
3	31.34	2.33	.35	44
4	34.00	1.73	.87	4
5	32.29	2.48	.45	31
6	31.97	2.65	.48	30
7	32.00	2.75	.39	51
8	31.53	2.37	.40	36
9	32.50	2.29	.81	8
10	32.69	3.02	.84	13
11	32.61	2.65	.62	18
12	32.00	2.61	.52	25
13	31.58	2.68	.30	81
14	31.72	2.66	.35	57
15	32.50	2.87	.40	52

TABLE 109
PERSONS OF ETHNIC GROUP 3 AND NUTRITIONAL CLASS 2 ANALYZED BY VARIOUS GEOGRAPHIC REGIONS

Table Group Numbers	(cm) Mean M	Standard Deviation σ	Standard Error S.E.M	Number N
Region	ARM CIRCUMFERENCE	Sample - A Male		
1	24.49	1.86	.35	28
2	24.00	2.19	.26	69
3	24.48	2.31	.29	65
4	25.20	1.80	.35	26
5	24.10	1.82	.33	31
6	23.65	1.95	.34	34
7	24.13	2.28	.41	31
8	24.10	1.83	.34	29
9	24.23	2.06	.38	30
10	23.67	2.06	.52	16
11	24.01	2.27	.38	35
12	24.60	2.56	.49	28
13	23.63	2.12	.24	79
14	23.68	2.33	.27	75
15	24.00	2.04	.26	60
		Females		
1	21.67	2.44	.55	20
2	22.07	2.04	.26	64
3	21.82	2.57	.39	44
4	20.59	1.40	.65	4
5	21.86	1.82	.33	31
6	21.78	2.11	.39	30
7	22.31	2.12	.30	51
8	21.60	2.30	.38	36
9	22.93	2.63	.93	8
10	22.84	1.80	.50	13
11	21.75	2.66	.63	18
12	22.04	3.28	.66	25
13	21.71	2.37	.26	81
14	22.03	2.31	.31	57
15	21.85	2.83	.39	52

TABLE 110
PERSONS OF ETHNIC GROUP 3 AND NUTRITIONAL CLASS 2 ANALYZED BY VARIOUS GEOGRAPHIC REGIONS

Table Group Numbers	Mean M	Standard Deviation σ	Standard Error S.E.M	Number N
Region	LEG CIRCUMFERENCE	Male Sample - A		
1	32.39	2.41	.46	28
2	32.16	2.14	.26	69
3	32.43	2.42	.30	65
4	33.27	2.26	.44	26
5	31.71	2.82	.51	31
6	31.94	2.47	.42	34
7	33.48	3.41	.61	31
8	32.90	2.70	.50	29
9	32.93	2.37	1.37	30
10	32.31	2.57	.64	16
11	33.03	3.23	.55	35
12	32.71	2.80	.53	28
13	32.20	2.49	.29	79
14	32.03	2.72	.31	75
15	32.22	2.30	.30	60
		Females		
1	31.20	2.34	.52	20
2	30.78	3.06	.38	64
3	30.84	2.66	.40	44
4	29.00	1.87	.94	4
5	30.13	2.35	.42	31
6	30.50	2.26	.41	30
7	21.29	2.36	.33	51
8	30.75	2.44	.41	36
9	31.88	3.26	1.15	8
10	32.62	1.90	.53	13
11	31.00	2.56	.60	18
12	31.76	3.27	.65	25
13	30.68	2.59	.29	81
14	30.82	3.17	.42	57
15	30.92	2.72	.38	52

TABLE 111
PERSONS OF ETHNIC GROUP 3 AND NUTRITIONAL CLASS 2 ANALYZED BY VARIOUS GEOGRAPHIC REGIONS

Table Group Numbers	(yrs) Mean M	Standard Deviation σ	Standard Error S.E.M	Number N
Region	AGE	Males Sample - A		
1	27.61	7.41	1.40	28
2	28.65	7.13	.86	69
3	27.54	6.64	.82	65
4	28.42	7.39	1.45	26
5	33.35	7.80	1.40	31
6	30.15	9.08	1.56	34
7	32.74	8.19	1.47	31
8	26.97	8.54	1.59	29
9	29.30	6.66	1.22	30
10	27.13	7.14	1.79	16
11	29.83	8.56	1.45	35
12	26.32	5.65	1.07	28
13	30.86	8.98	1.01	79
14	29.35	8.16	.94	75
15	28.82	8.52	1.10	60
		Females		
1	27.30	6.26	1.40	20
2	28.09	6.79	.85	64
3	28.09	5.84	.88	44
4	23.00	3.39	1.70	4
5	27.65	6.70	1.20	31
6	28.93	7.73	1.41	30
7	29.33	7.17	1.00	51
8	27.97	6.77	1.13	36
9	27.88	8.48	3.00	8
10	25.46	5.65	1.57	13
11	29.61	10.18	2.40	18
12	28.36	7.29	1.46	25
13	28.69	7.03	.78	81
14	29.02	6.89	.91	57
15	27.42	7.38	1.02	52

TABLE 112
PERSONS OF NUTRITIONAL CLASS 2 ANALYZED BY VARIOUS ETHNIC GROUPS

Table Group Numbers	Mean M	Standard Deviation σ	Standard Error S.E.M	Number N
EG	WEIGHT (lbs)	Males Sample - B		
1	125.27	18.98	3.12	37
2	127.72	19.10	1.13	288
3	127.77	17.49	.39	636
4	128.82	16.86	1.29	170
5	131.02	14.95	2.23	45
6	136.42	16.64	1.91	76
7	136.73	18.71	1.96	91
8	138.58	19.56	2.24	76
		Females		
1	109.38	16.32	2.68	37
2	107.32	19.90	1.10	325
3	107.98	18.48	.80	534
4	115.41	22.84	1.74	172
5	117.70	26.01	3.45	57
6	129.94	22.97	3.22	51
7	123.38	35.23	7.69	21
8	140.40	24.13	10.79	5
	NOSE WIDTH (mm)	Males		
1	34.05	3.20	.53	37
2	35.57	2.70	.16	288
3	35.31	3.15	.12	636
4	37.17	2.99	.23	170
5	38.39	2.79	.42	45
6	40.16	3.20	.37	76
7	40.26	3.34	.35	91
8	42.81	3.16	.36	76
		Females		
1	31.92	2.54	.42	37
2	32.50	2.40	.13	325
3	32.02	2.75	.12	534
4	35.47	2.55	.19	172
5	36.78	2.59	.34	57
6	38.41	3.33	.47	51
7	38.63	3.38	.74	21
8	38.19	2.42	1.08	5

TABLE 113
PERSONS OF NUTRITIONAL CLASS 2 ANALYZED BY VARIOUS ETHNIC GROUPS

Table Group Numbers	Mean M	Standard Deviation σ	Standard Error S.E.M	Number N
EG	TOTAL LEG LENGTH (cm)	Males Sample - B		
1	78.86	4.41	.72	37
2	78.74	4.44	.26	288
3	78.58	4.29	.17	636
4	79.23	4.48	.34	170
5	78.98	3.24	.48	45
6	81.71	3.76	.43	76
7	83.09	4.10	.43	91
8	84.12	4.41	.51	76
		Females		
1	72.35	3.37	.55	37
2	71.83	3.78	.21	325
3	72.44	4.04	.17	534
4	73.65	3.65	.28	172
5	74.35	4.65	.20	57
6	75.02	4.06	.57	51
7	76.19	3.11	.68	21
8	77.80	3.87	1.73	5
	TOTAL ARM LENGTH (cm)	Males		
1	72.14	4.05	.67	37
2	72.55	3.85	.23	288
3	72.98	3.67	.15	636
4	73.37	3.82	.29	170
5	73.52	3.50	.52	45
6	74.99	3.60	.41	76
7	75.79	4.03	.42	91
8	76.89	3.62	.42	76
		Females		
1	66.33	2.80	.46	37
2	65.68	3.63	.20	325
3	66.40	3.45	.15	534
4	67.12	3.21	.25	172
5	68.57	3.73	.50	57
6	69.23	3.68	.52	51
7	70.72	3.08	.67	21
8	70.21	2.79	1.25	5

TABLE 114
PERSONS OF NUTRITIONAL CLASS 2 ANALYZED BY VARIOUS ETHNIC GROUPS

Table Group Numbers EG	Mean M	Standard Deviation σ	Standard Error S.E.M	Number N
	STATURE	Sample - B Males		
1	163.57	6.96	1.14	37
2	163.61	6.31	.37	288
3	163.64	5.94	.24	636
4	164.08	6.28	.48	170
5	163.84	4.68	.70	45
6	166.72	5.60	.64	76
7	167.93	6.11	.64	91
8	168.93	6.48	.74	76
		Females		
1	152.27	5.80	.95	37
2	151.62	5.51	.31	325
3	152.40	5.75	.25	534
4	153.90	5.33	.41	172
5	154.37	5.55	.74	57
6	154.82	5.96	.84	51
7	156.62	5.20	1.13	21
8	159.40	4.45	1.99	5
	NOSE HEIGHT (mm)	Males		
1	54.14	4.04	.66	37
2	53.41	4.30	.25	288
3	53.44	3.34	.13	636
4	53.55	3.98	.31	170
5	52.36	5.05	.75	45
6	52.70	4.64	.53	76
7	52.10	4.59	.48	91
8	50.86	4.26	.49	76
		Females		
1	50.65	4.00	.66	37
2	50.34	4.17	.23	325
3	50.20	4.12	.18	534
4	50.40	4.59	.35	172
5	49.65	4.72	.62	57
6	49.65	4.52	.63	51
7	50.67	3.66	.80	21
8	51.00	1.41	.63	5

TABLE 115
PERSONS OF NUTRITIONAL CLASS 2 ANALYZED BY VARIOUS ETHNIC GROUPS

Table Group Numbers EG	Mean M	Standard Deviation σ	Standard Error S.E.M	Number N
	LEG CIRCUMFERENCE (cm)	Sample - B	Male	
1	31.78	2.73	.45	37
2	32.21	2.64	.16	288
3	32.42	2.61	.10	636
4	32.49	2.47	.19	170
5	32.87	2.15	.32	45
6	33.55	2.56	.29	70
7	34.05	2.68	.28	91
8	33.76	2.49	.29	76
			Females	
1	31.03	2.68	.44	37
2	30.72	2.76	.15	325
3	30.90	2.74	.12	534
4	31.95	2.90	.22	172
5	32.61	3.00	.40	57
6	33.59	2.29	.32	51
7	32.57	2.65	.58	21
8	34.00	3.48	1.55	5
	TOTAL FACE HEIGHT (mm)		Males	
1	120.52	5.99	.99	37
2	120.84	6.89	.41	288
3	120.33	6.37	.25	636
4	122.18	6.70	.51	170
5	120.85	7.13	1.06	45
6	124.58	7.16	.82	76
7	122.88	7.65	.80	91
8	122.32	7.34	.84	76
			Females	
1	114.79	6.05	.99	37
2	112.60	5.90	.33	325
3	111.99	6.22	.27	534
4	113.65	6.85	.52	172
5	115.62	7.19	.95	57
6	115.10	6.42	.90	51
7	116.73	7.46	1.63	21
8	120.91	4.26	1.91	5

TABLE 116
PERSONS OF NUTRITIONAL CLASS 2 ANALYZED BY VARIOUS ETHNIC GROUPS

Table Group Numbers EG	Mean M	Standard Deviation σ	Standard Error S.E.M	Number N
	HEAD LENGTH (mm)	Sample - B	Males	
1	182.54	6.21	1.02	37
2	182.67	7.28	.43	288
3	183.81	7.16	.28	636
4	185.09	7.69	.59	170
5	185.76	7.45	1.11	45
6	188.67	6.95	.80	76
7	188.70	6.87	.72	91
8	190.51	7.13	.82	76
			Females	
1	175.92	6.07	1.01	36
2	173.88	6.03	.34	325
3	175.45	6.39	.28	534
4	177.07	6.30	.48	172
5	179.35	7.58	1.00	57
6	182.20	6.79	.95	51
7	183.00	7.60	1.66	21
8	181.80	1.94	.87	5
	BIZYGOMATIC DIAMETER (mm)		Males	
1	133.78	4.49	.74	37
2	135.32	5.23	.31	288
3	136.36	3.40	.21	636
4	136.19	6.24	.48	170
5	136.82	5.85	.87	45
6	135.14	6.23	.72	76
7	135.98	5.70	.60	91
8	136.36	4.78	.55	76
			Females	
1	128.43	4.25	.70	37
2	128.05	4.79	.27	325
3	127.87	4.93	.21	534
4	128.58	4.80	.37	172
5	128.47	5.32	.70	57
6	130.22	4.56	.64	51
7	128.81	4.96	1.08	21
8	131.60	3.83	1.71	5

TABLE 117
PERSONS OF NUTRITIONAL CLASS 2 ANALYZED BY VARIOUS ETHNIC GROUPS

Table Group Numbers EG	Mean M	Standard Deviation σ	Standard Error S.E.M	Number N
	HEAD WIDTH (mm)	Sample - B	Males	
1	151.30	5.50	.90	37
2	150.55	5.65	.33	288
3	150.64	5.73	.23	636
4	150.04	5.64	.43	170
5	150.58	5.95	.89	45
6	148.37	5.69	.65	76
7	148.68	5.95	.62	91
8	147.26	5.40	.62	76
			Females	
1	144.72	5.84	.97	36
2	144.35	5.10	.28	325
3	144.20	5.19	.22	534
4	143.81	5.05	.39	172
5	142.98	5.82	.77	57
6	144.18	5.38	.75	51
7	142.24	6.02	1.31	21
8	140.80	2.14	.96	5
	BIGONIAL DIAMETER (mm)		Males	
1	98.10	6.65	.97	37
2	98.11	7.88	.28	288
3	99.52	5.97	.24	636
4	98.32	6.27	.39	170
5	97.81	5.45	.77	45
6	98.64	5.78	.75	76
7	98.92	6.15	1.31	91
8	99.66	6.25	.96	76
			Females	
1	91.58	4.01	.90	37
2	91.64	5.12	.33	325
3	92.51	5.36	.23	534
4	91.73	5.73	.43	172
5	92.29	5.10	.89	57
6	91.71	5.13	.65	51
7	91.60	3.94	.62	21
8	93.26	4.32	.62	5

TABLE 118
PERSONS OF NUTRITIONAL CLASS 2 ANALYZED BY VARIOUS ETHNIC GROUPS

Table Group Numbers	Mean M	Standard Deviation σ	Standard Error S.E.M	Number N
EG	BIACROMIAL DIAMETER (cm)		Sample - B	Males
1	36.49	1.64	.27	37
2	36.87	1.96	.12	288
3	37.28	1.83	.07	636
4	37.60	1.89	.15	170
5	38.11	1.73	.26	45
6	38.12	1.59	.18	76
7	38.60	1.62	.17	91
8	39.77	2.12	.24	76
				Females
1	33.23	2.33	.38	37
2	32.96	1.61	.28	325
3	33.34	1.67	.07	534
4	33.60	1.66	.40	172
5	33.78	1.37	.18	57
6	34.50	1.80	.25	51
7	35.00	2.15	.47	21
8	35.45	1.47	.66	5
	TRUNK HEIGHT (cm)			Males
1	53.40	3.32	.55	37
2	53.49	2.93	.17	288
3	53.95	2.85	.11	636
4	53.31	2.88	.22	170
5	53.38	2.59	.39	45
6	53.68	2.74	.31	76
7	53.65	2.84	.30	91
8	53.68	2.93	.34	76
				Females
1	50.42	2.76	.45	37
2	50.42	2.79	.16	325
3	50.84	2.68	.12	534
4	50.81	2.81	.21	172
5	50.64	2.15	.29	57
6	50.38	2.65	.37	51
7	50.63	2.55	.56	21
8	51.44	2.99	1.34	5

TABLE 119
PERSONS OF NUTRITIONAL CLASS 2 ANALYZED BY VARIOUS ETHNIC GROUPS

Table Group Numbers	Mean M	Standard Deviation σ	Standard Error S.E.M	Number N
EG	ARM CIRCUMFERENCE (cm)		Sample - B	Males
1	24.03	2.24	.37	37
2	23.94	2.20	.13	288
3	24.31	2.17	.09	636
4	24.36	2.07	.16	170
5	24.91	1.98	.30	45
6	25.27	2.34	.27	76
7	25.68	2.16	.23	91
8	26.49	2.65	.30	76
				Females
1	22.47	2.40	.39	37
2	21.86	2.55	.14	325
3	22.10	2.39	.10	534
4	22.85	2.89	.22	172
5	23.11	3.64	.48	57
6	25.30	3.47	.49	51
7	23.65	4.47	.97	21
8	24.22	3.07	1.37	5
	AGE (yrs)			Males
1	31.27	9.61	1.58	37
2	30.19	8.44	.50	288
3	28.93	8.50	.34	636
4	28.62	7.55	.58	170
5	26.36	6.28	.94	45
6	28.78	7.17	.82	76
7	28.33	7.73	.81	91
8	29.68	7.50	.86	76
				Females
1	27.35	6.19	1.02	37
2	30.13	8.37	.46	325
3	28.28	6.84	.30	534
4	28.84	7.79	.59	172
5	27.96	7.22	.96	57
6	30.39	7.75	1.09	51
7	32.48	7.68	1.68	21
8	25.00	4.38	1.96	5

TABLE 120
PERSONS OF ETHNIC GROUP 3 ANALYZED BY VARIOUS NUTRITIONAL CLASSES

Table Group Numbers	Mean M	Standard Deviation σ	Standard Error S.E.M	Number N
NC	WEIGHT (lbs)		Sample - C	Males
1	141.06	21.10	3.08	47
2	127.77	17.49	.39	636
3	123.55	17.81	1.47	147
4	118.73	14.82	3.16	22
				Females
1	128.33	23.40	3.61	42
2	107.98	18.48	.80	534
3	108.02	21.30	2.07	106
4	97.74	15.67	3.27	23
	NOSE WIDTH (mm)			Males
1	36.19	2.97	.43	47
2	35.31	3.15	.12	636
3	36.00	2.61	.22	147
4	36.24	2.50	.53	22
				Females
1	32.75	2.89	.45	42
2	32.02	2.75	.12	534
3	33.54	2.83	.28	106
4	33.40	3.06	.64	23

TABLE 121
PERSONS OF ETHNIC GROUP 3 ANALYZED BY VARIOUS NUTRITIONAL CLASSES

Table Group Numbers	Mean M	Standard Deviation σ	Standard Error S.E.M	Number N
NC	STATURE (cm)		Sample - C	Males
1	168.19	5.35	.78	47
2	163.64	5.94	.24	636
3	162.00	5.52	.46	147
4	163.05	7.39	1.58	22
				Females
1	155.76	4.54	.70	42
2	152.40	5.75	.25	534
3	151.79	5.96	.58	106
4	150.09	4.95	1.03	23
	NOSE HEIGHT (mm)			Males
1	56.96	3.98	.58	47
2	53.44	3.34	.13	636
3	53.08	4.04	.33	147
4	52.05	3.11	.66	22
				Females
1	53.10	4.16	.64	42
2	50.20	4.12	.18	534
3	50.29	4.03	.39	106
4	48.83	4.02	.84	23
	TOTAL FACE HEIGHT (mm)			Males
1	124.03	5.64	.82	47
2	120.33	6.37	.25	636
3	120.68	6.61	.55	147
4	121.58	5.59	1.19	22
				Females
1	114.57	6.72	1.03	42
2	111.99	6.22	.27	534
3	112.05	6.91	.67	106
4	113.69	6.93	1.44	23

TABLE 122
PERSONS OF ETHNIC GROUP 3 ANALYZED BY VARIOUS NUTRITIONAL CLASSES

Table Group Numbers	Mean M	Standard Deviation σ	Standard Error S.E.M	Number N
		Sample - C		
NC	BIGONIAL DIAMETER (mm)		Males	
1	100.73	5.32	.78	47
2	99.52	5.97	.24	636
3	98.45	6.54	.54	147
4	96.17	5.45	1.16	22
			Females	
1	95.00	4.91	.76	42
2	92.51	5.36	.23	534
3	91.23	4.72	.46	106
4	91.00	5.02	1.05	23
	LEG CIRCUMFERENCE (cm)		Males	
1	33.21	2.59	.38	47
2	32.42	2.61	.10	636
3	31.99	2.49	.21	147
4	31.59	1.67	.36	22
			Females	
1	32.48	3.04	.47	42
2	30.90	2.74	.12	534
3	30.86	2.90	.28	106
4	29.26	2.25	.47	23

TABLE 123
PERSONS OF ETHNIC GROUP 3 ANALYZED BY VARIOUS NUTRITIONAL CLASSES

Table Group Numbers	Mean M	Standard Deviation σ	Standard Error S.E.M	Number N
		Sample - C		
NC	BIACROMIAL DIAMETER (cm)		Males	
1	37.86	1.79	.26	47
2	37.28	1.83	.07	636
3	36.83	1.86	.15	147
4	36.55	2.42	.52	22
			Females	
1	33.97	1.89	.29	42
2	33.34	1.67	.07	534
3	32.97	1.61	.16	106
4	32.49	1.51	.32	23
	TRUNK HEIGHT (cm)		Males	
1	56.34	2.46	.36	47
2	53.95	2.85	.11	636
3	52.58	3.00	.25	147
4	53.60	3.64	.78	22
			Females	
1	52.20	2.85	.44	42
2	50.84	2.68	.12	534
3	50.10	2.45	.24	106
4	49.93	2.22	.46	23
	HEAD WIDTH (mm)		Males	
1	152.77	5.90	.86	47
2	150.64	5.73	.23	636
3	149.80	5.79	.48	147
4	151.27	5.12	1.09	22
			Females	
1	145.36	5.11	.79	42
2	144.20	5.19	.22	534
3	144.03	5.74	.56	106
4	143.43	5.51	1.15	23

TABLE 124
PERSONS OF ETHNIC GROUP 3 ANALYZED BY VARIOUS NUTRITIONAL CLASSES

Table Group Numbers	Mean M	Standard Deviation σ	Standard Error S.E.M	Number N
		Sample - C		
NC	TOTAL LEG LENGTH (cm)		Males	
1	80.62	3.64	.53	47
2	78.58	4.29	.17	636
3	77.69	3.92	.32	147
4	78.32	5.63	1.20	22
			Females	
1	74.40	3.49	.54	42
2	72.44	4.04	.17	534
3	72.09	4.27	.42	106
4	70.70	2.90	.60	23
	TOTAL ARM LENGTH (cm)		Males	
1	73.59	2.64	.39	47
2	72.98	3.67	.15	636
3	71.91	3.39	.28	147
4	72.28	4.88	1.04	22
			Females	
1	66.95	3.17	.49	42
2	66.40	3.45	.15	534
3	65.61	3.49	.34	106
4	65.40	3.24	.68	23
	HEAD LENGTH (mm)		Males	
1	189.91	6.58	.96	47
2	183.81	7.16	.28	636
3	183.50	6.46	.53	147
4	181.95	6.30	1.34	22
			Females	
1	179.69	7.02	1.08	42
2	175.45	6.39	.28	534
3	174.98	6.10	.59	106
4	172.61	5.78	1.21	23

TABLE 125
PERSONS OF ETHNIC GROUP 3 ANALYZED BY VARIOUS NUTRITIONAL CLASSES

Table Group Numbers	Mean M	Standard Deviation σ	Standard Error S.E.M	Number N
		Sample - C		
NC	BIZYGOMATIC DIAMETER (mm)		Males	
1	138.02	5.53	.81	47
2	136.36	3.40	.21	636
3	135.71	5.10	.42	147
4	136.09	5.22	1.11	22
			Females	
1	129.38	5.16	.80	42
2	127.87	4.93	.21	534
3	128.15	4.89	.48	106
4	124.96	5.81	1.21	23
	ARM CIRCUMFERENCE (cm)		Males	
1	25.26	2.53	.37	47
2	24.31	2.17	.09	636
3	23.90	2.15	.18	147
4	22.90	1.70	.36	22
			Females	
1	23.97	2.66	.41	42
2	22.10	2.39	.10	534
3	22.09	3.12	.30	106
4	21.33	2.30	.48	23
	AGE (yrs)		Males	
1	26.66	4.76	.69	47
2	28.93	8.50	.34	636
3	30.62	9.61	.79	147
4	33.82	9.88	2.11	22
			Females	
1	28.24	7.07	1.09	42
2	28.28	6.84	.30	534
3	29.50	8.76	.85	106
4	31.65	9.01	1.88	23

TABLE 126
INDICES BY VARIOUS NUTRITIONAL CLASSES

Table Group Numbers	Mean M	Standard Deviation σ	Standard Error S.E.M	Number N
NC	CEPHALIC INDEX	Sample - E		
*99	81.35	4.24	.11	1518
99	81.91	4.03	.10	1649
		Males		
1	80.74	3.74	.37	100
2	81.43	4.31	.13	1109
3	81.13	4.04	.24	274
4	82.25	4.69	.79	35
		Females		
1	81.45	3.60	.35	103
2	81.97	3.97	.11	1202
3	81.87	4.38	.25	302
4	81.73	3.96	.61	42
	$\sqrt[3]{\frac{STATURE}{WEIGHT}}$	Males		
1	32.02	1.55	.16	100
2	32.07	1.30	.05	1109
3	32.70	1.32	.08	274
4	33.03	1.26	.21	35
		Females		
1	30.83	1.91	.19	103
2	31.50	1.73	.05	1202
3	31.60	1.68	.10	302
4	31.81	1.55	.24	42
*99	32.66	1.33	.03	1518
99	31.48	1.74	.04	1649

*99 = Total Sample Means

TABLE 127
INDICES BY VARIOUS NUTRITIONAL CLASSES

Table Group Numbers	Mean M	Standard Deviation σ	Standard Error S.E.M	Number N
NC	LEG LENGTH / STATURE	Sample - E		
*99	48.24	1.59	.04	1518
99	47.60	1.50	.04	1649
		Males		
1	47.94	1.23	.12	100
2	48.27	1.57	.05	1109
3	48.29	1.74	.15	274
4	47.88	1.49	.25	35
		Females		
1	47.63	1.39	.14	103
2	47.57	1.48	.04	1202
3	47.75	1.61	.09	302
4	47.44	1.41	.22	42
	TRUNK HEIGHT / STATURE	Males		
1	33.36	1.41	.14	100
2	32.76	1.53	.05	1109
3	32.56	1.55	.10	274
4	33.02	1.53	.26	35
		Females		
1	33.10	1.59	.16	103
2	32.85	1.51	.05	1202
3	32.53	1.54	.09	302
4	32.71	1.55	.24	42
*99	32.77	1.54	.04	1518
99	32.80	1.53	.04	1649

*99 = Total Sample Means

TABLE 128
TOTAL NUMBER OF NON-CARIOUS TEETH BY GEOGRAPHIC REGION

Table Group Numbers	Mean M	Standard Deviation σ	Standard Error S.E.M	Number N
Region		Males		
1	17.89	8.34	.88	88
2	20.64	7.66	.56	181
3	21.19	7.44	.66	126
4	21.01	7.32	.99	54
5	23.26	7.25	.52	188
6	20.05	8.34	1.01	68
7	20.67	8.54	.90	88
8	20.96	8.06	1.04	60
9	22.02	6.63	1.09	37
10	22.65	7.17	1.33	29
11	18.37	7.82	.83	88
12	19.26	8.72	1.08	65
13	22.44	7.33	.55	172
14	23.55	7.35	.56	167
15	22.47	7.32	.71	106
		Females		
1	17.23	9.84	.97	101
2	17.71	8.48	.61	192
3	17.18	9.04	.87	107
4	19.71	8.74	1.47	35
5	18.36	9.06	.76	139
6	19.63	8.62	.77	124
7	19.48	8.82	.70	156
8	18.95	7.44	.80	85
9	13.52	9.23	2.01	21
10	21.89	6.61	1.05	39
11	16.05	8.89	1.02	75
12	18.40	8.43	.92	84
13	19.14	9.24	.64	204
14	21.82	7.66	.61	156
15	21.24	8.49	.73	132

TABLE 129
TOTAL NUMBER OF CARIOUS TEETH BY GEOGRAPHIC REGION

Table Group Numbers	Mean M	Standard Deviation σ	Standard Error S.E.M	Number N
Region		Males		
1	5.04	4.48	.47	88
2	4.50	4.09	.30	181
3	4.52	4.20	.37	126
4	3.38	3.36	.45	54
5	3.75	3.75	.27	188
6	3.91	3.20	.38	68
7	4.42	4.32	.46	88
8	3.86	3.55	.45	60
9	4.10	3.26	.53	37
10	4.10	3.90	.72	29
11	4.73	3.57	.38	88
12	3.87	3.57	.44	65
13	3.10	3.09	.23	172
14	3.07	3.03	.23	167
15	3.33	3.45	.33	106
		Females		
1	4.15	4.18	.41	101
2	4.47	4.00	.28	192
3	3.35	3.25	.31	107
4	3.14	2.48	.41	35
5	4.84	4.30	.36	139
6	3.82	4.53	.40	124
7	4.46	4.05	.32	156
8	5.18	3.94	.42	85
9	4.80	5.06	1.10	21
10	4.97	3.61	.57	39
11	4.94	4.06	.46	75
12	4.51	4.86	.53	84
13	3.96	3.65	.25	204
14	3.40	3.67	.29	156
15	3.12	3.17	.27	132

TABLE 130
TOTAL NUMBER OF TEETH MISSING BY GEOGRAPHIC REGION

Table Group Numbers	Mean M	Standard Deviation σ	Standard Error S.E.M	Number N
Region		Males		
1	8.25	8.03	.85	88
2	6.06	6.72	.50	181
3	5.58	6.44	.57	126
4	7.31	6.39	.87	54
5	4.47	5.50	.40	188
6	7.55	7.98	.96	68
7	6.47	7.82	.83	88
8	6.05	8.23	1.06	60
9	5.54	6.16	1.01	37
10	4.65	6.59	1.22	29
11	8.29	7.53	.80	88
12	8.01	8.30	1.02	65
13	5.81	6.71	.51	172
14	4.74	6.36	.49	167
15	5.64	6.15	.59	106
		Females		
1	9.83	10.40	1.03	101
2	9.09	9.02	.65	192
3	11.14	9.51	.91	107
4	8.62	9.12	1.54	35
5	8.43	8.69	.73	139
6	7.96	8.05	.72	124
7	7.51	8.14	.65	156
8	7.01	7.17	.77	85
9	12.85	9.99	2.18	21
10	4.35	5.28	.84	29
11	10.49	9.94	1.14	75
12	8.13	8.24	.90	84
13	8.24	9.69	.67	204
14	5.89	7.17	.57	156
15	6.97	8.44	.73	132

TABLE 131
TOTAL NUMBER OF CARIOUS PLUS MISSING TEETH BY GEOGRAPHICAL REGION

Table Group Numbers	Mean M	Standard Deviation σ	Standard Error S.E.M	Number N
Region		Males		
1	13.29	8.69	.92	88
2	10.56	7.93	.58	181
3	10.19	7.71	.68	126
4	10.70	7.46	1.01	54
5	8.22	7.37	.53	188
6	11.47	8.65	1.04	68
7	10.89	8.78	.93	88
8	9.91	8.60	1.11	60
9	9.64	6.56	1.07	37
10	8.75	7.48	1.39	29
11	13.03	8.19	.87	88
12	11.89	9.00	1.11	65
13	8.92	7.50	.57	172
14	7.82	7.44	.57	167
15	8.97	7.69	.74	106
		Females		
1	13.99	10.22	1.01	101
2	13.57	8.83	.63	192
3	14.58	9.21	.89	107
4	11.77	8.91	1.50	35
5	13.28	9.27	.78	139
6	11.79	8.91	.80	124
7	11.98	9.13	.73	156
8	12.18	8.06	.87	85
9	17.66	10.11	2.20	21
10	9.33	6.72	1.07	39
11	15.44	9.36	1.08	75
12	12.64	9.30	1.01	84
13	12.20	9.60	.67	204
14	9.30	8.08	.64	156
15	10.10	8.85	.77	132

TABLE 132
DENTAL COUNTS FOR PRISONERS BY GEOGRAPHIC REGION

Table Group Numbers	Mean M	Standard Deviation σ	Standard Error S.E.M	Number N
Region	TOTAL TEETH NON-CARIOUS			
1	10.33	9.84	4.01	6
2	21.48	8.37	1.61	27
3	18.89	8.17	.93	77
4	18.77	7.56	1.35	31
5	21.05	5.90	1.39	18
6	24.12	6.68	.84	63
7	19.52	8.77	2.01	19
8	20.00	4.00	2.82	2
9	20.95	7.27	1.15	40
10	25.85	5.96	2.25	7
11	22.34	5.34	1.04	26
12	21.20	7.07	1.41	25
13	28.63	3.44	1.03	11
14	24.13	6.15	1.58	15
15	26.07	5.05	.95	28
	TOTAL TEETH MISSING			
1	9.66	9.22	3.76	6
2	6.18	7.35	1.41	27
3	8.51	7.72	.88	77
4	7.83	7.15	1.28	31
5	4.88	3.91	.92	18
6	4.19	5.04	.63	63
7	7.10	6.27	1.43	19
8	5.00	4.00	2.82	2
9	5.40	6.16	.97	40
10	2.85	3.09	1.17	7
11	5.69	4.73	.92	26
12	5.48	5.56	1.11	25
13	1.81	3.01	.90	11
14	4.66	5.13	1.32	15
15	3.46	4.00	.75	28

TABLE 133
DENTAL COUNTS FOR PRISONERS BY GEOGRAPHIC REGION

Table Group Numbers	Mean M	Standard Deviation σ	Standard Error S.E.M	Number N
Region	CARIOUS TEETH			
1	1.83	1.46	.59	6
2	4.25	4.54	.87	27
3	4.44	4.63	.52	77
4	5.22	5.01	.90	31
5	5.61	5.03	1.18	18
6	3.36	3.48	.43	63
7	5.36	4.98	1.14	19
8	6.50	.50	.35	2
9	4.35	3.77	.59	40
10	3.28	3.28	1.24	7
11	3.23	2.70	.53	26
12	4.88	3.86	.77	25
13	1.27	1.13	.34	11
14	3.13	2.30	.59	15
15	1.57	1.91	.36	28
	TOTAL CARIOUS PLUS MISSING TEETH			
1	13.00	8.44	3.34	6
2	10.44	8.37	1.61	27
3	12.96	8.22	.93	77
4	13.06	7.58	1.36	31
5	10.44	6.33	1.49	18
6	7.55	6.71	.84	63
7	12.47	8.76	2.01	19
8	11.50	3.50	2.47	2
9	9.75	7.03	1.11	40
10	6.14	5.94	2.24	7
11	8.92	5.72	1.12	26
12	10.36	7.28	1.45	25
13	3.09	3.42	1.03	11
14	7.80	6.22	1.60	15
15	5.03	5.29	1.00	28

TABLE 134
TOTAL NUMBER OF MISSING TEETH BY ETHNIC GROUP

Table Group Numbers	Mean M	Standard Deviation σ	Standard Error S.E.M	Number N
EG		Males		
0	9.00	3.67	1.83	4
1	8.50	8.34	1.23	46
2	6.65	7.07	.38	343
3	5.71	6.81	.26	677
4	5.32	6.92	.50	187
5	7.00	7.44	1.01	54
6	7.20	7.66	.97	62
7	5.75	6.64	.76	76
8	5.26	5.58	.67	68
		Females		
0	11.00	3.00	2.12	2
1	7.74	9.11	1.24	54
2	8.94	9.10	.42	463
3	7.89	8.89	.33	705
4	7.47	8.25	.54	230
5	7.13	6.47	.74	76
6	10.44	10.42	1.22	72
7	9.17	7.99	1.28	39
8	3.14	2.95	1.11	7
9	2.00			1
		Prisoners		
1	1.00	1.41	.81	3
2	7.18	7.37	.96	58
3	5.76	6.27	.47	175
4	3.78	4.84	.75	41
5	4.07	5.69	1.57	13
6	5.42	5.52	.89	38
7	6.92	6.71	1.07	39
8	7.75	6.54	1.23	28

TABLE 135
TOTAL NUMBER OF NON-CARIOUS TEETH BY ETHNIC GROUP

Table Group Numbers	Mean M	Deviation σ	Error S.E.M	Number N
EG		Males		
0	16.50	6.80	3.40	4
1	18.95	8.48	1.25	46
2	20.54	7.87	.42	343
3	21.88	7.68	.29	677
4	22.15	8.27	.60	187
5	19.75	8.17	1.11	54
6	19.38	8.11	1.03	62
7	21.94	6.95	.79	76
8	23.02	6.60	.80	68
		Females		
0	12.50	4.50	3.18	2
1	19.12	8.77	1.19	54
2	17.86	8.94	.41	463
3	19.47	8.81	.33	705
4	20.08	8.21	.54	230
5	19.88	8.10	.93	76
6	17.26	10.00	1.17	72
7	17.74	8.13	1.30	39
8	24.71	5.56	2.10	7
9	16.00			1
		Prisoners		
1	23.66	2.92	1.68	3
2	21.44	7.54	.99	58
3	21.87	7.87	.59	175
4	24.56	6.18	.96	41
5	23.46	6.65	1.84	13
6	21.15	6.31	1.02	38
7	20.23	7.91	1.26	39
8	18.82	7.60	1.43	28

TABLE 136
TOTAL NUMBER OF CARIOUS PLUS MISSING TEETH BY ETHNIC GROUP

Table Group Numbers	Mean M	Standard Deviation σ	Standard Error S.E.M	Number N
EG		Males		
0	15.50	6.80	3.40	4
1	12.32	8.76	1.29	46
2	10.76	8.15	.43	343
3	9.50	7.88	.30	677
4	9.02	8.40	.61	187
5	11.66	8.45	1.14	54
6	12.00	8.37	1.06	62
7	9.81	7.57	.86	76
8	8.66	6.58	.79	68
		Females		
0	19.50	4.50	3.18	2
1	11.96	9.01	1.22	54
2	13.55	9.30	.43	463
3	11.86	9.25	.34	705
4	11.00	8.61	.56	230
5	11.43	8.42	.96	76
6	14.13	10.38	1.22	72
7	14.46	8.29	1.32	39
8	7.28	5.55	2.09	7
9	16.00			1
		Prisoners		
1	6.33	3.86	2.23	3
2	10.31	7.67	1.00	58
3	9.53	7.92	.59	175
4	7.14	6.08	.95	41
5	7.69	6.86	1.90	13
6	10.81	6.32	1.02	38
7	11.51	8.15	1.30	39
8	13.03	7.71	1.45	28

TABLE 137
TOTAL NUMBER OF CARIOUS TEETH BY ETHNIC GROUP

Table Group Number	Mean M	Standard Deviation σ	Standard Error S.E.M	Number N
EG		Males		
0	6.50	7.26	3.63	4
1	3.82	3.34	.49	46
2	4.08	3.88	.20	343
3	3.78	3.64	.13	677
4	3.69	4.00	.29	187
5	4.66	3.59	.48	54
6	4.79	3.69	.46	62
7	4.06	3.33	.38	76
8	3.39	3.44	.41	68
		Females		
0	8.50	1.50	1.06	2
1	4.22	3.26	.44	54
2	4.60	4.32	7.20	463
3	3.95	3.81	.14	705
4	3.59	3.29	.21	230
5	4.30	3.84	.44	76
6	3.69	4.06	.47	72
7	5.28	3.77	.60	39
8	4.14	3.09	1.16	7
9	14.00			1
		Prisoners		
1	5.33	3.68	2.12	3
2	3.12	3.34	.43	58
3	3.77	3.83	.28	175
4	3.36	3.14	.49	41
5	3.61	4.18	1.15	13
6	5.39	4.68	.76	38
7	4.58	4.89	.78	39
8	5.32	5.05	.95	28

TABLE 138
DENTAL COUNTS BY NUTRITIONAL CLASS

Table Group Numbers	Mean M	Standard Deviation σ	Standard Error S.E.M	Number N
NC	NUMBER OF CARIOUS TEETH		Males	
1	5.58	3.70	.37	100
2	3.75	3.63	.10	1108
3	3.98	4.01	.24	274
4	3.68	3.90	.65	35
			Females	
1	5.57	4.41	.43	103
2	3.89	3.77	.10	1202
3	4.64	4.52	.25	302
4	4.23	3.59	.55	42
			Prisoners	
2	3.82	3.94	.22	310
3	4.61	4.54	.49	83
4	3.00	2.00	1.41	2
	NUMBER OF CARIOUS PLUS MISSING TEETH			
			Males	
1	11.30	5.94	.59	100
2	9.62	7.96	.23	1108
3	10.85	8.78	.53	274
4	10.77	9.56	1.61	35
			Females	
1	12.59	7.99	.78	103
2	12.20	9.19	.26	1202
3	13.19	9.50	.54	302
4	11.38	9.97	1.53	42
			Prisoners	
2	9.71	7.54	.42	310
3	10.56	8.10	.88	83
4	7.50	4.50	3.18	2

TABLE 139
DENTAL COUNTS BY NUTRITIONAL CLASS

Table Group Numbers	Mean M	Standard Deviation σ	Standard Error S.E.M	Number N
NC	TOTAL TEETH NON-CARIOUS		Males	
1	20.02	6.06	.60	100
2	21.75	7.72	.23	1108
3	20.52	8.46	.51	274
4	20.65	9.33	1.57	35
			Females	
1	18.69	7.57	.74	103
2	19.16	8.80	.25	1202
3	18.24	9.10	.52	302
4	20.07	9.63	1.48	42
			Prisoners	
2	21.98	7.40	.41	310
3	20.62	8.08	.88	83
4	24.50	4.50	3.18	2
	TOTAL TEETH MISSING		Males	
1	5.72	4.62	.46	100
2	5.85	6.95	.20	1108
3	6.87	7.59	.45	274
4	7.08	7.42	1.25	35
			Females	
1	7.01	7.05	.69	103
2	8.31	8.86	.25	1202
3	8.54	9.23	.53	302
4	7.14	9.25	1.42	42
			Prisoners	
2	5.88	6.46	.36	310
3	5.96	6.16	.67	83
4	4.50	2.50	1.76	2

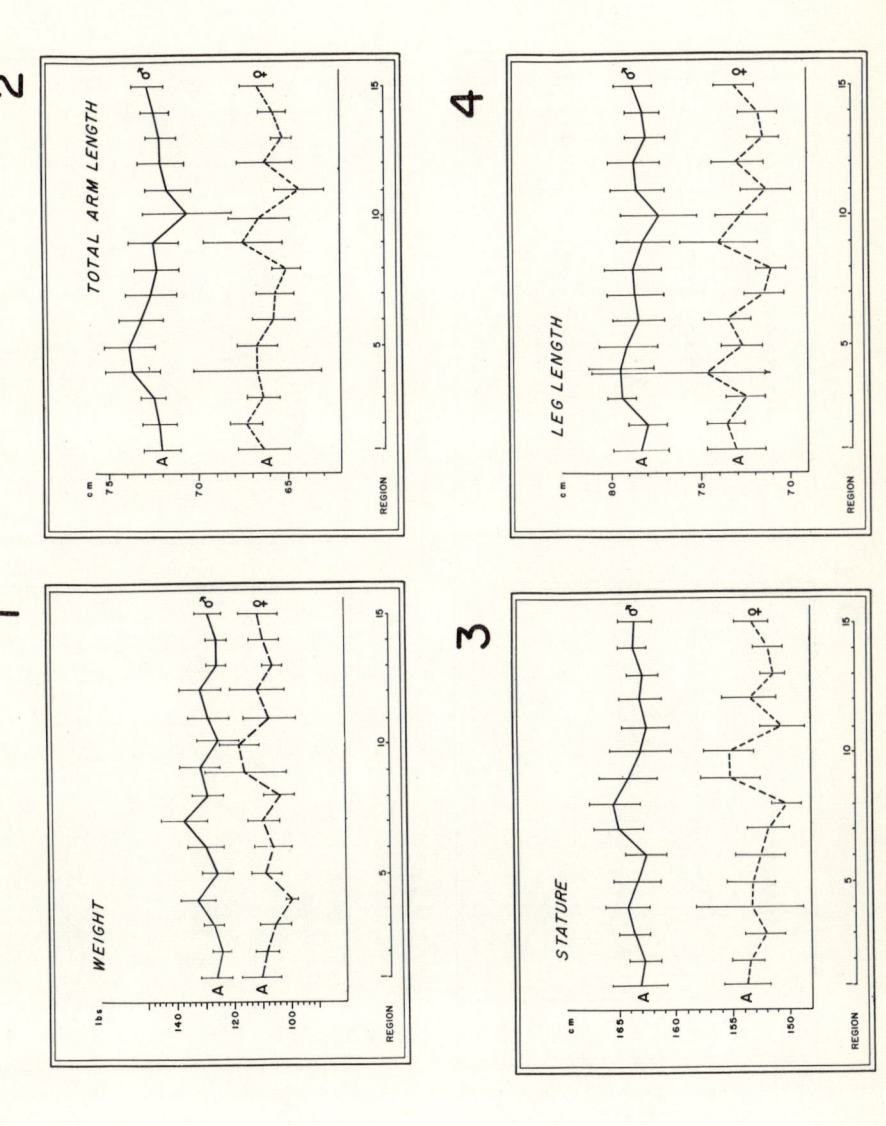

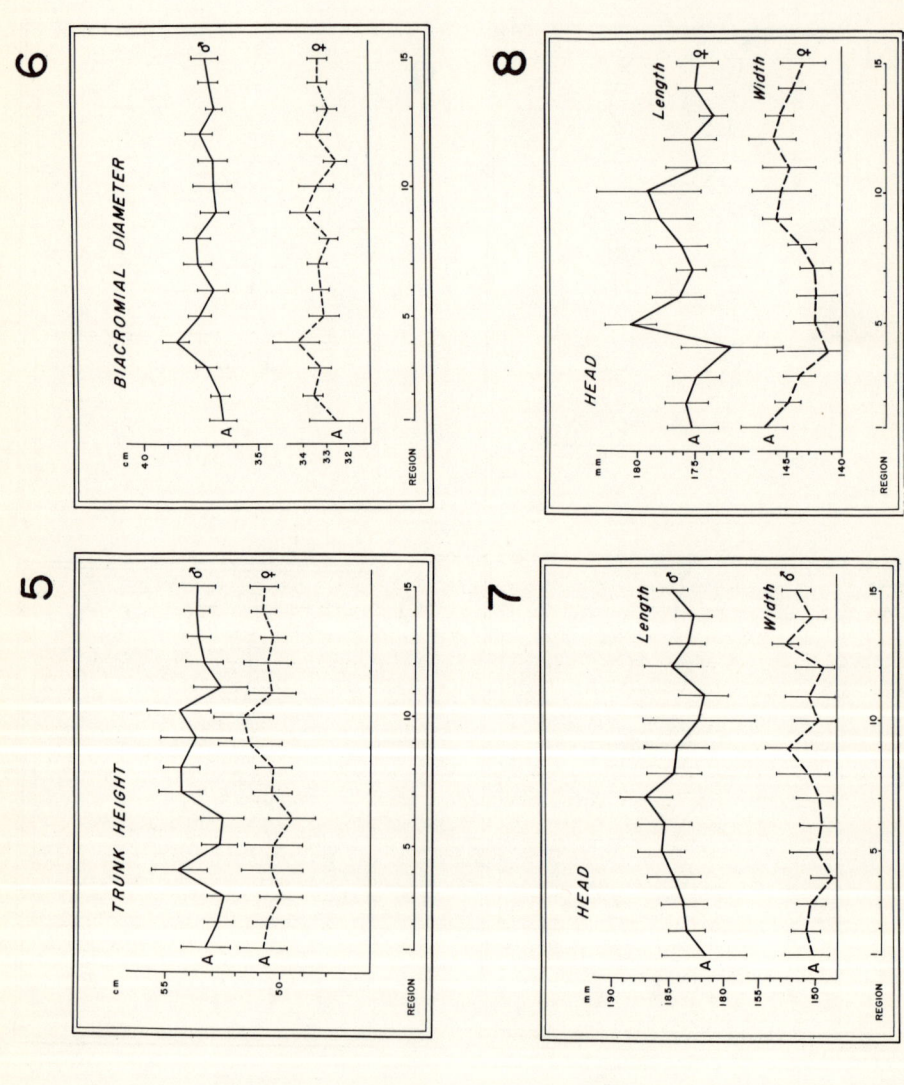

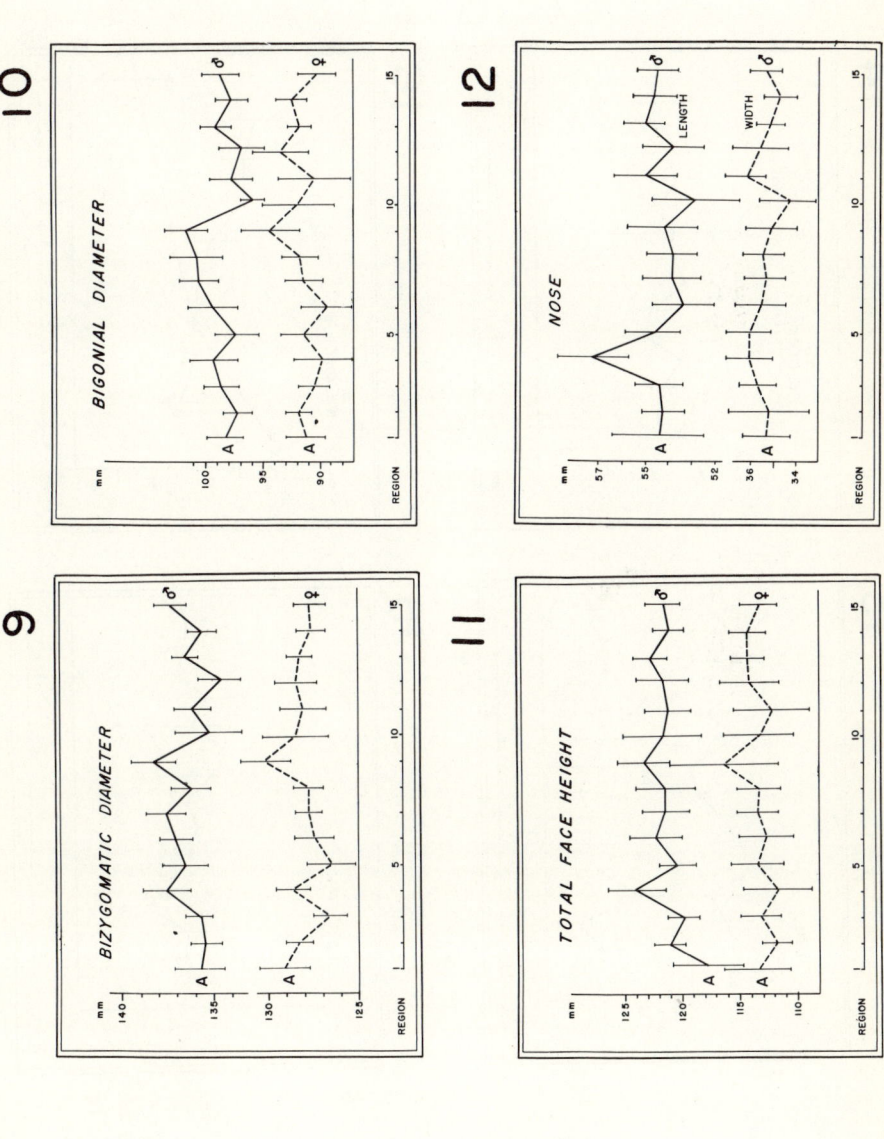

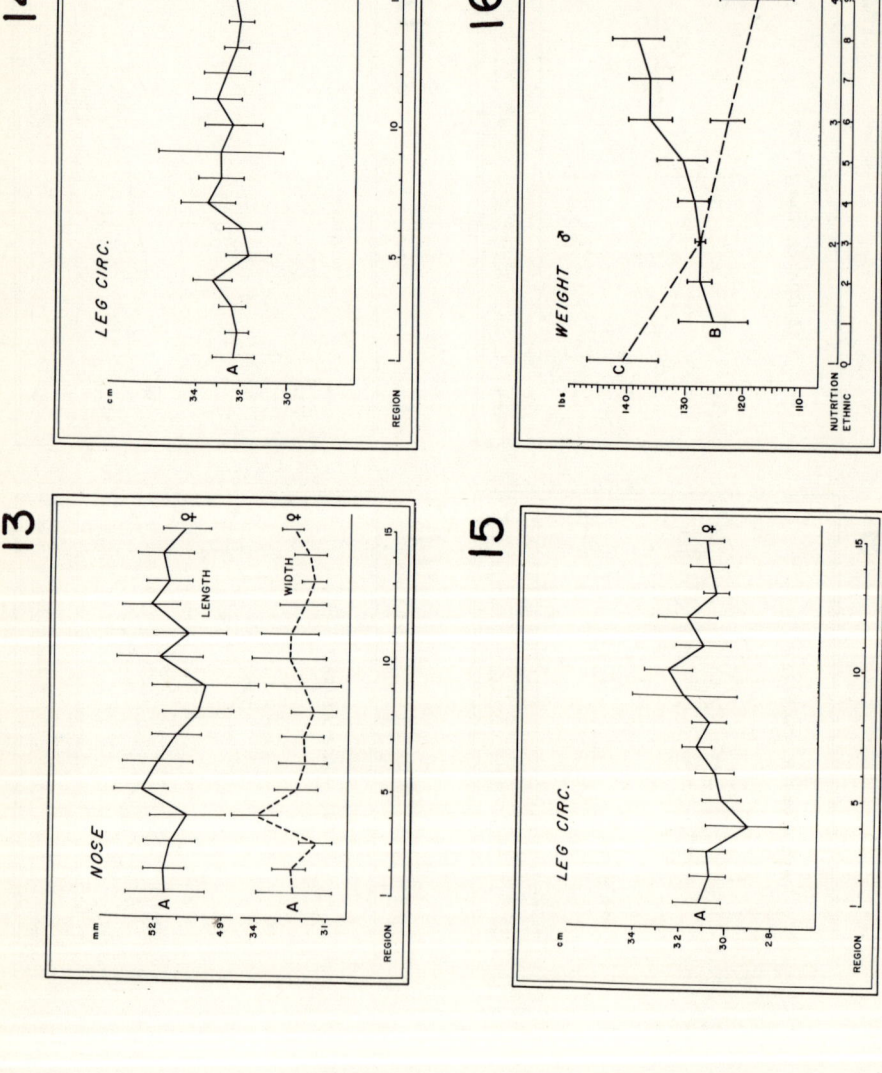

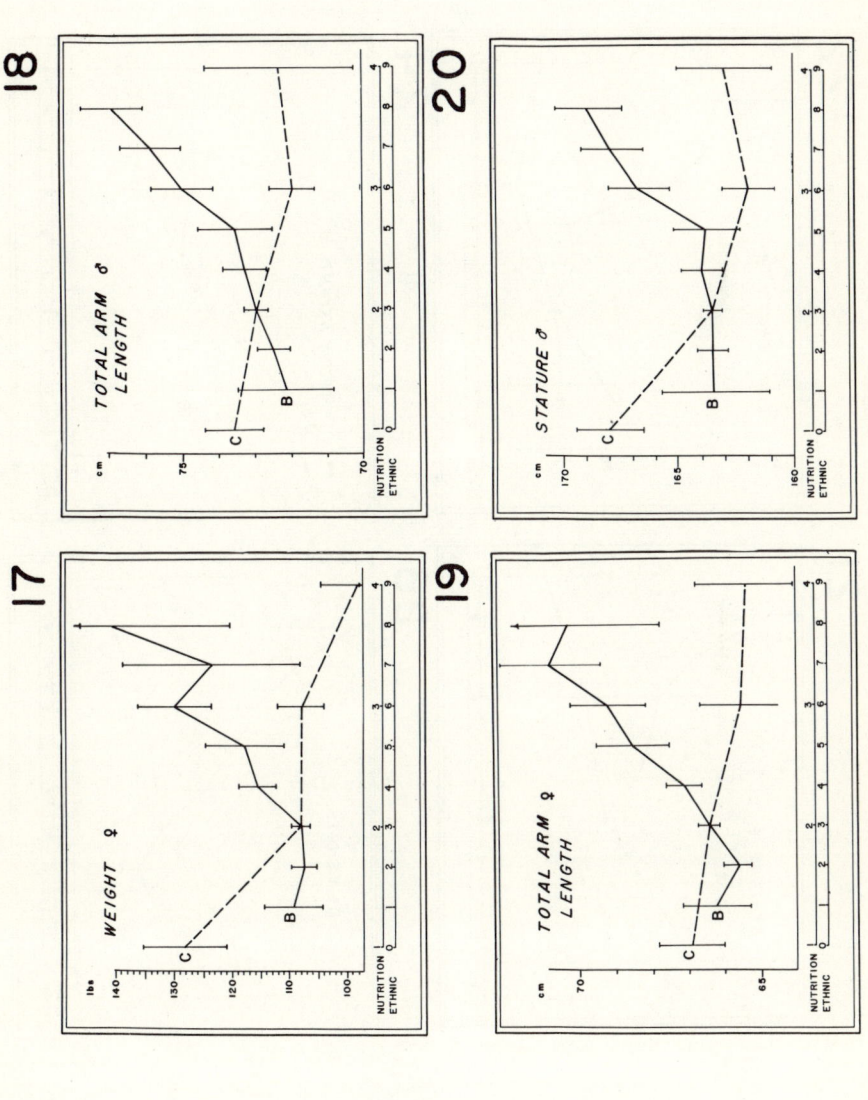

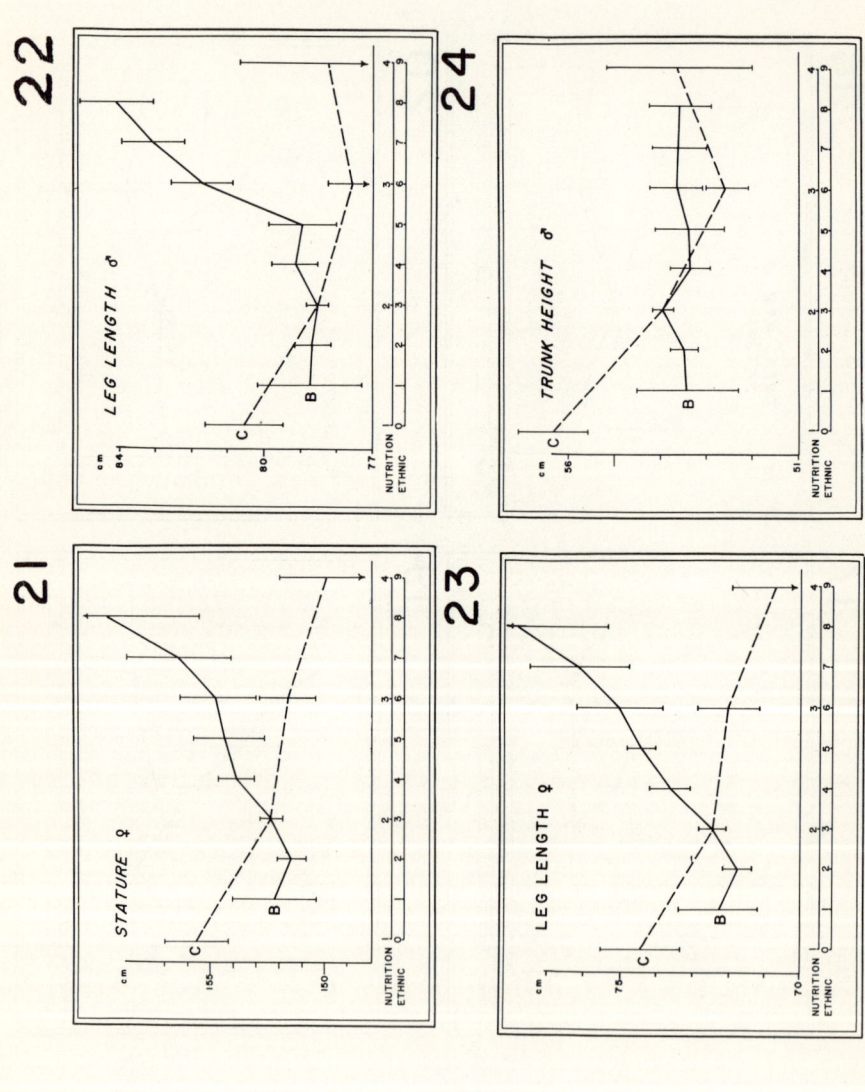

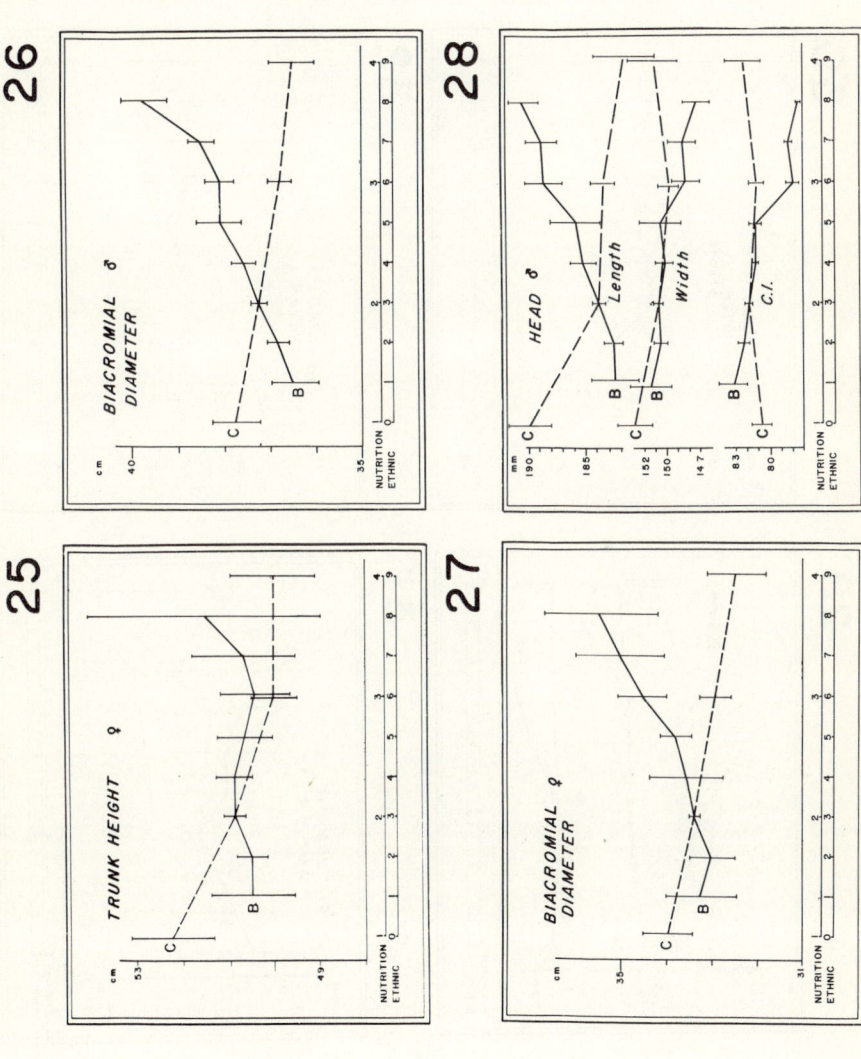

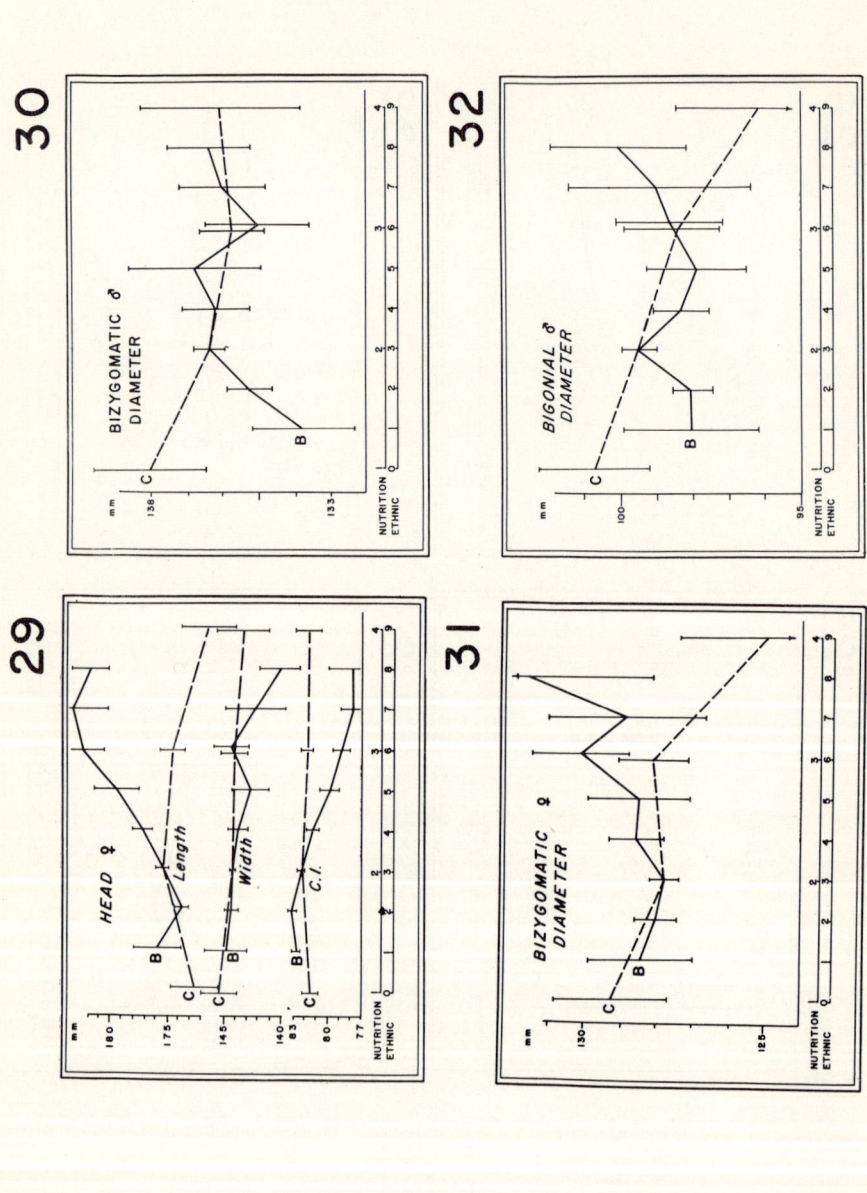

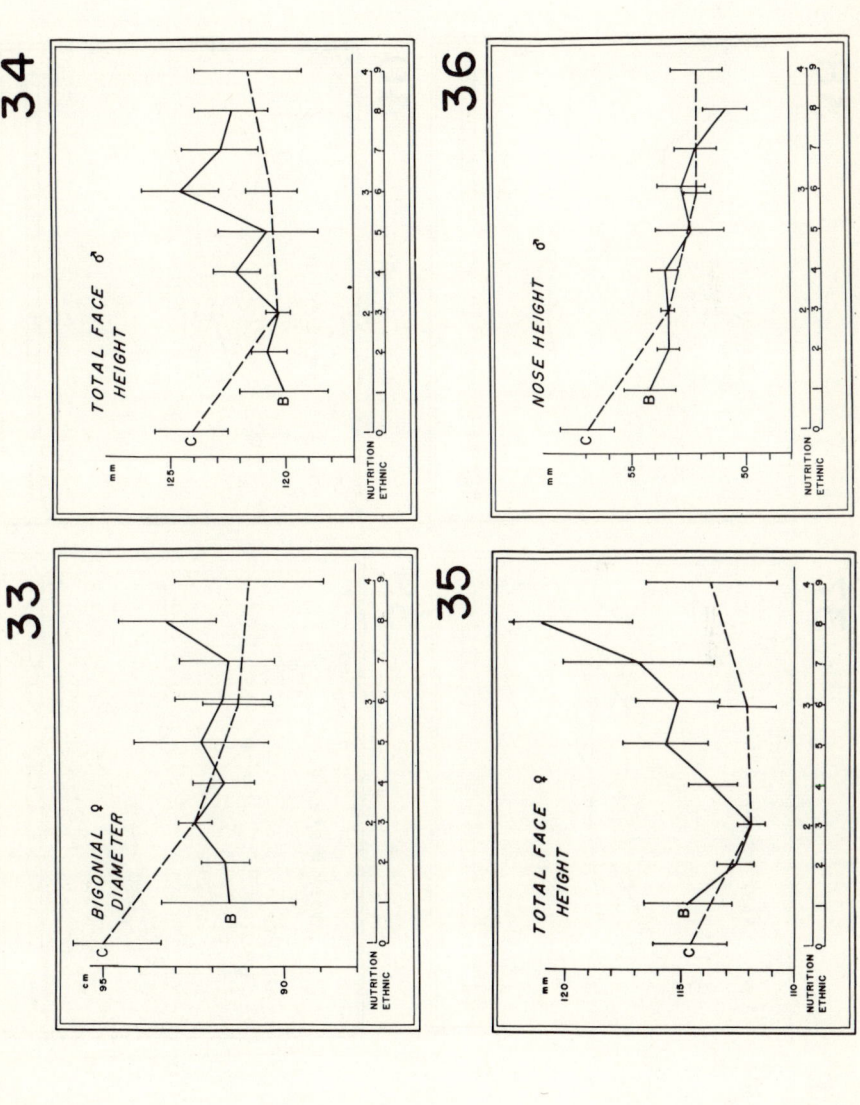

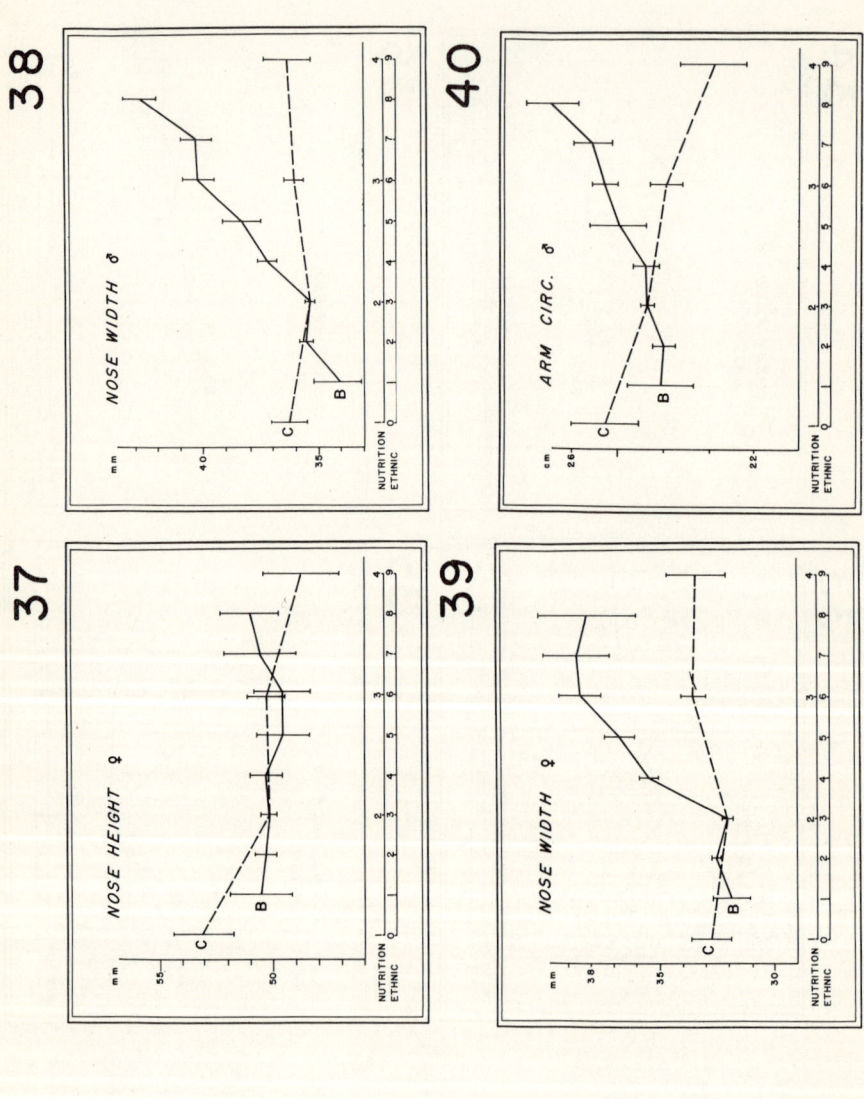

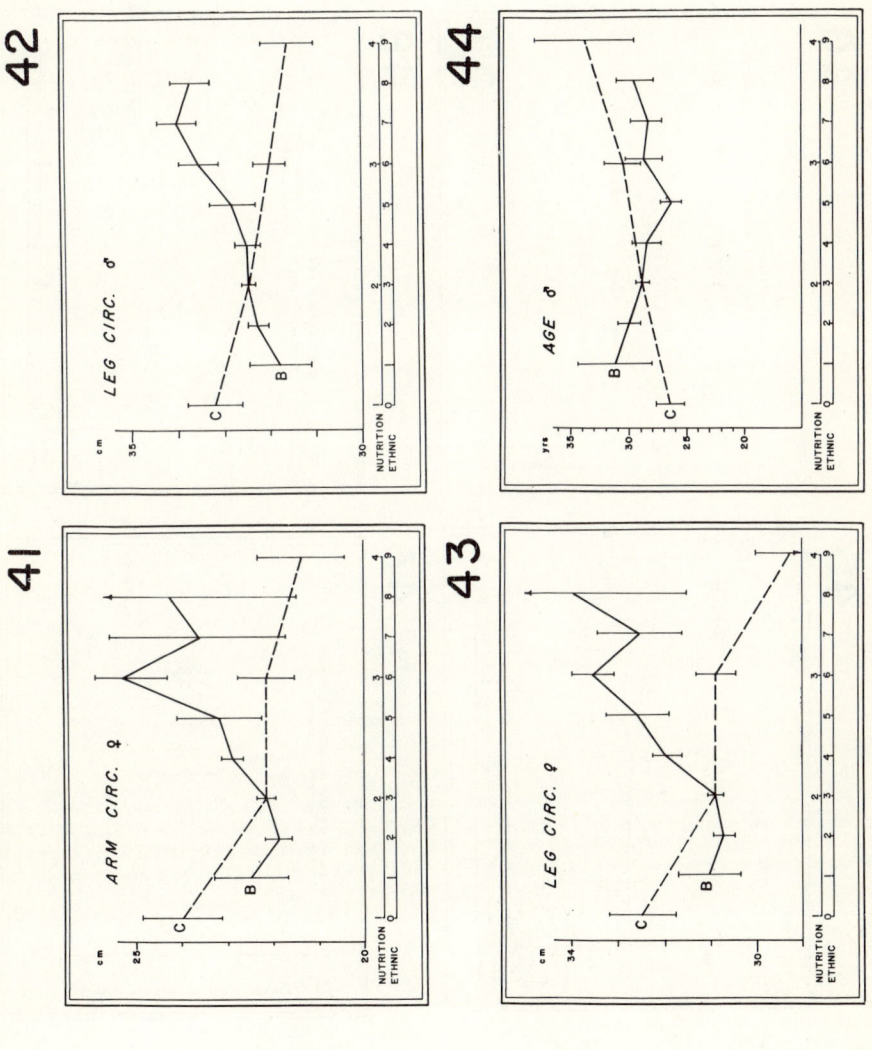

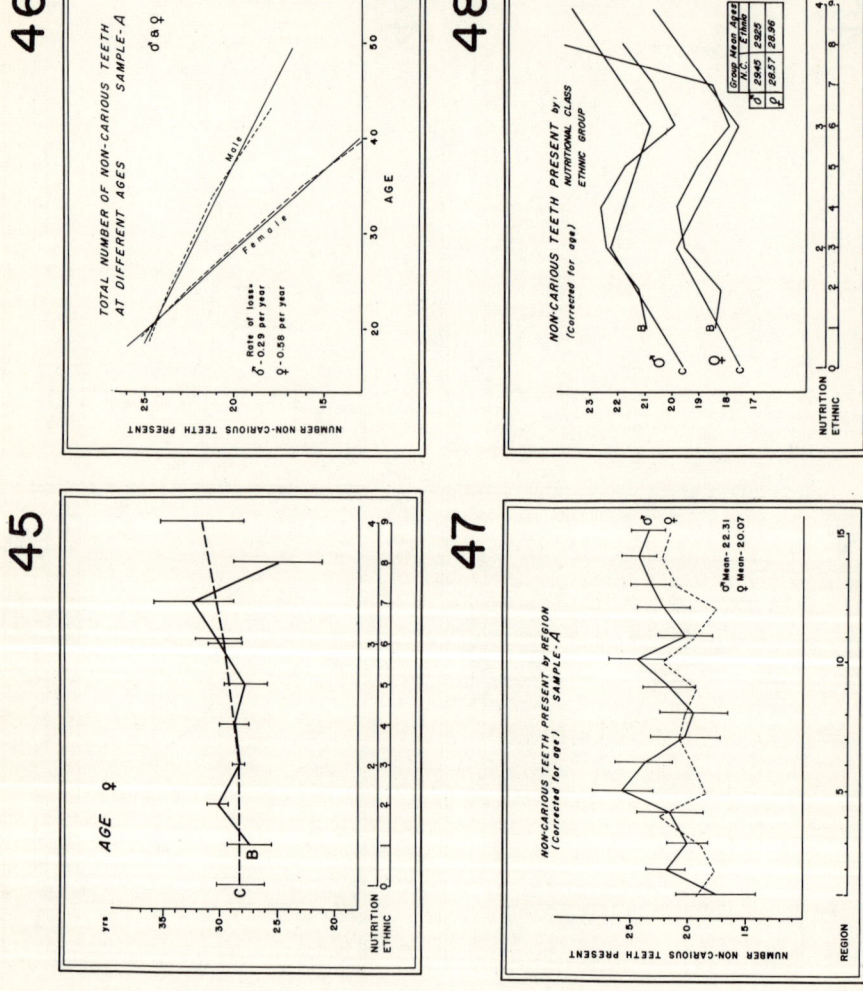

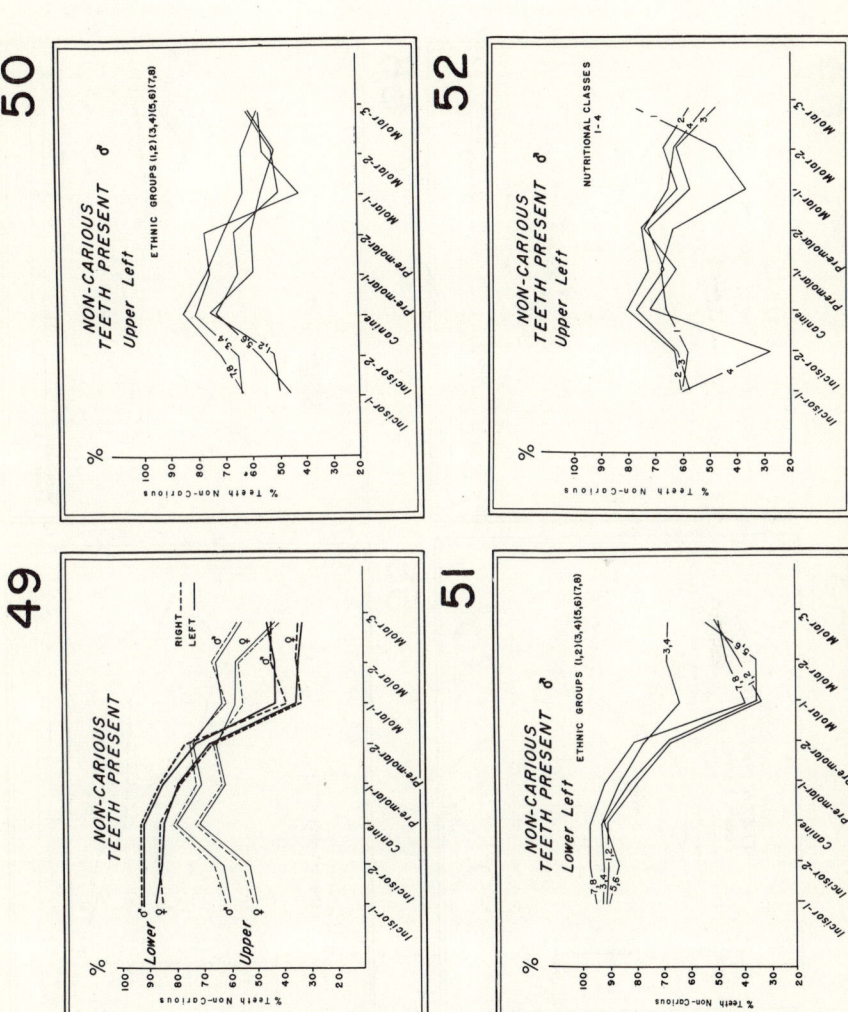

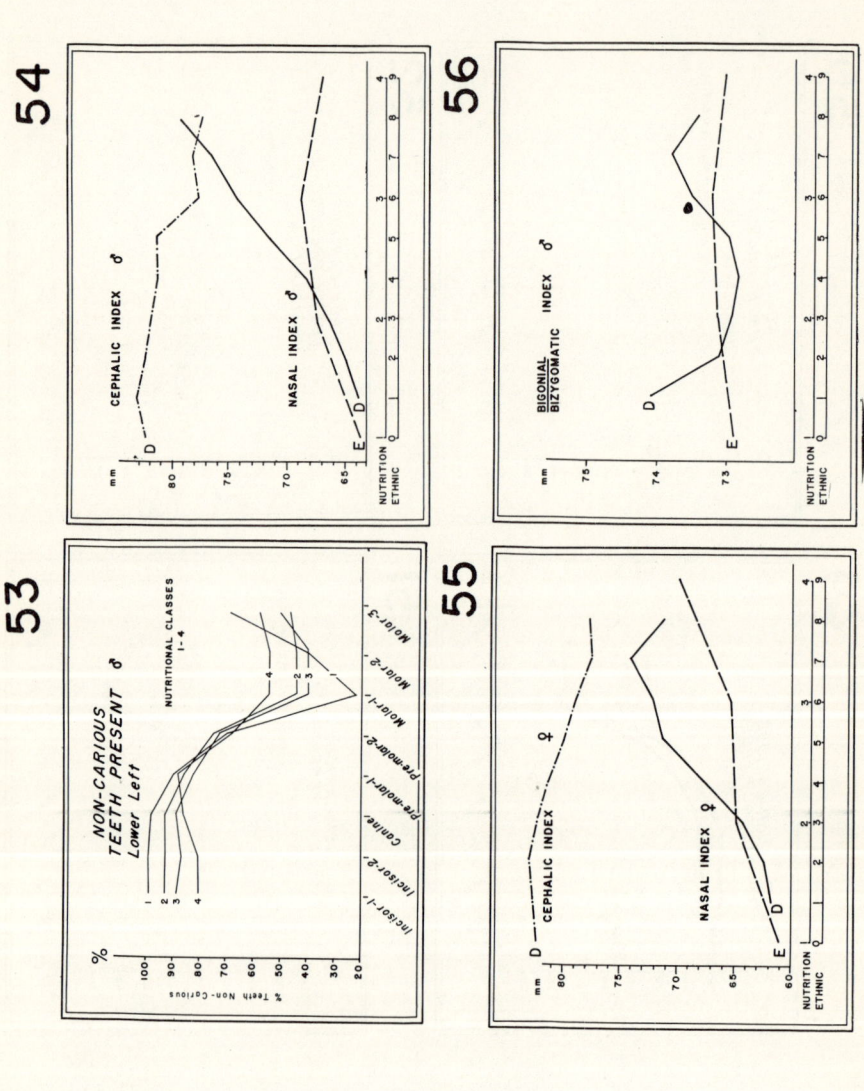

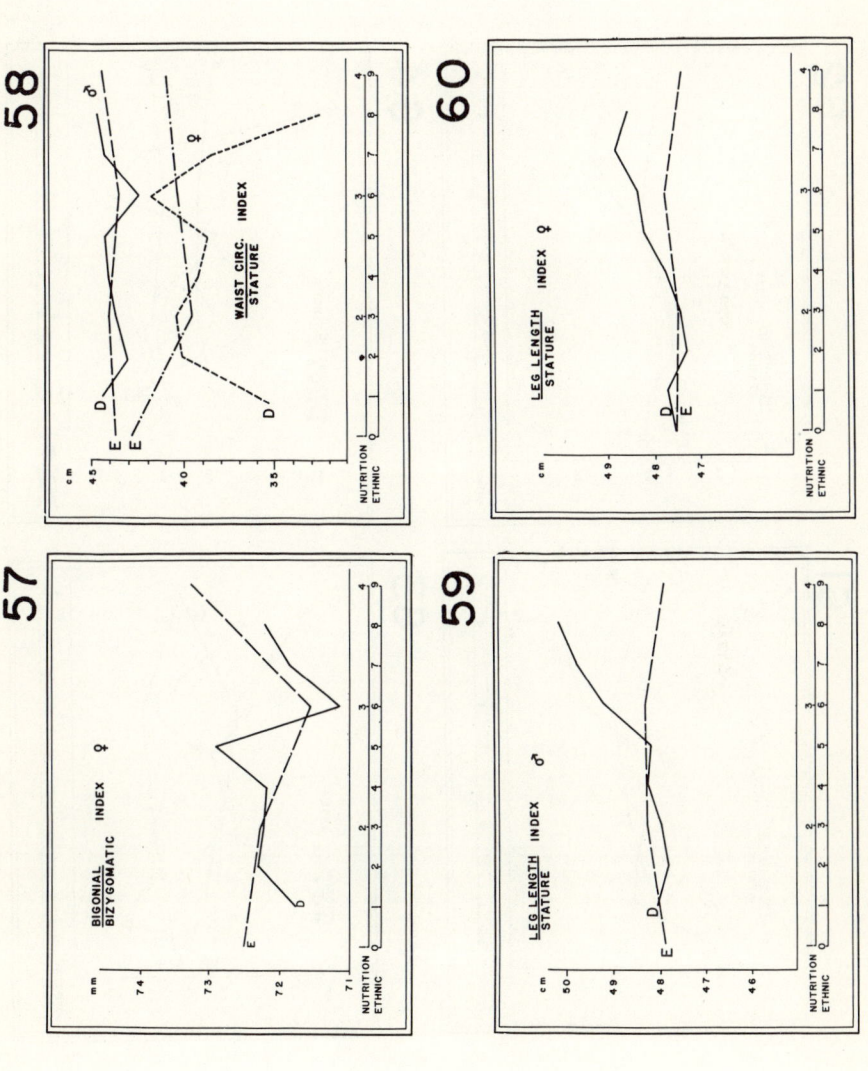

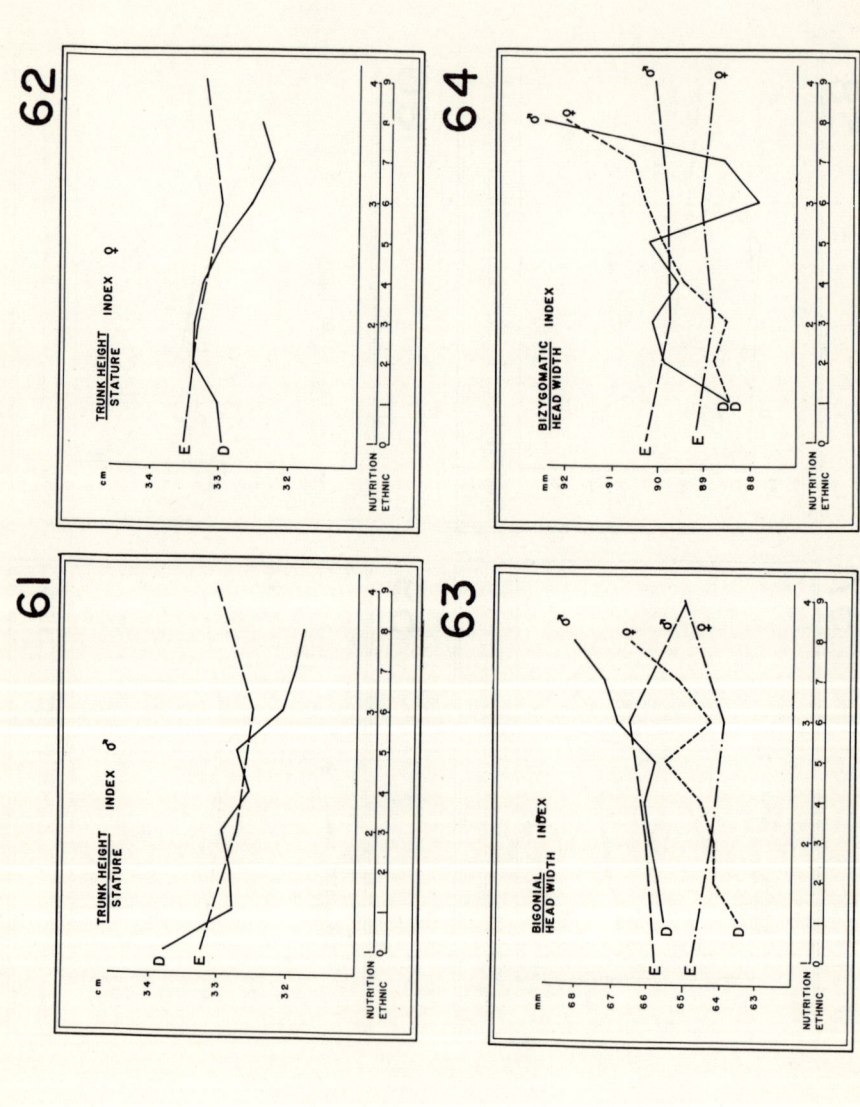

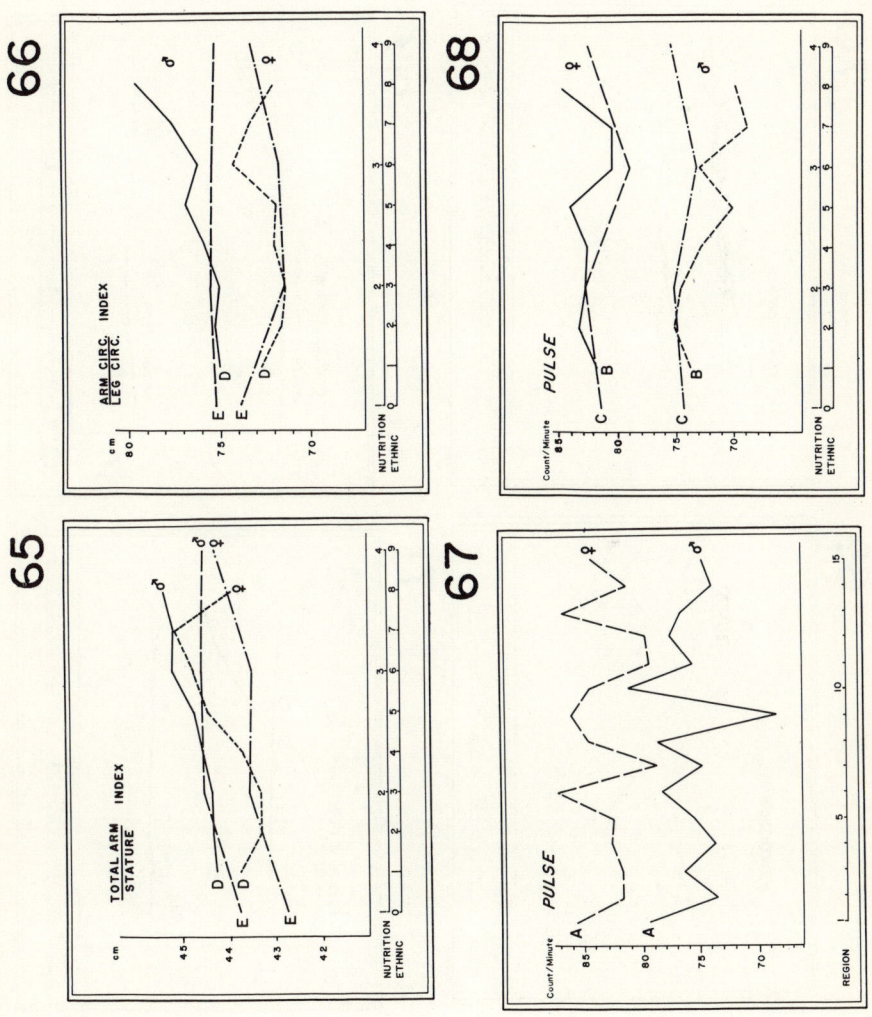

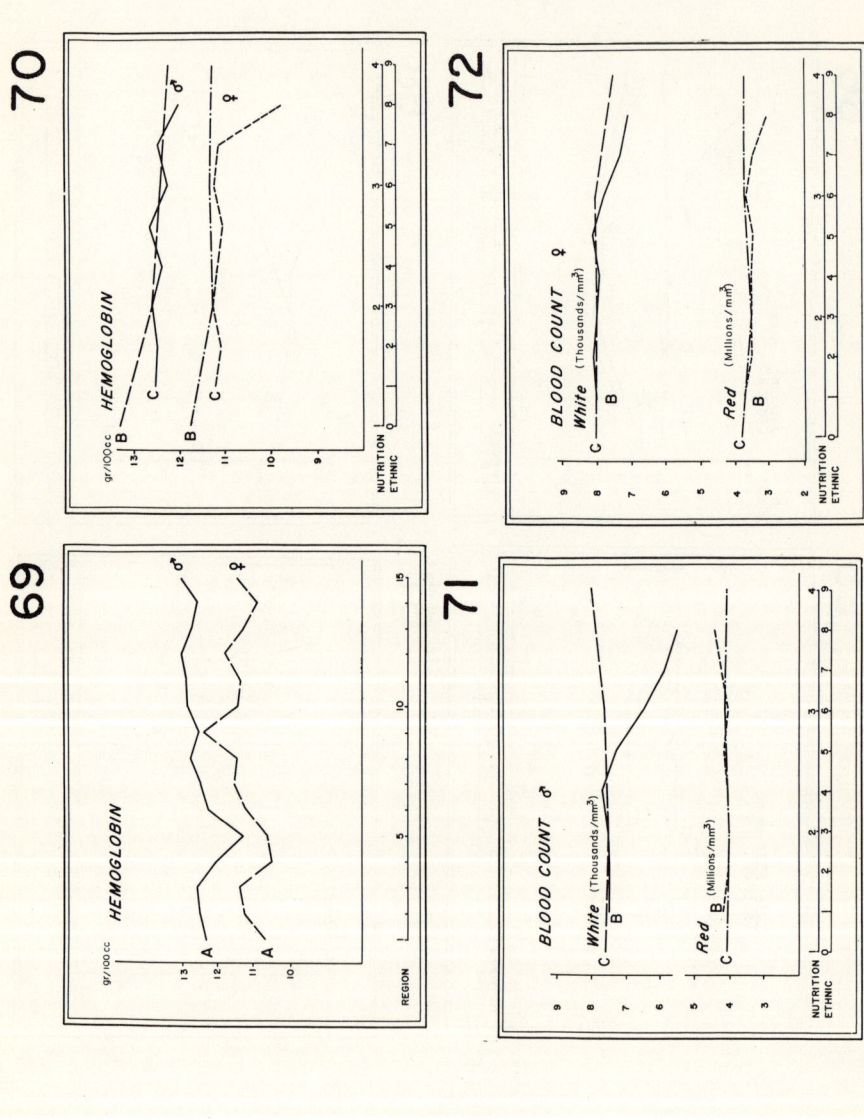

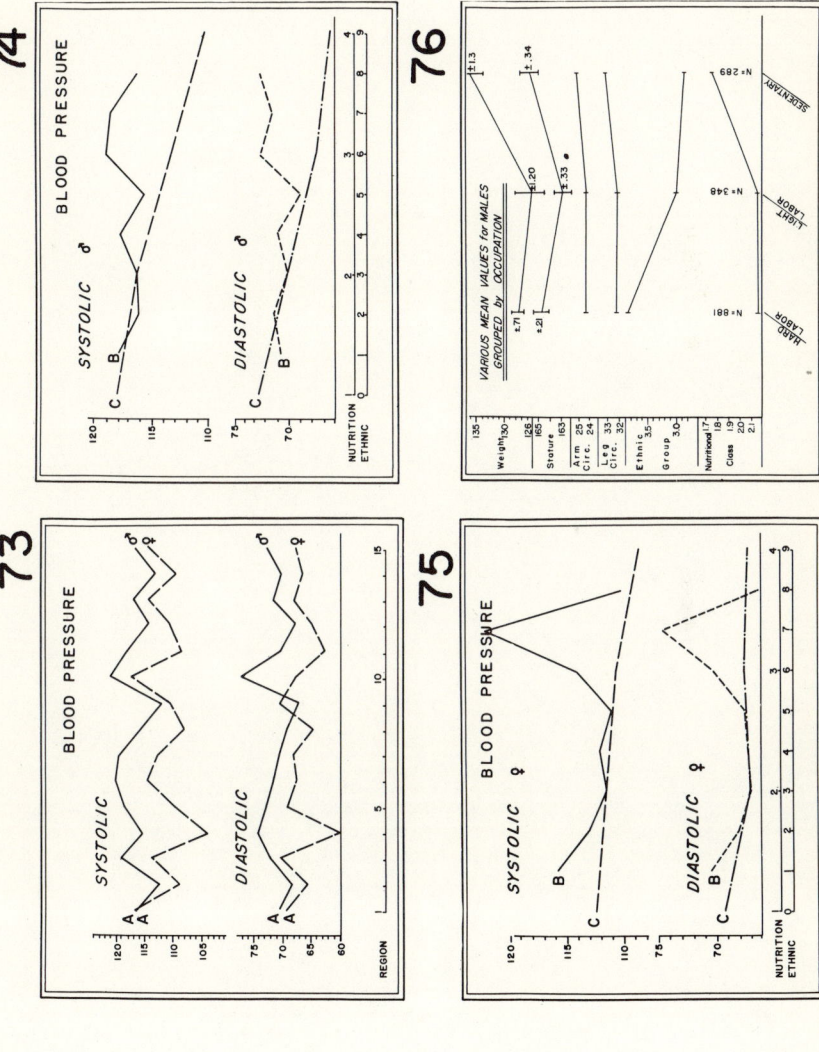